WELCOME to
The Taste of Scotland Guide 1990

J M B MacMillan MBE MC *Chief Executive*

At a time when the High Streets of every major town are being clogged with the dull uniformity and shallow mediocrity of fast food chains, it becomes increasingly important to be able to identify and enjoy the caring attention and individualism of those who serve the more discerning public.

The function of a guide is to inform. To present the reader with a short list of recommended establishments and to provide sufficient information about the premises, the food and the prices to make choice easy.

The reader should be absolved from the tedium of trying out dozens of different establishments before finding one that meets requirements.

This Guide is aimed at the discerning diner who enjoys good food, prepared from the best quality fresh produce, which is cooked with skill and imagination and presented and served by well

trained, knowledgeable and agreeable Guides come in all shapes, sizes and prices. So too do the public.

It is a refreshing feature of the human race that we have such a wide range of likes and dislikes, fads and fantasies. Each of us, however, is an expert on what he or she likes to eat.

It is for that reason, amongst others, that the Taste of Scotland Guide lists such a wide range of eating places. Within this volume you will find everything from that rarity nowadays, the cosy village tea room specialising in home-baking, through every level of restaurant and hotel to the grand de luxe five star hotels of international repute.

The area in between is a rich one; with something for everyone at every price level.

If there is a particular category in which Scotland excels it is surely in its Country House hotels. Almost all are proprietor managed, many are architectural gems with interiors reflecting the comfort and grandeur of a disappearing era.

Here one is very much the personal, and special, guest of the proprietor. Welcome is warm, food is excellent, service is courteous and the cares of the world are a long way off.

Equally outstanding are the many smaller proprietor run restaurants in cities, towns and countryside. There was a time when Scotland had all too few of these. But not now. Many are acclaimed internationally, most can hold their own with the best in their price group anywhere in Europe.

There really has been a revolution in catering standards in Scotland and you can enjoy some wonderful meal experiences.

Do try them.

Jack MacMillan

1

CONTENTS

TASTE OF SCOTLAND introduced a modified logo in 1989. Some establishments may still display the old symbol. Current members are identified by the 1990 Certificate of membership which should be on display.

The Taste of Scotland Scheme Ltd
is sponsored by:

The Scottish Tourist Board

The Highlands & Islands Development Board

The Scottish Milk Marketing Board

The Scotch Quality Beef & Lamb Association Ltd

The Scottish Salmon Board

HOW TO USE THIS GUIDE

Sample entry

location number →

KILLIECRANKIE
112   E6

← grid reference

address & tel no
etc →

Killiecrankie Hotel
by Pitlochry
Perthshire
PH16 5LG
Tel: 0796 3220
Fax: 0796 2451

On old A9, 3 miles north of Pitlochry. ← how to find it

description →

A converted dower house, set in four
acres of well-kept gardens overlooking the
historic Pass of Killiecrankie. Furnished to
a high standard to reflect the expected
small country house atmosphere and
comfort requirements of the most
fastidious guest.

any seasonal limitations → Open late Feb to mid Nov

Rooms: 12 with private facilities ← accommodation
Breakfast from 8 am
Bar Lunch 12.30 - 2 pm (a)
Bar Supper 7 - 9.30 pm (b) ← meal times & prices
Dinner 7 - 8.30 pm (d)

specimen inclusive terms
quoted on per person →
per night basis

No smoking in dining room.
Bed & breakfast £29 - £32.50
Dinner B & B £45 - £48.50

Traditional Scottish menu featuring ← specimen food specialities
speciality soups, smoked haddock flan,
Tay salmon, fresh Buckie fish, Angus
beef, Scotch lamb, venison, game and
cheeses.

comparative ratings →

STB 2 Crown Commended
RAC 2 Star H
AA   2 Star HB

Credit cards: 1, 3 ← credit cards accepted
Proprietors: Colin & Carole Anderson

Entries

- Establishments selected by Taste of Scotland
  are listed in this Guide in alphabetical order
  under the nearest town or village.
- Island entries are shown alphabetically by
  island or island group, e.g. Skye or Orkney.
- A full list of hotels etc is given in alphabetical
  order in the index at the end of the Guide.

Special diets or requirements

- Vegetarian meals are more readily available
  nowadays, but we advise that you mention
  this requirement when making your booking.
- Other special needs, such as diet or facilities
  for disabled guests should also be arranged in
  advance.

Pets
- Pets are accepted in some establishments with forewarning – but do check this also – there may be a small charge.

Wines and spirits
- Except where otherwise stated, all hotels and restaurants are licensed for the sale of wines, spirits, beers etc.
- Most unlicensed establishments will welcome your taking your own wine, but again please enquire in advance.

Bar lunches
- Nowadays lunch-time eating has become much less formal except in city centre hotels and restaurants. Bar snacks are more usual in some smaller establishments and rural hotels – so if you wish a full meal it is best to check.

HOW TO AVOID DISAPPOINTMENT
- Make an advance reservation whenever possible.
- Mention you are using this Guide.
- Remember that many dishes are seasonal and that members will even then only offer them if they can obtain top quality produce to cook and offer to visitors.
- Check the availability of a full lunch if this is what you want, as many establishments may only offer bar lunches or snacks.
- Confirm that credit cards are accepted.

COMMENTS
Taste of Scotland welcomes comments.

If you have an unsatisfactory meal, we would always advise you to speak to the restaurant or hotel manager or proprietor at the time.

Write to the Taste of Scotland Scheme if this fails to solve the problem.

But do let us hear of your good experiences too!

For your convenience a comment slip is included at the back of this Guide.

GRADING AND CLASSIFICATION
The Scottish Tourist Board operates a grading and classification system. It offers reassurance on both the range of facilities and their quality.

Many of the establishments in this Guide have been inspected and this is shown in their entries. Some entries are shown as 'Award Pending' at the time of going to press.

The classifications – from 'Listed' to '5 Crowns' – are awarded according to the range of facilities available. Grading is solely concerned with quality. The grades awarded – 'Approved', 'Commended' or 'Highly Commended' – are based upon a wide variety of items, from the appearance of the buildings and gardens, to the quality of the furnishings.

PRICES
Users of the Guide should always check prevailing prices.

Estimated prices, as at November 1989, for a three-course meal, excluding drinks, are:

(a)	under £5.00
(b)	£5.00 - £8.00
(c)	£8.00 - £12.00
(d)	£12.00 - £15.00
(e)	£15.00 - £20.00
(f)	£20.00 +

Please note these prices are *for guidance only* and should be checked on booking or arrival.

Similarly, many members given due notice will offer vegetarian meals or special diets to meet medical requirements.

Inclusive terms are listed as a guideline. Where a price range is given, the lower price normally indicates the rate per person sharing a double room and the higher price the rate for a single room or a higher quality room.

Times of food service are listed to show first and last orders, unless otherwise indicated.

A warm welcome from the Scots . . .

Perhaps the first picture of Scotland is of its scenic attractions – the grandeur of its hills and lochs or the drama and the spectacle of Edinburgh, its capital city. Scotland certainly has beautiful landscapes and it offers an even more valuable attraction: friendly people.

It might be the cosy scale of the cities, towns and villages or a rural tradition of communities supporting each other, but you will find as you travel around that the Scots are eager to help and to ensure you have a good time during your stay. In fact, in the Scottish Highlands in olden times, no stranger who came to the door of a house (no matter how humble) was ever turned away. This tradition of hospitality was part of the Highland way of life.

You will find this echoed in today's hotels and restaurants. Sample the cuisine of any of the establishments featured in this guide and you will find out for yourself that Scotland can provide an impressive range of ingredients for outstanding meals. But fine produce, well-prepared, tastes all the better when service is friendly and helpful – another Scottish speciality. From a friendly 'good morning' at breakfast time to advice on a malt whisky nightcap, the Scots are at your service – in establishments ranging from the smallest B&B to luxury country hotels; whether offering simple afternoon tea or lavish dinners.

We look forward to meeting you in Scotland and we know you'll enjoy our food!

CREDIT/CHARGE CARDS

1 Access/
   Mastercard/
   Eurocard
2 American Express
3 Visa
4 Carte Bleu
5 Diners Club
6 Mastercharge

See entry page . . . 68

The Scottish Highlands and Islands
– where all the signs point to peace and contentment

Starting with Argyll and the Isles . . .

From the Mull of Kintyre to Oban and beyond, Argyll stretches serenely across mountains, forests, glens and lochs. Like a necklace around it lie the Isles: Mull, Coll, Tiree, Iona, Colonsay, Jura, Islay, Gigha, Arran, Cumbrae and Bute.

Here you can visit some of Britain's most beautiful gardens: all kinds of flowers flourish in the gentle Gulf Stream climate. You can play golf amid some of the finest scenery in Europe; visit prehistoric standing stones; go cruising in waters Saints and Vikings have sailed; walk wooded mountain trails; and enjoy unrivalled hospitality.

The Heart of the Highlands . . .

embraces Mallaig, Fort William, Inverness, Nairn and the Spey Valley. It's a region of superlatives: Britain's highest mountain, Ben Nevis; Britain's deepest loch, Loch Morar; Britain's oldest monster, Nessie (she may also be the shyest but could well pop out to see you); and Britain's biggest inland waterway, the Caledonian Canal. Here, naturally, you'll have a superlative holiday, whether you're visiting castles, beaches, wildlife centres or the sites of ancient battlefields.

The Northern Highlands and Islands . . .

Within the broad scope of the Northern Highlands and Islands you'll find far-flung islands: Skye and the Inner and Outer Hebrides. On the mainland you'll discover the dramatically varied scenery of Ross and Cromarty, Caithness and Sutherland.

This is a land of remarkable contrasts. In the course of a day you can come across towering mountains, gentle moors, quiet beaches, stone-age remains and magnificent castles. You can enjoy boat trips, visit bird sanctuaries, go hill-walking or fish for record-breaking skate and halibut. And at the end of the day, you can frequently enjoy a *Ceilidh*, where the music and dancing continue into the wee small hours.

Orkney and Shetland . . .

Just about where ancient mariners thought the world ended, the Orkneys start. And beyond the Orkneys, only 200 miles from the coast of Norway, lie the Shetland Isles. The nearness of Scandinavia has influenced life in these islands down the centuries. Listen carefully to the locals: you'll find their accents owe more to the Viking than the Pict.

Explore the countryside, the ragged cliffs and sandy beaches: you'll see the work of the wild Atlantic and the North Sea everywhere. (You'll also find the work of early man in the ancient forts and burial mounds that dot the landscape.)

Above all, be ready to make new friends. If you were expecting to find these islands peopled by inward-looking folk, wrapped in splendid isolation, you'd be wrong. Orcadians and Shetlanders have been welcoming visitors from over the seas since time immemorial. Make this year the year they welcome you.

How do you get there?

Easily – by road, rail or air. Excellent roads bring you into the Highlands, some leading you to drive-on, drive-off ferries which connect you to the main islands. For train-lovers, the Inter-City service goes to Inverness, and the tracks in the Highlands lead you along some of the most beautiful rail journeys in the world.

Scottish Salmon – *one of nature's greatest foods*

Scottish Salmon is the King of Fish and part of Scotland's heritage. With its powerful body, sleek lines and its neat scales glistening with an iridescent sheen, it is quite simply magnficent.

Once, Scottish rivers held such abundant stocks of wild salmon that rich and poor alike could feast on them at will. Poached in vast copper kettles, they adorned the laird's table. Pickled, smoked and salted, they graced the captain's table on his distant voyages under sail. It is even said that a clause in Perth apprentices' indentures limited the number of salmon meals to no more than three per week.

Wild Scottish Salmon caught by rod or net have always been a seasonal delicacy, but several factors have caused the numbers landed to decline year after year. As they became rarer, so Scottish Salmon became relatively more expensive.

Scottish Salmon reared by painstaking husbandry in the security of the clear, clean inshore waters of the Scottish lochs and voes are however available all year round. It is the one luxury food which does not cost the earth.

Nutritionists agree on the value of salmon in the diet. A 4 oz portion has under 200 calories when steamed or poached. It contains protein, calcium and iron, as well as vitamins A and D, thiamin and riboflavin. Its natural oil includes two fatty acids resembling polyunsaturated vegetable oils. Current medical opinion suggests that these may help reduce the risk of heart disease by altering the way in which the blood clots, making it less able to stick to the arterial walls.

Scottish Salmon – *the pleasure can be yours*

Scottish Salmon is available all year round. It's one of life's affordable luxuries.

Scottish Salmon is delivered fresh with minimal handling to the counters of fishmongers and market stalls, shops and supermarkets, throughout many parts of the world.

Today more international chefs serve Scottish Salmon than ever before. It is proudly served at five star restaurants in London, Paris and New York.

Airlines, hotel chains and restaurants which care about their customers choose Scottish Salmon for all the benefits it brings them.

Scotch Whisky –
Spirit of Scotland

Scotch whisky is the national drink of Scotland. It is also the natural drink of Scotland, made only from the purest natural ingredients – golden barley, clear water and cool Scottish air.

Scotch whisky can only be called Scotch if it is distilled and matured in Scotland – by law it must be left to mature for a minimum of three years, but in practice most Scotch whisky is left to mature for much longer.

Few would venture to assert the precise moment at which Scotch whisky was first distilled. What is certain is that the ancient Celts practised the art, and had an expressive name for the fiery liquid they produced – 'uisge beatha' – the water of life.

For generations the Scots kept their whisky to themselves, distilling it in homes and farmhouses throughout the Highlands, Islands and glens alike. Then came the Government determined to tax it.

For more than 150 years, the wily Scots continued to distil their whisky, smuggling it down to the towns and cities, and outwitting the hated excise officers and revenue men, who are today the stuff of legend.

However, by the mid-19th century, most distilleries had legalised their businesses, and the foundations of today's Scotch whisky industry were laid.

There are four main stages in the pot still process – malting, mashing, fermentation and distilling. First the barley is steeped in water and then allowed to germinate, before being dried in a peat-fired kiln, the smoke of which contributes to the flavour and aroma of the final product.

Next, hot water is added to the ground malted barley in a mash tun to convert the starch into sugar. Then the mixture is transferred to a fermenting vat where yeast is added and fermentation converts the sugar into alcohol.

Finally, in the distinctively shaped swan-necked copper pot stills, distillation of the new spirit takes place. Most malt whisky is distilled twice, and only when the spirit reaches a high enough standard is it filled into oak casks and stored in cool dark warehouses where the long process of maturation takes place.

Unlike grain whiskies, malt whiskies vary enormously from one distillery to the next and one geographical region to another. The flavour of a malt depends on the water used, the distillation technique unique to that distillery, the size and type of cask, and the atmospheric temperature and humidity during maturation. There are over 100 different distilleries in Scotland, each producing its own distinctive malt whisky. The distilleries are divided geographically into Highland, Lowland, Islay and Campbeltown malts.

Highland malts are often subdivided into five further categories: the most famous whisky producing area is Speyside where some of the best known Highland malts are produced – Glenfiddich, Macallan, Cardhu, Glen Grant, Tamdhu and The Glenlivet to name but a few. The four other types of Highland malt are Eastern, Northern (of which Glenmorangie is probably the best known), Perthshire, e.g. Glenturret, and the Islands, which include Highland Park on Orkney and Talisker on Skye.

Islay malts range from the lighter peated Bunnahabhain and Bruichladdich through to the more heavily peated Laphroaig and Bowmore. Although close to Islay, on mainland Kintyre, the two remaining Campbeltown malts, Springbank and Glenscotia, have a distinctive style of their own, while Lowland Scotland is more associated with grain whisky production. However, there are ten malt whisky distilleries in that region, which extends as far south as Bladnoch in Wigtown.

Bunnahabhain
Bunnahabhain
Bunnahabhain
Bunnahabhain
Bunnahabhain
Bunnahabhain
Bunnahabhain
Bunnahabhain
Bunnahabhain

(Bū-na-ha-venn)

SINGLE
MALT
SCOTCH
WHISKY

AGED
12
YEARS

From the Isle of Islay, a soft mellow malt whisky of great
character and distinction
More characters. More character.

See Glassmaking at Caithness Glass

Perth

Visit the Caithness Glass Visitor Centre and Factory.
Factory Shop and Restaurant. Monday to Saturday 9.00am to 5.00pm.
Sunday 1.00pm to 5.00pm. (Sundays, Easter to end Sept. open 11.00am)
Glassmaking – Monday to Friday 9.00am to 4.30pm.
Car and Coach Parking.

Caithness Glass PLC, Inveralmond, Perth PH1 3TZ. Tel: 0738 37373.
On the north side of Perth on the A9.
Also at Wick, Oban and King's Lynn.

CAITHNESS GLASS
PRESTIGE AWARDS

In 1988, Caithness Glass PLC, one of Scotland's foremost glass manufacturers and designers, launched the Caithness Glass Prestige Award Scheme.

The object was to give recognition to existing high standards in the hotel and catering trade in Scotland and, by so doing, encourage others to emulate the winners.

The awards were restricted to establishments which are members of the Taste of Scotland Scheme and thus already identified as leaders in their particular category. The public was invited to help the judging panel by nominating hotels and restaurants in which they had experienced particularly good standards of food and service.

Taste of Scotland is pleased to record and congratulate the 1989 award winners in each category. These were:

Best Country House Hotel:	Cromlix House Kinbuck, near Dunblane
Best Town Hotel:	North West Castle Hotel Stranraer
Best Formal Restaurant:	The Cross Kingussie
Best Informal Restaurant:	Ostlers Close Cupar
Best Bar Lunch:	Smugglers Restaurant Glenturret Distillery, Crieff
Best Overall Excellence:	Auchterarder House Auchterarder

The trophies are held for one year and competed for again in the following year.

We invite you once again to help us select the 1990 winners by submitting nominations.

In 1990 the categories under competition are:

> *Best Hotel*
>
> *Best Restaurant*
>
> *Best Country House Hotel*
>
> *Best Hospitality & Welcome*
>
> *Best Newcomer to Taste of Scotland*

The sixth trophy will be awarded at the discretion of the Judging Panel to an establishment identified as worthy of special merit.

You will find details and nomination coupons on page 148 of this Guide, but letter and/or postcards are equally acceptable.

Closing date for entries: 15 September 1990.

The trophy symbol is shown against the winners' entries in the Guide.

Cheeses of Scotland

Meals play a very important part in the enjoyment of a holiday. One of the pleasures in life is food and Scotland can provide an excellent variety. The cheeses of Scotland are often full of flavour and texture and the discovery of a new variety can add such pleasure at the end of a meal.

As you travel around take the opportunity to look out for the different cheeses available and try them; you will find cheeses to suit every palate. A cheese, or a piece from a large cheese makes a very acceptable gift to take home to a friend or relative. On the islands of Orkney, Arran and Islay, individual Dunlop cheeses are made and the Orkney cheeses come in three types — white, coloured and smoked. Most of the cheddar cheese is made on the mainland along with a wide range of soft cheeses.

The range of soft Scottish cheese is now extensive and ingredients such as oatmeal, nuts, whisky, pepper and fruits are blended with local cheese to give a unique experience of one of Scotland's oldest industries. See how many Scottish cheeses you can find in shops and cheeseboards as you travel round Scotland and make your holiday a real *"Taste of Scotland"*.

This is the symbol of quality for Scottish Cheddar and Dunlop Cheese.

Here are some names to look our for —
"Crowdie, Caboc, Lothian, Pentland, Arran, Islay, Orkney, Gruth Dhu, Langskaill, Peat Smoked, Highland Herb, Highland Choice, Galic, Crowdie and Cream.

Aerial view of Dunoon, Argyll

△ New Lanark

Tarbert, Loch Fyne ▽

Loch Achray & Ben Venue

△ *Loch Vaa, near Aviemore*

Isle of Islay ▽

△ *Burghead Harbour, near Elgin*

Glengorm Castle, Isle of Mull ▽

△ *Edinburgh: Atholl Crescent*

Campbeltown ▽

△ Smailholm Tower, near Kelso

Kintyre ▽

Kirkcudbright Harbour

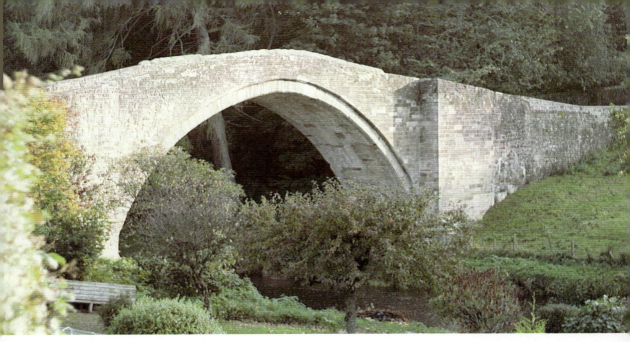

△ *Auld Brig o' Doon, Alloway*

Loch Nan Uamh, Arisaig ▽

△ *Glasgow: George Square*

Younger Botanic Gardens, Benmore, by Dunoon ▽

Kilchurn Castle, Loch Awe

Scotch Beef and Lamb

Scotland is world famous for producing the best Beef and Lamb in the world. For hundreds of years our farmers have, through selective breeding and good husbandry, successfully produced the high quality meat that the modern consumer demands. Scotch Beef is available in a wide selection of assorted cuts, and modern butchery methods have added new varieties to the range on offer. These require much less preparation and make a convenience food that is highly nutritious.

The recent formation of the Guild of Scotch Quality Meat Suppliers has further ensured that the high quality standards of Scotch Beef and Lamb are maintained throughout the production chain through to the consumer.

By ensuring that strict new specification standards are enforced and regular inspections of quality marked carcasses are carried out, consumers are guaranteed a new standard of excellence and eatability of Scotch Beef and Lamb.

Scotch Lamb is recognised as a high quality meat, being tender, with a fine, delicate flavour.

Co-operation between producers, processors and retailers, is resulting in the production of increasingly leaner, high yielding lambs which the modern consumer requires, and which enables the retailer to offer an increasingly wider range of new lamb products in addition to the traditional and boneless cuts familiar to everybody.

When buying lamb, the meat should be firm, fine grained, pinky brown in colour, with a light covering of creamy white fat.

Scotch Beef and Scotch Lamb, with their melting tenderness and superb flavour will make mouth-watering meals even with the simplest of cooking methods. Often the differences between the names of the cuts from region to region make it confusing for the visitor to Scotland. However, help is always near at hand in the Scottish butchers as they welcome enquiries and are always pleased to give advice on the most suitable cuts for a variety of dishes.

ABBEY ST BATHANS

Abbey St Bathans Tearoom & Interpretative Centre
Duns
Berwickshire
TD11 3TX
Tel: 036 14 237

From Cocksburnpath (A1), 6 miles. From Duns – Grantshouse rd to Cranshaw/Gifford rd, 4 miles; signposted Abbey St Bathans.

Former estate workshop and stable, attractively renovated with murals depicting life in the valley from the bronze age to the present day. Trout farm, interesting gallery with resident potters, walks through ancient oak woods. Beautiful secluded valley but well worth the visit. A self-service coffee/tea room.

Open May to Sept. Open Sundays only in Oct.
Lunch 11 am - 5 pm (a)
Unlicensed.

Smoked trout salad, home-made soups, pâté and quiche. Freshly made sandwiches, traditional home-baking.

No credit cards
Proprietor: W S J Dobie

ABERDEEN
2 E8

Ardoe House Hotel
Blairs
South Deeside Road
Aberdeen
AB1 5YP
Tel: 0224 867355

B9077, 3 miles west of Aberdeen.

An elegant silver-grey granite mansion with lofty turrets and inscriptions of heraldry. Only four minutes from Europe's oil capital in Aberdeen set in beautifully wooded parkland commanding a magnificent view of Royal Deeside.

Open all year
Rooms: 19 with private facilities
Breakfast 7.30 - 9.30 am
Bar Lunch 12 - 2 pm (a)
Lunch 12 - 2 pm (b)
Dinner 7 - 9.30 pm (d)
No dogs.
Bed & breakfast £40 -£65
Dinner B & B £55 - £80.50
STB 5 Crown Commended
Credit cards: 1, 2, 3, 5, 6

Caledonian Thistle Hotel
Union Terrace
Aberdeen
AB9 1HE
Tel: 0224 640233
Telex: 73758
Fax: 0224 641627
City centre

The hotel overlooks Union Terrace Gardens in the business and tourist centre of Aberdeen. The elegant restaurant and cocktail bar are luxuriously furnished and offer traditional standards of service, hospitality and cuisine. For the less formal – try Elrond's Cafe bar and restaurant providing an interesting and reasonably priced meal.

Open all year
Rooms: 80 with private facilities
Breakfast 7 - 10 am
Bar Lunch 12 - 2.30 pm (a)
Lunch 12.30 - 2 pm (c)
Dinner 6.30 - 10 pm
Bed & breakfast £30 - £77.75
Dinner B & B £39.50 - £93.70
Fresh local game, poultry and locally caught fish are featured on all menus.
STB 5 Crown Commended
RAC 4 Star
AA 3 Star B
Credit cards: 1, 2, 3, 4, 5, 6 + Trumpcard

Craighaar Hotel
Waterton Road
Bucksburn
Aberdeen
AB2 9HS
Tel: 0224 712275

Turn off A96 at Greenburn Drive. Follow to end then turn left up Waterton Road.

Privately-run hotel with friendly atmosphere, has a long-established custom from local business community. Renowned for fresh produce prepared and presented imaginatively by skilled chefs.

Open all year
Rooms: 41 with private facilities
Breakfast 7 - 10 am
Bar Lunch 12 - 2 pm (b)
Bar Supper 6.30 - 10 pm (b)
Dinner 7 - 9.30 pm (d)
No dogs.
Bed & breakfast from £38
Dinner B & B from £53
Gairloch scallops and crab claws with shallots and cream flavoured with basil then served in a puff-pastry shell. Medallions of Highland venison with shallots and juniper berries flamed with gin.
RAC 2 Star
Credit cards: 1, 2, 3, 5

Craiglynn Hotel
36 Fonthill Road
Aberdeen
AB1 2UJ
Tel: 0224 584050

Midway between Union Street and King George IV Bridge. Car park access from Bon Accord Street.

Craiglynn, an impressive granite building with many unique features is run in a relaxed yet efficient manner. The theme being "Victorian elegance with modern comforts". Dinner menus are decided upon daily and always offer an interesting choice of dishes carefully cooked using local produce when available. Dinner reservations essential for non-residents.

Open all year
Rooms: 9,1 with private facilities
Breakfast 7.30 - 9 am
Dinner 7 - 7.30 pm (c)
Reservations required for non-residents.
No smoking in dining room.
No dogs.
Bed & breakfast £17 - £21
Dinner B & B £27.50 - £31.50
Leek and potato soup, grilled Dee salmon, apple and bramble crumble . . . A sample of the many and varied dishes frequently offered.
STB 2 Crown Commended
Credit cards: 1, 2, 3, 5
Proprietors: Chris & Hazel Mann

New Marcliffe Hotel
51-53 Queens Road
Aberdeen
AB9 2PE
Tel: 0224 321371

Direct access north and south from A92.

Relaxing and comfortable accommodation with a sophisticated surrounding. Elegant table settings and a quietly efficient service. West end rendezvous for the business community and visitors to the city. Carvery lunches and à la carte dinner. The "in-season" produce of Scotland's fields, moors, rivers and seas is cooked with flair in traditional and innovative ways.

Open all year except 26 Dec, 1 and 2 Jan.
Rooms: 27 with private facilities
Breakfast 7.30 - 9.30 am
Bar Lunch 12 - 2.30 pm (b)
Bar Supper 6.30 - 9.30 pm (b)
Dinner 7 - 9.45 pm (d)
No dogs.
Bed & Breakfast from £50
Dinner B & B from £65
STB 4 Crown Commended
AA 3 Star L.
Credit cards: 1, 2, 3, 5, 6
Proprietors: Stewart & Sheila Spence.

Stakis Tree Tops Hotel

Springfield Road
Aberdeen
AB9 2QH
Tel: 0224 313377
Telex: 73794
Fax: 0224 312028

Situated at west end of Aberdeen off A92 road to Dundee.

Elegant, modern hotel with split-level Regency-style restaurant. Set in wooded landscaped gardens with indoor swimming pool and leisure complex. The chef makes intelligent use of fresh local produce.

Open all year

Rooms: 113 with private facilities
Breakfast 7 - 10 am; Sun 8 - 10.30 am
Lunch 12.30 - 2 pm (b).
Dinner 7 - 10 pm (c).
High Tea on request. Taste of Scotland applies to Garden Restaurant only.
Bed & breakfast from £49.
Dinner B & B from £29 (min. 2 nights stay).

Menu features local produce, including local game, fish and beef. Salmon.

STB 5 Crown Commended.
RAC 4 Star.
AA 4 Star.

Credit cards: 1, 2, 3, 4, 5, 6

Westhill Hotel

Westhill
Aberdeen
AB3 6TT
Tel: 0224 740388
Telex: 739925
Fax: 0224 744354

On A944 7 miles west of Aberdeen city centre.

Situated in pleasant suburban surroundings this modern hotel is only 15 minutes drive from the centre of Aberdeen. The hotel has 52 bedrooms (all en-suite facilities), lounge, cocktail and public bars, restaurant and function suite. Recently refurbished "Castles Restaurant" is highly popular and serves excellent local and international cuisine.

Open all year

Rooms: 52 with private facilities
Breakfast 7.30 - 9.30 am
Bar Lunch 12 - 2 pm (a)
Lunch 12 - 2 pm (b)
Bar Supper 5.30 - 9.30 pm (a)
Dinner 7 - 10 pm (c)
Dinner not served on Christmas Day.
Facilities for the disabled.
Bed & breakfast £29 - £42
Dinner B & B £41 - £54
Weekend breaks 2 nights Dinner B&B £65 per person.

Prime Aberdeen Angus steaks grilled or in special sauces and seasonal fresh fish caught locally, all with fresh local produce.

STB 3 Crown Approved
RAC 3 Star M
AA 3 Star

Credit cards: 1, 2, 3, 5

ABERDOUR
3   **G6**

Hawkcraig House

Aberdour
Fife
KY3 0TZ
Tel: 0383 860335

Hawkcraig Point, Aberdour.

Elma Barrie has earned a fine reputation for this old ferryman's house at water's edge, overlooking harbour, Inchcolm Island and 12th century abbey. Seals and seabirds abound, yet only 30 minutes from Edinburgh by road or rail. Gleneagles and St Andrews equally accessible from this favoured corner of Scotland, rich in history, castles and stately houses.

Open Feb to mid Dec

Rooms: 2 with private facilities
Dinner 7 - 9 pm (d)
Breakfast and lunch (c) by arrangement.
Open to non-residents – booked meals only. Take your own wine.
No smoking.
Unlicensed.
Bed & breakfast from £13
Dinner B & B from £25

Home cooking par excellence, using prime Scottish produce.

STB 2 Crown Commended

No credit cards

Proprietor: Elma Barrie

ABERFELDY
4   **F6**

Guinach House

by The Birks
Aberfeldy
Perthshire
PH15 2ET
Tel: 0887 20251

On A826, south-west outskirts of Aberfeldy, on road to 'The Birks' Guinach is signposted from Urlar Road.

Luxurious country house hotel in its own secluded garden grounds, with friendly atmosphere and glorious views of the Perthshire Highlands. Superb cuisine and wines are served in the elegant dining room at candle-lit tables.

Open 20 Mar to late Oct.

Rooms: 6 with private facilities
Breakfast 8.30 - 9.30 am
Dinner 7.30 - 8 pm (d)
Guests are requested not to smoke in the dining room.
Bed & breakfast from £27.50
Dinner B & B from £42.50.

Four-course dinners, imaginative menus incorporating Scottish specialities – fresh Tay salmon, pan-fried trout, haunch of Atholl venison, medallions of Scotch lamb, prime beef. Full Scottish breakfast.

STB 3 Crown Highly Commended
RAC Acclaimed
AA Selected

No credit cards

Proprietors: R A & M A Lorge

CREDIT/CHARGE CARDS	
1	Access/Mastercard/Eurocard
2	American Express
3	Visa
4	Carte Bleu
5	Diners Club
6	Mastercharge

Buffers
Station Square
Aboyne
Aberdeenshire
Tel: 033 98 86747

Main Deeside road.

Situated in the old Station Square of
Aboyne on Royal Deeside. This is a cosy
restaurant offering simple well cooked
food from the freshest of produce.

Open all year

Breakfast 8 - 10.30 am (a)
Lunch 10.30 - 2.30 pm (a)
High Tea 2.30 - 6.30 pm (a)

Facilities for the disabled

No credit cards

Proprietor: Fiona Cox

ABERFOYLE
5   F5

Forest Hills Hotel
Kinlochard
by Aberfoyle
Stirling
FK8 3TL
Tel: 08777 277

*4½ miles from Aberfoyle on B829 to Loch
Lomond.*

Country house hotel and country club on
timeshare estate in the beautiful
Trossachs area. Extensive leisure centre.
Imaginative food and wines with a
wonderful selection of malts. All rooms
with private facilities, satellite TV,
telephone and tea-making facilities.

Open all year.

Rooms: 16 with private facilities
Breakfast 8.15 - 9.30 am
Bar Lunch 12 - 2 pm except Sun + Sat (a)
Lunch 12.30 - 2 pm Sun only (b)
Dinner 7.30 - 9 pm (c)
No dogs in public rooms.
Bed & breakfast from £30
Dinner B & B from £40

*Salmon, trout, venison, grouse, pheasant
and other game. Delicious steaks and
Scottish lamb. Roasts of pork and beef.
Exciting chef's specialities.*

STB 4 Crown Commended

Credit cards: 1, 2, 3, 5

ABERLADY
6   G7

Kilspindie House Hotel
Main Street
Aberlady
East Lothian
EH32 0RE
Tel: 087 57 682

On A198 in centre of Aberlady village.

Kilspindie House is a small hotel
personally run by the Binnie family for the
last 22 years. Centrally situated in the
conservation village of Aberlady, the hotel
is only 20 minutes' drive from Edinburgh
and within easy reach of East Lothian's
tourist attractions.

Open all year

Rooms: 26 with private facilities
Breakfast 7.30 - 9.15 am
Bar Lunch 12 - 2.15 pm (a)
Lunch 12 - 2.15 pm (b)
High Tea 5 - 6 pm
Dinner 7.30 - 8.30 pm (c)
Bar meals 12 - 9 pm during summer
Bed & breakfast from £24
Dinner B & B from £34

*Trout Rob Roy, Steak Balmoral, Scampi
Maison. Accent on local produce.*

STB 4 Crown Commended
RAC 2 Star
AA 2 Star

Credit cards: 3, 5, 6

Proprietor: Raymond Binnie.

Altnaharra Hotel
Altnaharra
Sutherland
IV27 4UE
Tel: 054 981 222

A836, 21 miles north of Lairg

One of Scotland's most famous fishing
hotels situated in the heart of beautiful
Sutherland offering comfort and warmth.
Open to non-residents and non-sporting
guests. Specialising in all requirements for
the angler and outdoor enthusiast with an
emphasis on comfort and cuisine.

Open Mar to Nov.

Rooms: 20 with private facilities
Breakfast 7.45 - 9 am
Bar Lunch 12 - 2.15 pm (b)
Dinner 7.30 - 8.30 pm (c)
No smoking in dining room
Bed & breakfast rates on application
Dinner B & B from £40

*Scottish beef, lamb, fresh salmon (subject
to availability), home-made soups and
desserts.*

Credit cards: 1, 3

Proprietor: Paul Panchaud

Craw's Nest Hotel

Anstruther
Fife
KY10 3OS
Tel: 0333 310691
Telex: 727049

Centre of Anstruther on A917 coast road, south of St Andrews.

This is very much a family owned and run hotel in what was originally an old Scottish manse, with recent additions. Well placed for the many interesting towns and harbours of the East Neuk of Fife, and offering straight forward presentation of good local produce, especially fish.

Open all year.

Rooms: 50 with private facilities
Breakfast 8 - 10 am
Bar Lunch 12.15 - 1.50 pm (a)
Lunch 12.15 - 1.50 pm (a)
High Tea 4.30 - 6 pm
Dinner 7 - 8.45 pm (c)
Bed & breakfast from £25
Dinner B & B from £32

Roast Aberdeen Angus, Craw's Nest stuffing; local scampi; Pittenweem haddock, fresh salmon, crab, prawns in season.

RAC 3 Star
AA 3 Star

Credit cards: 1, 2, 3, 4, 5, 6

Proprietor: I Birrell

CREDIT/CHARGE CARDS

1 Access/Mastercard/Eurocard
2 American Express
3 Visa
4 Carte Bleu
5 Diners Club
6 Mastercharge

Invercreran Country House Hotel

Glen Creran
Appin
Argyll
PA38 4BJ
Tel: 063 173 414/456

Just off Oban-Fort William road A828 at head of Loch Creran, 14 miles north of the Connel Bridge.

Superlatives are often overused. But not here. This is a gem of a place, strikingly different. A uniquely styled modern mansion house luxuriously appointed and with truly magnificent views of the hills and glens. Marie and John Kersley with their family have created a haven of total relaxation and enjoyment.

Open all year

Rooms: 7 with private facilities
Breakfast 8.15 - 9.15 am
Lunch 12 - 2 pm (b)
Dinner 7 - 8.15 pm (e)
No smoking in the restaurant.
No dogs.
Bed & breakfast £30 - £40
Dinner B & B £50 - £60

Emphasis on locally landed seafood, selection of finest Scottish meat and game, prepared with close attention to detail and presentation.

STB 4 Crown Commended
BTA Commended

Credit card: 1, 3

Proprietor: John Kersley

Byre Restaurant

Redford
Carmyllie
Arbroath, Angus
DD11 2QZ
Tel: 02416 245

B961 Dundee to Brechin route.

Original stone-built byre on a dairy farm. The unpretentious restaurant occupies the full length of the building opening into a peaceful garden where tables are available for service also. Home-made jams, marmalade and honey together with a variety of cakes are for sale. The restaurant is also decorated with a selection of pottery and house plants.

Open Mar to Dec and at weekends in Jan and Feb.

Morning coffee 10 am - 12 noon.
Bar Lunch 12 - 2 pm (a)
Lunch 12 -2 pm (b)
High Tea 4.30 - 6.30 pm

Home-made steak pie, steak bridie, bannocks and cheese, Arbroath smokie flan, Scotch broth. Clootie dumpling.

No credit cards

Proprietor: Anne Law

Carriage Room Restaurant

Montrose Road
Arbroath
Angus
DD11 5RA
Tel: 0241 75755

On the Montrose road ½ mile north of Arbroath.

The Carriage Room is a large, opulent, purpose-built, sixty-seater restaurant. There is a comfortable lounge and bar area luxuriously furnished where pre-dinner drinks and after-dinner coffee are served.

Open all year except one week in January.

Bar Lunch 12 - 2 pm (a) } except Sun,
Lunch 12 - 2 pm (b) } Mon, Sat (a)
Dinner 7.15 - 9.30 pm (d)

Pheasant, pigeon, venison, fish and shellfish, heather honey and Armagnac ice cream.

Credit cards: 1, 2, 3, 5

Proprietor: Stephen Collinson

Loch Duich Hotel
Ardelve
by Kyle of Lochalsh
IV40 8DY
Tel: 059 985 213

7 miles from Kyle of Lochalsh/Skye ferry on the A87 from Fort William and Inverness (via Loch Ness).

Dramatically situated at the junction of three sea lochs overlooking ancient Eilean Donan Castle and the mountains of Kintail and Skye. This award-winning hotel wants to entice you to experience the joy of its situation, the warmth of its welcome and the delights of its delicious, carefully prepared food.

Open mid Mar to Nov and for bookings only Nov to mid Mar.

Rooms: 18, 17 with private facilities
Breakfast 8.30 - 9.30 am
Bar Lunch 12.30 - 1.45 pm (a)
Dinner 7 - 9 pm (c)
Earlier breakfast easily arranged.
Bed & breakfast £15 - £18
Dinner B & B from £30

Potato and Stilton soup, smoked haddock loaf, queenie scallop crumble, oysters and mussels, wild salmon, local langoustines, lobster, crab, wild duck, pigeon, venison, heather lamb, walnut tart.

AA   1 Star + Rosette.

No credit cards

Proprietor: R C Stenson

Ardentinny Hotel
Loch Long
near Dunoon
Argyll
PA23 8TR
Tel: 036 981 209
Fax: 036 981 345

M8 to Gourock, Ferry to Dunoon, A815 then A880 – or drive round Loch Lomond.

Old coaching inn circa 1720 fully modernised but retaining many old features. Lovely gardens to the sea and lying in the mountainous Argyll Forest Park. The hotel dining room and buttery very popular with yachtsmen, fishers and walkers. All bedrooms with private facilities and good views of the loch or mountains.

Open Mar to Nov.

Rooms: 11 with private facilities
Breakfast 8.30 - 9.30 am
Bar Lunch 12 - 3 pm (a)
Sunday Brunch 12 - 3 pm
Bar Supper 6.30 - 9.30 pm
Dinner 7.30 - 9 pm (d)
No smoking in dining room
Bed & breakfast £23 - £32
Dinner B & B £32 - £50

Stronchullin steaks, lobster salads, prawn soup, Glenfinnart venison casserole, Loch Long langoustine, Argyll lamb with heather honey, sweets prepared daily, speciality coffees with Ardentinny mints.

STB   3 Crown Commended

AA   2 Star H

Credit cards: 1, 2, 3, 5

Proprietors: John & Thyrza Horn,   Hazel Hall

The Arisaig Hotel
Arisaig
Inverness-shire
PH39 4NH
Tel: 06875 210

At the edge of Arisaig village on A830 Fort William to Mallaig road, 10 miles before Mallaig on Loch Nan Ceall.

Coaching inn from early 18th century with additions through Victorian times until now. On the roadside on the sea shore at the edge of village. Run by the Stewarts as large family home furnished in keeping with style of building. Open fires in public rooms – all home comforts in bedrooms.

Open all year.

Rooms: 15, 6 with private facilities
Breakfast 8.30 - 10 am
Bar Lunch 12.30 - 2 pm (a)
High Tea 5 - 6.30 pm
Dinner 7.30 - 8.30 pm (d)
No smoking in main dining room.
Bed & breakfast £20 - £35
Dinner B & B £33.50 - £54

Local seafood, lobster, prawns, clams, halibut, turbot etc. Home-made soups and puddings. Traditional breakfast with Mallaig kippers.

AA   2 Star H

No credit cards

Proprietors: George, Janice & Gordon   Stewart

Auchrannie Country House Hotel
Auchrannie Road
Brodick
Isle of Arran
KA27 8BZ
Tel: 0770 2234

One mile north of Brodick Ferry Terminal and 400 yards from Brodick Golf Club.

Nestling among Scots pines this delightful country house has been tastefully refurbished to highest standards. All rooms have private facilities. The renowned Garden Restaurant offers varied menus with particular emphasis on fresh local produce including seafood. A haven of comfort and charm from which to enjoy the splendours of Arran.

Open all year.

Rooms: 12 with private facilities
Breakfast 8.30 - 9.30 am; 9 - 10 am Sun
Lunch 12.30 - 2.30 pm (b)
High Tea 6 - 6.30 pm (children only)
Dinner 6.30 - 10 pm (d)
No dogs.
Bed & breakfast £18.50 - £35.50.
Dinner B & B £31 - £48.50.

Free range fowl. Fresh local dishes such as wild salmon, trout and marinated scallops.

STB   4 Crown Commended

Credit cards: 1, 3

Proprietor: Iain Johnston

Glenisle Hotel
Lamlash
Isle of Arran
KA27 8LS
Tel: 07706 559/258

Via car ferry from Ardrossan, Ayrshire (50 minutes), or Clonaig on Kintyre (30 minutes).

The Glenisle Hotel is centrally situated in the sleepy 'laid back' bayside village of Lamlash. Seafront location with attractive garden. Restaurant with unique cocktail lounge – the Talisman Bar – featuring wooden carvings from that famous Clyde steamer. The hotel is centrally heated and open fires keep it extra cosy.

Open all year.

Rooms: 13 with private facilities
Breakfast 8.30 - 9.30 am
Lunch 12 - 2 pm (a)
Dinner 6.30 - 9 pm (b)
Bed & breakfast £16 - £21
Dinner B & B £24.50 - £29.50
STB   4 Crown Commended
Credit cards: 1, 3
Proprietor: Alice Toomey

Shedock Farm

Shiskine
Isle of Arran
KA27 8EW
Tel: 0770 86 261

String road, Brodick to Blackwaterfoot (B880).

Traditional farmhouse built in 1885 specialising in pony-trekking holidays. Situated in the Shiskine valley at the heart of the Isle of Arran. A working farm of approx 270 acres facing out over the Mull of Kintyre.

Open Apr to late Sep.

Rooms: 5
Breakfast from 9 am
Dinner from 6 pm (b)
Unlicensed
Bed & breakfast from £12
Dinner B & B from £16

No credit cards

Proprietor: Jan MacAlister

AUCHENCAIRN
16 16

Balcary Bay Hotel

Auchencairn
near Castle Douglas
Kirkcudbrightshire
DG7 1QZ
Tel: 055664 217/311

Off A711 Dalbeattie to Kirkcudbright.

Family-run country house hotel in secluded and delightful situation on the shores of the bay, standing in three acres of garden. All rooms with colour TV, tea/coffee facilities, telephone, hairdryer. Ideal base for all leisure activities or a relaxing holiday with good food and wine.

Open Mar to Nov

Rooms: 13, 12 with private facilities
Breakfast 8.30 - 9.45 am
Bar Lunch 12 - 2 pm (a)
Lunch 12 - 2 pm (c) - by prior arrangement
Dinner 7 - 9 pm (c)
Bed & breakfast £22 - £33
Dinner B & B £35 - £45
Seasonal and 3 or 7 day reductions.

Fresh local seafood including Solway salmon and lobster cooked in a variety of ways. Galloway beef and lamb.

STB 4 Crown Commended
RAC 3 Star R
AA   3 Star HL

Credit cards: 1, 3

Proprietor: Ronald & Jean Lamb

AUCHTERARDER
17 F6

Auchterarder House

Auchterarder
Perthshire
PH3 1DZ
Tel: 0764 63646/7
Fax: 0764 62939

B8062 Auchterarder-Crieff road

Ian and Audrey Brown have created a magnificent small luxury hotel from this fine old mansion house which stands in 17½ acres of mature lawns and wooded grounds. There are sumptuous public rooms and the Chef creates imaginative dishes with fresh local produce and presents them with flair.

Open all year.

Rooms: 11 with private facilities
Breakfast, lunch and dinner when required.
No children.
Bed & breakfast £70 - £100
Dinner B & B rates on application

Emphasis on Scottish food and local produce. Reservations essential.

STB 5 Crown Highly Commended

Credit cards: 1, 2, 3, 4, 5, 6

Best Overall Excellence 1989

Proprietors: Ian & Audrey Brown

Cairn Lodge

Orchil Road
Auchterarder
Perthshire
PH3 1LX
Tel: 0764 62634

In the village of Auchterarder.

Attractive country house with five comfortable bedrooms each with colour TV offering every opportunity to relax and enjoy an extended stay or just an overnight stop. Elegant restaurant, quiet leisurely atmosphere, a meal of the highest quality complemented by a good selection of fine wines and malt whisky. Enjoy a truly warm welcome at the Cairn Lodge.

Open all year except 26 Dec, 1 and 2 Jan

Rooms: 5 with private facilities
Breakfast 8 - 9.30 am
Bar Lunch 12 - 2 pm (a)
Lunch 12 - 2 pm (c)
Dinner 7 - 9.30 pm in summer; 7 - 9 pm in winter
No dogs.
Bed & breakfast £45.50 - £75
Dinner B & B rates on application.

Seasonal specialities – seafood, game, local produce.

STB 4 Crown Commended
RAC Highly Acclaimed

Credit cards: 1, 2, 3

Proprietor: Gilberto Chiodetto

The Gleneagles Hotel

Auchterarder
Perthshire
PH3 1NF
Tel: 0764 62231
Telex: 76105
Fax: 0764 62134

½ mile west of A9, 8 miles north of Dunblane.

A magnificent hotel of international reputation. A resort in itself. A spectacular Scottish 'palace' in rolling Perthshire countryside. Five restaurants, each using the best Scottish produce, range from the relaxed Dormy House Grill (open April to October) to the exquisite Conservatory, while traditional afternoon tea is also served. The Gleneagles Hotel is Britain's only country hotel to receive the AA's highest accolade of five red stars.

Open all year

Rooms: 236 with private facilities
Breakfast 7.30 - 10.30 am
Lunch 12 - 3 pm (f)
Dinner 7 - 10 pm (f)
Country Club Brasserie and Equestrian Centre Restaurant & Bar - residents and members only. 'Braids' Champagne Bar open from 6.30 pm.
Bed & breakfast £76 - £107
Dinner B & B £89.75 - £134.50

RAC 5 Star
AA   5 Star

Credit cards: 1, 2, 3, 5, 6 + Carte Blanche

AUCHTERMUCHTY
18 F6

Ardchoille Farm Guest House
Dunshalt
Auchtermuchty
KY14 7EY
Tel: 0337 28414

Just outside Dunshalt village on B936, 1½ miles south of Auchtermuchty.

Donald and Isobel Steven welcome you to Ardchoille – a spacious, well appointed centrally heated farmhouse, with superb views of the Lomond hills. Twin-bedrooms have colour TV and tea/coffee trays with home-made butter shortbread. Large comfortable lounge. Attractive dining room where delicious freshly prepared meals are served with flair and imagination. Excellent base for touring, golfing or just relaxing. Guests welcome to take own wine.

Open all year
Rooms: 3 with private facilities
Breakfast 7.30 - 9.30 am
Dinner 6.30 - 8 pm (d)
Breakfast earlier by arrangement.
Packed lunches to order.
No smoking in dining room.
Residents only.
Unlicensed.
No dogs.
Bed & breakfast £16 - £20
Dinner B & B from £28.50

Auchtermuchty broth, Pittenweem sole in a sweet green pepper sauce, roast leg of Scotch lamb with apricot and walnut stuffing, fresh orange souffle – Grand Marnier with home-made vanilla ice-cream.

STB 3 Crown Commended
No credit cards
Proprietors: Donald & Isobel Steven.

AULTBEA
19 D4

Drumchork Lodge Hotel
Aultbea
Ross-shire
IV22 2HU
Tel: 044 582 242

Off A832, on hillside above Aultbea.

This quiet, friendly family run hotel is situated on the hillside above the village and commands spectacular views over Loch Ewe. The famous Inverewe Gardens are only six miles away and there are many interesting walks in the area.

Welcoming peat, log and coal fires during the winter months.

Open all year (restricted service during winter).

Rooms: 11 with private facilities
Breakfast 8.30 - 9 am
Bar Lunch 12 - 2 pm (a)
Bar Supper 5.30 - 8 pm (b)
Dinner 7 - 8 pm (d)
Bed & breakfast from £27
Dinner B & B from £38

Home-made soups. Locally caught fish and shellfish. Scottish prime meats and venison. Home-made desserts a speciality.

STB 3 Crown Commended
RAC 2 Star
AA 2 Star

Credit cards: 1, 3.
Proprietors: Cooper Family.

AVIEMORE
20 E6

Stakis Coylumbridge Resort Hotel
Coylumbridge
Aviemore
Inverness-shire
PH22 1QN
Tel: 0479 810661
Telex: 75272
Fax: 0479 811309

30 miles south of Inverness and 75 miles north of Perth on A9.

The Coylumbridge Resort Hotel, situated in the heart of the Scottish Highlands is the ideal centre for outdoor leisure and sporting pursuits. There are two indoor heated pools, a sauna, whirlpool, multi-gym and games room. Two tennis courts, putting green, children's adventure play area, clay and pistol shooting and archery.

Open all year
Rooms: 176 with private facilities
Breakfast 7.30 - 10.30 am
Lunch 12.30 - 2 pm (b)
High tea (children) 4.30 - 6 pm
Dinner 6.30 - 9.15 pm (c)
All day bistro 12 noon - 10 pm (a)
Room rate £58
Dinner B & B £31 (min. 2 nights stay)

Medallions of stag in a sloe gin sauce. Baked Scottish sea trout. Woodlands pheasant.

STB 4 Crown Commended
Credit cards: 1, 2, 3, 5

Stakis Four Seasons Hotel
Aviemore
PH22 1PF
Tel: 0479 810681
Telex: 75213
Fax: 0479 810862

Country location adjacent to Aviemore Centre.

Stakis Four Seasons Hotel is one of the finest in the scenic Spey Valley. This luxurious hotel provides the ideal base for a visit to Aviemore – Britain's premier leisure resort. Tastefully decorated bedrooms provide the ultimate in comfort; the charming cocktail bar is the perfect place to relax after an active day; and only the best of cuisine can be enjoyed in the elegant Four Seasons Restaurant. Hotel's own first class leisure centre. A lovely place to stay.

Open all year
Rooms: 89 with private facilities
Breakfast 8 - 10 am
Lunch 12.30 - 2.30 pm (b)
Dinner 7 - 9.30 pm (d-f)
Bed & breakfast from £49
Dinner B & B from £35 (min. 2 nights stay)

Highland game platter, smoked salmon roulade. Salmon and dill butter, Scottish venison, fillet of Angus beef.

STB 5 Crown Highly Commended
AA 4 Star
Credit cards: 1, 2, 3, 5

The Winking Owl
Main Road
Aviemore
Inverness-shire
PH22 1RH
Tel: 0479 810646

400 yards north of railway station in town's main street.

Restaurant in converted farm cottage standing in its own grounds, set back from the road in the village's main street. Cosy dining room and cocktail bar with popular pub on first floor (but away from dining room). Friendly, family-run business renowned for good food and value for money.

Open all year except mid Nov to mid Dec.
Dinner 6.15 - 9.30 pm (c-d)

Taste of Scotland applies to restaurant only.

▶

Local salmon, venison and game in season, Scottish lobster and scallops when available. Beef, pork, lamb, home-made soups, pâtés, bread and fresh vegetables are presented in a wide range of dishes.
Credit cards: 1, 2, 3, 5
Proprietor: W McConnachie

AYR
21   H5

Burns Byre Restaurant
Mount Oliphant Farm
Alloway
Ayr
KA6 6BU
Tel: 0292 43744

Signposted off A77 south of Ayr to Corton, opposite turn-off to Alloway.

Enjoy Scottish food in the warm and intimate setting of the original byre of Mount Oliphant Farm, with its unspoiled and traditional farmhouse surroundings. Savour the authentic background of Robert Burns' home in his early years (1766-77). Informal atmosphere together with the highest standards of traditional and modern Scottish cuisine.

Open all year

Light lunch 12.15 - 2 pm
Lunch 12.15 - 2 pm (b)
Dinner 7 - 9.30 pm (e)
Credit cards: 1, 2, 3, 5
Proprietor: Duncan Baird

Burns Monument Hotel
Alloway
Ayr
KA7 4PQ
Tel: 0292 42466

In Alloway village on B7024, 2 miles south of Ayr town centre.

An elegant and charming historic hotel located in the famous Alloway village. Splendidly situated in its own grounds with landscaped gardens along the banks of the River Doon with the backdrop of Burns Monument and Auld Brig of Doon. Locally renowned restaurant using only the best of fresh local produce.

Open all year

Rooms: 9, 8 with private facilities
Breakfast 8 - 9.30 am; 8 - 10 am Sun
Bar Lunch 12 - 2.15 pm (a)
Lunch 12 - 2.15 pm (b)
High Tea 5 - 9.45 pm
Dinner 7 - 9.45 pm (d)
Bed & breakfast £20 - £25
Dinner B & B from £30 - £35

Imaginative cuisine featuring locally caught seafood, with meat, game and poultry from the hotel's farm. Fresh Ayrshire potatoes in season, locally produced haggis.
STB   4 Crown Commended
RAC   2 Star
AA   2 Star
Credit cards: 1, 2, 3, 5
Proprietor: Robert Gilmour

Fouters Bistro Restaurant
2A Academy Street
Ayr
KA7 1HS
Tel: 0292 261391

Town centre, opposite Town Hall & Tourist Information Centre.

Situated in the vaults of an old bank, the place exudes a warm and friendly almost Provence-like atmosphere. The best available local produce is prepared with the care it deserves, and served with panache. The welcome is genuine, the food is superb. Do reserve in advance.

Open all year

Lunch 12 - 2 pm (b)
Dinner 6.30 - 10.30 pm; 7 - 10 pm Sun (d)
Ayrshire pheasant with game sauce. Red deer with orange and Glayva butter sauce. Local guinea-fowl with redcurrant and green peppercorn sauce. Smoked chicken and venison. Seafood a speciality.
Credit cards: 1, 2, 3, 4, 5, 6
Proprietors: Laurie & Fran Black

The Hunny Pot
37 Beresford Terrace
Ayr
KA7 2EU
Tel: 0292 263239

In the town centre of Ayr close to Burns' Statue Square.

This is a small but popular and attractive coffee shop and health food restaurant run personally by Felicity Thomson. Pine furniture and a Pooh Bear theme give the place character.

Open all year.

Meals served all day from 10 am - 10 pm (a)
Unlicensed.
No smoking area in restaurant.
All home-made soups, scones, brown sugar meringues, cakes and dish of the day. Puddings include seasonal fruit crumbles, hazelnut meringue cake. Scottish cheeses with oatcakes.
No credit cards
Proprietor: Felicity Thomson

Pickwick Hotel
19 Racecourse Road
Ayr
KA7 2TD
Tel: 0292 260111
Fax: 0292 611295

On A719 Ayr-Dunure road, ½ mile from Ayr Town Centre.

A magnificent period character building set in its own extensive landscaped gardens and featuring a traditional Dickensian theme characteristic of its name. The hotel is family run and features 15 excellent bedrooms, all with full private facilities. Conveniently close to Ayr Town Centre and all Ayr's amenities, and only a few minutes' walk from the sea-front. Large beer garden.

Open all year

Rooms: 15 with private facilities
Breakfast 7.30 - 9.30 am
Bar Lunch 12 - 2.15 pm (a)
Lunch 12 - 2.15 pm (b)
High Tea 5 - 6.30 pm (b)
Bar Supper 5 - 9.45 pm (b)
Dinner 7 - 9.45 (d)
Bed & breakfast from £27.50
Dinner B & B from £40

Fresh local seafood. Home-made soups and sweet trolley. Fresh prime local beef and poultry. Menu changed daily according to availability of fresh produce.
STB   Award Pending
RAC   3 Star
AA   3 Star
Credit cards: 1, 2, 3, 5, 6
Proprietor: Robert S Gilmour

The Stables Restaurant & Coffee House
Queen's Court
Sandgate
Ayr
KA7 1BD
Tel: 0292 283704

Immediately behind the Tourist Information Centre in the Sandgate.

In the centre of Ayr is a tiny Georgian Courtyard which is a haven of little shops with a tea garden. The Stables were built of local stone probably in the late 1760s. The restaurant (evenings only) could best be described as ethnic Scottish. The Coffee House offers lighter fare.

Open all year except evenings in November

►

Dinner 6.30 - 10 pm except Sun, Mon (c-d)
Coffee shop open 10 am - 10 pm (a-b) but closed all Sun, and Mon evening. No smoking area - daytime only.
Mussels in syboe butter, lamb roasted with apricot and rosemary, venison and juniper pie, cranachan and local cheeses. Wines from Moniack Castle and English vineyards.
Credit cards: 1, 2, 3, 4, 5, 6
Proprietor: Ed Baines

BALLACHULISH
22   F4

The Ballachulish Hotel
Ballachulish
Argyll
PA39 4JY
Tel: 08552 606
On A828 at the Ballachulish Bridge.
The Ballachulish Hotel commands an inspiring panorama over Loch Linnhe to the peaks of Morvern and Ardgour. In this friendly family-owned hotel, careful restoration and refurbishment have ensured a skilful blend of traditional style with modern international standards. Gracious baronial lounges lead to an elegant cocktail bar and the Loch View Restaurant.
Open all year
Rooms: 30 with private facilities
Breakfast 8 - 9.30 am
Bar Meals 12.30 - 10 pm (a)
Dinner 7 - 10 pm (d)
Unlicensed
Bed & breakfast £19.50 - £27
Dinner B & B £32.50 - £39.50
Local fresh seafoods and salmon. Prime Scottish beef, venison and lamb.
STB   4 Crown Commended
RAC   3 Star
AA   3 Star
Credit cards: 1, 3
Proprietors: The Young Family

BALLATER
23   E7

Craigendarroch Hotel & Country Club
Braemar Road
Ballater
Royal Deeside
AB3 5XA
Tel: 03397 55858
Telex: 739952
Fax: 03397 55447

On A93 42 miles west of Aberdeen, near Braemar.
This luxury resort hotel, in the heart of the Scottish mountains, boasts three restaurants all run by twice Scottish chef of the year, Bill Gibb. The fine cuisine complements the splendour of the hotel and countryside surrounding Craigendarroch's hillside location. However, only The Oaks and Lochnagar Restaurants are open to non-residents, the other facilities are for members and residents only.
Open all year
Rooms: 50 with private facilities
Breakfast 7.30 - 10 am
Lunch 12 - 2.30 pm (c)
Dinner 5.30 - 10 pm (e)
Cafe Jardin: members and residents only
The Oaks: Lunch 12.30 - 2 pm (c); Dinner 7.30 - 10 pm (e-f)
Lochnagar: Dinner 7.30 - 10 pm
Bed & breakfast from £40
Dinner B & B from £52.50
STB 5 Crown Highly Commended
RAC 4 Star
AA   4 Star H
Credit cards: 1, 2, 3, 5

The Green Inn
9 Victoria Road
Ballater
AB3 5QQ
Tel: 0338 55701

In centre of Ballater on village green.
Granite-built former temperance hotel now a small licensed restaurant with three letting bedrooms. Emphasis on fresh food. Local produce used as much as possible. Scottish dishes always available.
Open 8 Feb to late Oct
Rooms: 3 with private facilities
Breakfast 8 - 9 am
Lunch 12.30 - 2 pm (b)
Dinner 7 - 9.30 pm (d)
Breakfast - residents only
Bed & breakfast from £15
Dinner B & B rates on application
Fisherman's platter (lunch only), fresh salmon, sweet herring, prawns. Venison with port and redcurrant sauce. Fillet of salmon with hollandaise sauce. Ham 'n' haddie.
STB 3 Crown Commended
AA   1 Knife & Fork
Credit cards: 1, 3, 6
Proprietor: A C S Hamilton

Moorside House
26 Braemar Road
Ballater
AB3 5RI
Tel: 0338 55492

200 yards from centre of village, on main road (A93) leading out of Ballater towards Braemar.
This family run award-winning establishment is a former manse built over one hundred years ago, situated in the burgh of Ballater on Royal Deeside. Set in three-quarters of an acre of garden and lawns, it is ideally suited for hill-walking, fishing, golfing or touring the Highlands.
Open mid Mar to mid Nov
Rooms: 9 with private facilities
Breakfast 8.30 - 9 am
Dinner from 7 pm except Sun
No smoking in dining room and lounge
Residents only
Bed & breakfast from £12
Dinner B & B from £22
Baked loin of Ayrshire pork in sweet mustard sauce. Grampian chicken in sherry and celery sauce. Grapefruit ceilidh. Wide choice at breakfast.
STB 3 Crown Commended
RAC Acclaimed
AA   Listed
Credit cards: 1, 3
Proprietors: Ian & Ann Hewitt

BALQUHIDDER
24   F5

Monachyle Mhor Farm
Balquhidder
Lochearnhead
Perthshire
FK19 8PQ
Tel: 08774 622
On A84 north of Callander.
Monachyle Mhor Farmhouse is set in the beautiful Braes o' Balquhidder home of Rob Roy McGregor. Its unique position overlooks Lochs Voil and Doine, whilst the conservatory allows guests to dine and still enjoy the glorious view in the long summer evenings. Your host's 'fetish' – cuisine and comfort!
Open all year
Rooms: 4 with private facilities
Breakfast from 8.30 am
Lunch 12 - 2 pm (a-b)
High Tea 3 - 6 pm (a)   ▶

Dinner 7.30 - 9 pm (c)
Unlicensed.
No dogs.
Bed & breakfast from £14.50
Dinner B & B from £22.50

Monachyle venison envelopes, made with puff pastry, marinated in red wine, with juniper berries and garlic.

STB 3 Crown Commended
Scottish Farmhouse Holidays

No credit cards

Proprietor: Jean Lewis

Horse Mill Restaurant (National Trust for Scotland)
Crathes Castle
Banchory
Kincardineshire
AB3 3QJ
Tel: 033044 525

Off A93 3 miles east of Banchory

An attractive and relaxed restaurant situated in a converted horse mill close to the picturesque 16th century Crathes Castle, famous for its painted ceilings, fine furniture and beautiful 3¾ acre walled garden, considered to be among the finest in Britain. The grounds extend to 600 acres, with 15 miles of well marked woodland trails.

Open Easter to late Oct

Lunch 12 - 5.30 pm (a-b)
High Tea 3 - 5.30 pm (a)
Dinner (c) booked parties only
No dogs.
Facilities for the disabled.
No smoking in restaurant.

Coffee or tea with home-baked scones and cakes. Lunch from an à la carte menu includes home-made soup, traditional dishes and sweets, or freshly made sandwiches and salads.

Credit cards: 1, 3

Invery House Hotel
Bridge of Feugh
Banchory
Kincardineshire
AB3 3NJ
Tel: 03302 4782
Telex: 73737
Fax: 03302 4712

B974 - 1 mile south of Banchory.

Set in 30 acres of wooded grounds on the banks of the River Feugh on Royal Deeside. A member of Prestige Hotels,

with golf, fishing and shooting arranged for guests. Furnished throughout to a very high standard with antiques and paintings. Imaginative food prepared with great care and presented with panache.

Open all year except 4 to 8 Jan.

Rooms: 14 with private facilities
Breakfast 7.30 - 10 am
Lunch 12.15 - 2 pm (d)
Dinner 7.30 - 9.45 pm (f)
Bed & breakfast from £65 - £80
Dinner B & B from £85

Venison with brambles, game pie, baked sea trout, lobster, salmon en croute.

STB 5 Crown Highly Commended
RAC 4 Star
AA 4 Star HBL

Credit cards: 1, 2, 3, 5, 6

Proprietors: Stewart & Sheila Spence

Raemoir House Hotel
Banchory
Kincardineshire
AB3 4ED
Tel: 03302 4884
Telex: 73315
Fax: 03302 2171

On A890 Royal Deeside.

Beautiful historic house set in 3,500 acres of wooded grounds and parkland. Many rooms and suites face south overlooking the nine-hole mini golf course and tennis court, and have tapestried walls and antique furniture. This family-owned hotel is proud of its Scottish cuisine carefully prepared by award winning chefs.

Open all year

Rooms: 28 with private facilities
Breakfast 7.30 - 9.45 am
Bar Lunch 12.30 - 2 pm (a)
Lunch 1 - 2 pm Sun only (b) or by arrangement
Dinner 7.30 - 9 pm (e)
Bed & breakfast from £50
Dinner B & B from £68.50

Cream of pheasant soup, game consommé. Smoked salmon florettes, venison, game, fish pâtés and terrines. Poached Dee salmon, roast venison, grouse, Aberdeen Angus beef, rosetted Scottish lamb.

STB 4 Crown Commended
RAC 3 Star C
AA 3 Star L
BTA Commended

Credit cards: 1, 2, 3, 5, 6

Proprietor: Kit Sabin

Auchen Castle Hotel & Restaurant
Beattock
Moffat
Dumfriesshire
DG10 9SH
Tel: 06833 407

Direct access from A74, one mile north of Beattock Village.

Gracious country house spectacularly situated in 50 acres with fine shrubs and trees. Ten of the 25 bedrooms are in a modern wing. Ideally situated for the Border Country. 55 miles south of Edinburgh and Glasgow.

Open all year except Christmas and New Year.

Rooms: 25 with private facilities
Breakfast 7.30 - 9.30 am
Bar Lunch 12 - 2 pm (a)
Dinner 7 - 9 pm (d)
Bed & breakfast from £20
Dinner B & B from £27

Local lamb, poultry, beef and pork. Game in season. Salmon and shellfish.

STB 4 Crown Commended
AA 3 Star H

Credit cards: 1, 2, 3, 5, 6

Proprietor: Hazel Beckh

Priory Hotel
The Square
Beauly
Inverness-shire
IV4 7BX
Tel: 0463 782309
Fax: 0463 782531

A862 12 miles north-west of Inverness.

The Priory is a bustling local hotel with a reputation for particularly good food and efficient friendly service. Situated in the main square in Beauly – close to the ancient Priory ruins. The hotel is an ideal base for touring the beautiful north and west of Scotland.

Open all year

Rooms: 12 with private facilities
Breakfast from 7 am

▶

Bar Lunch 12 - 2 pm (a)
Lunch 12 - 2 pm (a)
High Tea 5.30 - 7 pm
Bar Supper 5.30 - 9 pm (a)
Dinner 5.30 - 9 pm (d)
Food available all day.
Bed & breakfast £21.75 - £25.95
Dinner B & B from £28

Haggis, chef's pâté, Orkney herring. Salmon, trout, Scotch lamb, Aberdeen Angus beef, speciality whisky steaks. Extensive sweet trolley. Vegetarian dishes.

STB   4 Crown Commended
RAC   2 Star
AA   2 Star
Credit cards: 1, 2, 3, 5, 6

Proprietors: Stuart & Eveline Hutton

BENBECULA
28   ISLE OF   D1

Dark Island Hotel
Liniclate
Isle of Benbecula
Western Isles
PA88 5PJ
Tel: 0870 2414/2283

Benbecula lies between North and South Uist (Western Isles).

This unusually named hotel is of modern low ranch style construction and is acclaimed as one of the best hotels in the Hebrides. There is a comfortable and spacious residents' lounge and a dining room which caters for everything from intimate dinners to major functions. An ideal spot for exploring the adjacent islands. Fishing, golf, birdwatching and interesting archaeological sites.

Open all year
Rooms: 42, 35 with private facilities
Breakfast 7.30 - 9.30 am
Bar Lunch 12 - 2 pm (a)
Lunch 12 - 2 pm (b)
High Tea 5 - 6.30 pm
Dinner 6.30 - 9 pm (c)
Bed & breakfast from £30
Dinner B & B from £40

Lobster, crab, scallops and venison.

STB   4 Crown Commended
Credit cards: 1, 3

Proprietor: Stephen Peteranna

BIGGAR
29   G6

Shieldhill Country House Hotel
Quothquan
Biggar
Lanarkshire ML12 6NA
Tel: 0899 20035
Telex: 777308
Fax: 0899 21092

This historic country house hotel dating back to 1199, situated amidst rolling hills and farmlands has been restored to its former elegance using Laura Ashley's rich Venetian collection of fabrics and wallpapers. All guest rooms have private bathrooms, some with added extras such as fireplaces, four-posters and jacuzzis.

Open Mar to Dec. Closed from Christmas Day.
Rooms: 9 with private facilities
Breakfast 8 - 10 am
Bar Lunch 12 - 2.30 pm (c)
Lunch 12 - 2.30 pm (d)
Dinner 7 - 10 pm (f)
No smoking in restaurant.
No children.
No dogs.
Bed & breakfast from £82
Dinner B & B from £100

Fillet of veal stuffed with strawberries on a strawberry and sage cream sauce. Roast saddle of venison with a raspberry essence topped with a ginger and cream sauce.

STB   4 Crown Highly Commended
Credit cards: 1, 2, 3, 4, 5, 6

Proprietors: C Dunstan & J Greenwald

BLAIR ATHOLL
30   E6

Woodlands
St Andrews Crescent
Blair Atholl
Perthshire PH18 5SX
Tel: 0796 81 403

A9 north of Pitlochry (7 miles).

Cheerful and comfortable, Woodlands was built in 1903 and maintains most original features including service bells. No TV in bedrooms. Good selection of freshly made real teas always available. Guests introduced over a glass before dinner. Leisurely breakfasts with freshly baked bread. Most important house feature – no hurry! All this while gazing at Ben-y-Vrackie!

Open all year

Rooms: 4
Breakfast 8 - 9 am
Dinner from 7 pm (c) or by arrangement
Unlicensed.
Bed & breakfast from £12.50
Dinner B & B from £20

Rannoch venison in red wine and juniper berries. All home-made preserves – including rowan jelly. Lewis salmon, jugged Buckie kippers. Nut soups and vegetarian dishes.

STB   Listed Commended
No credit cards
Proprietor: Dolina MacLennan (Herdman)

BLAIR DRUMMOND
31   F5

Broughton's Restaurant
Blair Drummond
Stirling
FK9 4XE
Tel: 0786 841897

Less than 1 mile west of Blair Drummond on A873.

Broughton's Country Cottage Restaurant is devoted to the service of good food and wine in a relaxed atmosphere. All dishes are prepared by Chef/Proprietor Helen Broughton and her staff from the finest local produce with most of the vegetables and herbs from the garden. The lunch menu offers several lighter alternatives. Caithness Glass/Taste of Scotland Newcomer of the Year Award 1988. AA top 500.

Open all year except last 2 wks in Jan and first 2 wks in Feb.
Lunch 12 - 2 pm (a)
Dinner 7 - 10 pm except Sun (d)
Closed Mon
Dinner - last orders 10 pm. No smoking in restaurant.

Local game, jugged hare, ghillies venison, sea trout cooked in sorrel with hollandaise sauce, duck Gressingham, Arbroath smokie ramekin. Vegetarian dishes always available.

AA   Rosette
Credit cards: 1, 3
Best Newcomer 1988
Proprietor: Helen Broughton

BOTHWELL
32   **G5**

The Grape Vine Restaurant & Lounge Bar
27 Main Street
Bothwell
Lanarkshire
G71 8RW
Tel: 0698 852014

½ mile off M74 (East Kilbride turn-off).

Situated in the centre of a picturesque conservation village, yet within easy access of the motorway. Whether you are looking for a light meal in the bar, or a more leisurely experience in the glass-domed restaurant, both are available all day. With the emphasis on fresh local produce, carefully and creatively prepared under the guidance of proprietor, Colin Morrison.

Open all year except limited period Christmas and New Year.
Lunch 12 - 5 pm (b)
Dinner 5 - 10.30 pm (d)

Local venison, trout, salmon and cheeses featured.

Credit cards: 1, 2, 3
Proprietor: Colin Morrison

BRAEMAR
33   **E6**

Braemar Lodge
Glenshee Road
Braemar
Aberdeenshire
AB3 5YQ
Tel: 03397 41627

On main A93 Perth - Aberdeen road, on the outskirts of Braemar.

Recent, stylish renovation of an Edwardian shooting lodge in extensive grounds looking down Glen Clunie to Glenshee. Individually designed bedrooms with views of the mountains. Wood panelled bar with log fires. Elegant restaurant for which Marian Campbell produces traditional and innovative dishes using the finest Scottish produce.

Open all year except Apr and Dec
Rooms: 8, 6 with private facilities
Breakfast 8.30 - 9 am
Lunch by arrangement (c-d)
Dinner 7 - 8.30 pm (d)
No smoking in dining room
No dogs.
Bed & breakfast £19.50 - £27.50

Dinner B & B rates on application
Menu changes daily: Angus steak parcel, trout in Isle of Mull vermouth, smoked venison etc. All-Scottish cheeseboard.
STB   3 Crown Commended
AA   2 star

Credit cards: 1, 3
Proprietors: Trevor & Marian Campbell

BRIDGE OF CALLY
34   **F6**

Bridge of Cally Hotel
Bridge of Cally
by Blairgowrie
Perthshire
PH10 7JJ
Tel: 025 086 231

6 miles north of Blairgowrie, on A93 road to Braemar.

Family owned former coaching inn set in the Perthshire hills. Noted for good food. Full central heating, with a log fire in the bar during the winter months. Free fishing. Golf, pony trekking and skiing are within easy reach.

Open all year except Nov
Rooms: 9, 6 with private facilities
Breakfast 8.30 - 9.30 am
Bar Lunch 12 - 2 pm (a)
Lunch 12 - 2 pm (a)
Dinner 7 - 8.30 pm (c)
Bed & breakfast from £19
Dinner B & B from £29.50
STB   3 Crown Commended
RAC   2 Star R

Credit cards: 1, 3, 5
Proprietors: Hugh & Mary Sharrock

BRIDGE OF EARN
35   **F6**

Rockdale Guest House
Dunning Street
Bridge of Earn
Perth
PH2 9AA
Tel: 0738 812281

A90 – ½ mile from M90 – 4 miles south of Perth.

Bridge of Earn has best of both worlds. Country surroundings but only four miles from Perth. An ideal situation for touring or a golf break as there are plenty of the well-known beautiful courses all within approx. 30 miles. Family run guest house. A caring attitude to guests' comforts.

Open all year
Rooms: 8, 1 with private facilities
Breakfast 7.45 - 9 am
High teas available at weekends.
Dinner 5.30 - 7 pm (b)
Dinner bookings essential for non-residents. Restricted hotel licence.
Bed & breakfast £11.50 - £14.50
Dinner B & B £18.50 - £21.50
Reduced winter rates on request.

Traditional roasts and home-made soups. Well-known for its Scottish breakfasts.
STB   2 Crown Commended
No credit cards
Proprietor: Adele Barrie

BRORA
36   **C6**

Links Hotel
Golf Road
Brora
Sutherland
KW9 6QS
Tel: 0408 21225

Off A9 at Brora.

This hotel overlooks James Braid's 18-hole links course at Brora. Breathtaking view over golf links and along beautiful Moray Firth coast. Golfers in seventh heaven with Golspie, Tain and Royal Dornoch all nearby and, of course, the Brora Links on the doorstep. A wealth of interest locally with fairytale Dunrobin Castle, woolmills and a distillery to visit as well as magnificent walks and drives.

Open all year.
Rooms: 22 with private facilities
Breakfast 8 - 9.30 am
Bar Lunch 12 - 2 pm (a)
Lunch 12 - 2 pm (b)
Dinner 7 - 9 pm (d)
Bed & breakfast from £32.50
Dinner B & B from £43

Fresh Sutherland lamb and salmon. Aberdeen Angus beef. Traditional local soups and fish dishes. Breakfast of Loch Fyne kippers or Arbroath smokies.
STB   4 Crown Commended
RAC   3 Star
AA   3 Star

Credit cards: 1, 2, 3, 5
Proprietors: C Richards, T & S Pearson

BUCKIE
37   D7

The Old Monastery Restaurant
Drybridge
Buckie
Banffshire
AB5 2JB
Tel: 0542 32660

3 miles south of Buckie, narrow lane above Drybridge.

The monks chose wisely their Morayshire retreat, with breathtaking western seascape views to the distant Sutherland mountains. Traditional hospitality continues on the plate and in the glass, drawing from the bountiful local larder and Spey Valley distilleries, and served in unique surroundings. Lunch in Cloisters Bar, Dinner in the Chapel.

Open all year except 2 wks in Nov and 3 wks in Jan.

Bar Lunch 12 - 2 pm (a)
Lunch 12 - 2 pm (b)
Dinner 7 - 9.30 pm (d)
Closed Sun + Mon.
No smoking area in restaurant.

Moray fish feast, lobster, venison, Aberdeen Angus steaks, Spey salmon, soft fruits, Scotch lamb, crab, sea trout and local trout, home-made soups and sweets, e.g. iced ginger souffle with Glayva.

Credit cards: 1, 2, 3, 5

Proprietors: Douglas & Maureen Gray

BURRELTON
38   F7

Burrelton Park Hotel
High Street
Burrelton
Perthshire
PH13 9NX
Tel: 08287 206

On A94 Perth to Coupar Angus road.

Not so much an hotel, more a restaurant with superb accommodation, where personal attention and service enhance first class food. Set in the village of Burrelton, a farming community renowned for its soft fruit and potato growing. A perfect centre for daily touring, north, south, east and west. For the sports enthusiast the best golfing, fishing (salmon), shooting, skiing and walking.

Open all year
Rooms: 6 with private facilities
Breakfast 7 - 10 am
Bar meals served all day 11 am - 11 pm
Dinner 6.30 - 10 pm (c)
No smoking area in restaurant
Bed & breakfast from £22.50
Dinner B & B from £30

A multitude of "specials" on the blackboard daily. Vegetarian specialists. Chef special salmon coullibac – rice risotto layered with fresh salmon encased in puff pastry with light scallop sauce.

STB   Award Pending

Credit cards: 3

Proprietors: Malcolm & Karen Weaving

CAIRNDOW
39   F4

Loch Fyne Oyster Bar
Cairndow
Argyll
PA26 8BH
Tel: 04996 217/264

Head of Loch Fyne A83.

Simple oyster bar in converted old farm building serving local produce including oysters, langoustines, crab, fresh salmon. Own smokehouse provides smoked salmon, trout, eel, mussels, etc. Also seafood shop in smokehouse. Short, very carefully selected, wine list. The restaurant has been expanded to around 80 seats. There is now a bar where customers may sit and enjoy their food and wine.

Open Mar to Oct

Menu available throughout the day: 9 am - 8.30 pm

Oysters on crushed ice in half shell, baked oysters in parsley and garlic butter, langoustines, poached salmon, sea fish platter, finnan haddock in milk, Loch Fyne kippers.

Credit cards: 1, 3

Proprietors: Andrew Lane & John Noble

CALLANDER
40   F5

Bridgend House Hotel
Bridgend
Callander
Perthshire
FK17 8AH
Tel: 0877 30130

On A81 – 100 yards from Callander main road.

This 17th century building, comfortably appointed, with its garden offering a magnificent view of Ben Ledi, yet within three minutes' walk of the town centre. Bedrooms en-suite, extensive menu in the à la carte restaurant – including a choice of traditional Scottish dishes. Open fire in lounge, central heating throughout.

Open all year.

Rooms: 7, 5 with private facilities
Breakfast 8 - 9.30 am
Bar Lunch 12 - 2.30 pm (a)
Dinner 7 - 9 pm (c)
High Teas – parties only at 5 pm
Bed & breakfast £12.50 - £24.50
Dinner B & B £23 - £35

A wide range of food from traditional Scottish soup, prime roast beef and lamb to local salmon and Atholl Brose. Haggis a speciality.

AA   1 Star HL

Credit cards: 1, 2, 3, 5, 6

Proprietors: Sandy & Maria Park

Highland House Hotel
South Church Street
Callander
Perthshire
FK17 8BN
Tel: 0877 30269

Just off A84 in town centre.

Small Georgian house beautifully furnished offering warm and comfortable accommodation. Intimate bar with wide range of malt whiskies. Tasteful dining room and lounge. Immaculate bedrooms with drink-making facilities. Full central heating in all rooms. The proprietors strive to offer a warm welcome and personal service to all guests.

Open Mar to Nov
Rooms: 10, 4 with private facilities
Breakfast 8.30 - 9 am
Dinner from 7 pm (c)
No smoking area in restaurant
Bed & breakfast from £13.50
Dinner B & B from £25   ▶

Home-made soups, pâtés, kippers, herring. Fresh local produce including salmon, trout, venison. Delicious desserts. Personally prepared by proprietors, Keith and Pat Cooper.

STB 3 Crown Commended
RAC Acclaimed
AA   Listed

No credit cards

Proprietors: Keith & Pat Cooper

Roman Camp Hotel
Callander
Perthshire
FK17 8BG
Tel: 0877 30003

Signposted off main route through Callander (A84).

Originally built in 1625 as a hunting lodge, this charming Country House hotel on the edge of the Trossachs is a superb centre from which to tour. It is set in 20 acres of beautiful gardens which sweep down to the River Teith. The public rooms are gracious and relaxing, and the dining room enjoys a fine reputation for good food.

Open all year

Rooms: 14 with private facilities
Breakfast 8 - 9.30 am
Lunch 12 - 2 pm (d)
Dinner 7 - 9 pm (f) 4 courses
No smoking in dining room
Facilities for the disabled
Bed & breakfast from £40
Dinner B & B from £60

Local fresh fish – salmon, trout – and seafood. Game in season.

STB 4 Crown Commended
RAC 3 Star
AA   3 Star

Credit cards: 1, 2, 3, 4, 5, 6

Proprietors: Eric & Marion Brown

CREDIT/CHARGE CARDS

1 Access/Mastercard/Eurocard
2 American Express
3 Visa
4 Carte Bleu
5 Diners Club
6 Mastercharge

CAMPBELTOWN
41   H3

Seafield Hotel
Kilkerran Road
Campbeltown
Argyll
PA28 6JL
Tel: 0586 54385

On the shores of Campbeltown Loch – 4 minutes walk from town centre.

Victorian villa built by the founders of Springbank Distillery and reputed to be the first house in Campbeltown fitted with a bath! Has a garden court annexe in the walled garden at the rear of the hotel, offering quiet peaceful accommodation.

Open all year

Rooms: 9 with private facilities
Breakfast 7.30 - 9 am
High Tea 5 - 6 pm
Dinner 7 - 8 pm (c)
Bed & breakfast £19 - £25
Dinner B & B £29.50 - £35.50

Local fresh seafoods and salmon. Scottish beef, lamb and game.

STB 3 Crown Commended
RAC 2 Star

Credit cards: 1, 3

Proprietors: Alastair & Elizabeth Gilchrist

White Hart Hotel
Main Street
Campbeltown
Argyll
PA28 6AN
Tel: 0586 52440/53356

Mull of Kintyre.

Well established town hotel centrally situated in busy fishing port/market town. Ideal base for the famous Machrihanish golf links, the Mull of Kintyre and Campbeltown Loch.

Open all year

Rooms: 20 with private facilities
No Parking
Breakfast 7.30 - 9 am
Bar Lunch 12 - 2 pm (a)
Lunch 12 - 2 pm except Sun (a)
High Tea 5.30 - 6.30 pm
Dinner 7 - 9.30 pm (c); 7 - 8.30 pm Sun Mar to Oct.
Restaurant closed Sun – Nov to Mar.
Bed & breakfast from £25
Dinner B & B rates on application.

Serving the best of local fresh seafood, game and meat products.

Credit cards: 1, 3, 6

Proprietors: P Stogdale & B Kennedy

CARRADALE
42   G3

Carradale Hotel
Carradale
Argyll
PA28 6RY
Tel: 058 33 223

On A842, 9 miles north of Campbeltown, Argyll.

Sixty years in same family ownership, the hotel is situated in the fishing village of Carradale, and stands in its own gardens above the quaint harbour. The hotel offers squash courts, sauna, solarium. Full central heating. Golf course next to the hotel and safe, sandy beaches nearby.

Open Mar to Oct

Rooms: 20, 18 with private facilities
Breakfast 8.30 - 9 am
Bar Lunch 12.30 - 2 pm (a)
High Tea from 5.30 pm
Dinner 7 - 8.45 pm (c)
No smoking area in restaurant.
Bed & breakfast £17 - £25
Dinner B & B £29 - £37

Kintyre Hill lamb, Carradale oak-smoked salmon, house kippers.

STB 3 Crown Commended
AA   2 Star

Credit cards: 1, 3, 6

Proprietors: John & Katherine Martin

CARRBRIDGE
43   E6

Dalrachney Lodge Hotel
Carrbridge
Inverness-shire
PH23 3AT
Tel: 047984 252
Fax: 047984 383

Just off A9 south of Inverness and north of Aviemore.

Victorian Hunting Lodge in 14 acres of peaceful surroundings, Dalrachney is a careful blend of old and new. Relax by the log-fire in cosy 'Stalkers' Bar or in à la carte 'Lodge' Restaurant which has gained a reputation for fine food and service. Excellent selection of wines, liqueurs and malts.

Open all year

Rooms: 11 with private facilities
Breakfast 8 - 9.30 am
Bar Lunch 11 - 4 pm (a-b)
Bar Supper 4 - 11 pm (a-b)
Dinner 6 - 9 pm (d)   ▶

No smoking area in restaurant.
Bed & breakfast from £25
Dinner B & B from £35

Home-made soups, pâtés and desserts. Spey Valley salmon, Highland venison, beef, Scotch lamb beautifully prepared and served with fresh vegetables in season.

STB 4 Crown Commended
AA   2 Star
Credit cards: 1, 2, 3
Proprietor: Helen Swanney

Ecclefechan Bistro
Main Street
Carrbridge
Inverness-shire
PH23 3AJ
Tel: 047 984 473

Main road, Carrbridge, on Carrbridge bypass off A9 north of Aviemore.

Informal family run bistro invoking the best of the Auld Alliance: Scottish food in a French atmosphere, freshly prepared the way you like it, from scones to scallops, steaks to strudel – and coffee that tastes like coffee.

Open all year
Open for meals 10 am - 10 pm (a-c)
Closed all day Tuesday
Facilities for the disabled.

Venison in claret, Hebridean skink, haggis and clapshot, local smoked salmon, Scottish prawns with dill. Ecclefechan tart, Blairgowrie raspberry trifle.

No credit cards
Proprietors: Duncan & Anne Hilditch

The Keeper's House Private Hotel
Carrbridge
Inverness-shire
PH23 3AT
Tel: 047 984 621

North end of Carrbridge on A938 opposite golf course.

Small unlicensed country hotel of charm and character with a warm, friendly atmosphere, set in two acres. Fine traditional menus using fresh local produce, home-grown fruit and free-range eggs and a varied selection of vegetarian meals by arrangement. An ideal centre to explore the many delights of the Spey Valley.

Open 20 Dec to late Oct
Rooms: 5, 4 with private facilities
Breakfast from 8.30 am
Dinner 7 pm.
No smoking area in dining room and lounge.

Residents only.
Bed & breakfast £14 - £15
Dinner B & B £20 - £23.50

Fine Scottish lamb, beef, pork and salmon. Home-made desserts and preserves made from home-grown fruit. Kippers and haddock on the breakfast menu.

STB 2 Crown Commended
No credit cards
Proprietor: Penny Rawson

Mountain Thyme Country House
Beananach
Carrbridge (Spey Valley)
Inverness-shire
PH23 3AP
Tel: 047 984 696

One mile west of Carrbridge village.

Experience Scottish hospitality in this 19th century former Highland estate house. Standing in attractive gardens, embraced by mountain and moorland it offers comfortable accommodation in well-appointed rooms. Choose home-cooked fare from menus including local and garden produce. Enjoy the ambience of a more leisurely era.

Open late Dec to Oct
Rooms: 5 with private facilities
Breakfast 8.15 - 8.45 am
Dinner 7 pm (b)
No smoking in dining room
Bed & breakfast £14 - £16
Dinner B & B from £20 - £25

Featured regularly on the menu – home-made soups, fresh local trout and venison; Aberdeen Angus roast beef, calorie-laden sweets, Scottish cheeses, free-range eggs.

STB 3 Crown Commended
RAC Acclaimed
AA   Listed
No credit cards
Proprietor: Margaret Pearson

CASTLE DOUGLAS
44   H5

Longacre Manor Hotel
Ernespie Road
Castle Douglas
Dumfries-shire
DG7 1LE
Tel: 0556 3576

On A75 on northern boundary of Castle Douglas.

Charming small hotel, personally run, offering warm welcome and service.

Situated in 1½ acres of woodland gardens with magnificent views to Screel and Galloway hills. Television, direct dial telephone, radio and tea-making facilities in each room. Premises are fully central heated.

Open all year
Rooms: 4 with private facilities
Breakfast 8.30 - 9 am
Dinner 7.30 - 8.30 pm (b)
Bed & breakfast from £19
Dinner B & B from £28

Daily changing menu using locally produced fish, beef, lamb, pork and game with fresh vegetables. Home-made desserts a speciality.

STB 4 Crown Commended
No credit cards
Proprietors: Elizabeth & Walter Meldrum

CLEISH
45   NEAR KINROSS   G6

Nivingston House
Cleish
Kinross-shire
KY13 7LS
Tel: 05775 216

2 miles from junction 5 on M90.

Victorian mansion of 12 acres of gardens commanding superb views over local countryside. Log fires burn in the winter and candles flicker in the evenings. Nivingston House uses the best local produce and their gold medal-winning chef accompanies these with delightful unusual sauces.

Open all year
Rooms: 17 with private facilities
Breakfast 7.45 - 10 am
Bar Lunch 12 - 2 pm (a)
Lunch 12 - 2 pm (c)
Dinner 7 - 9 pm (e)
Bed & breakfast from £34
Dinner B & B from £51

STB 4 Crown Commended
AA   3 Star + Rosette
BTA   Commended
Credit cards: 1, 2, 3, 6
Proprietors: Allan & Pat Deeson

COLONSAY
ISLE OF
46   F2

Isle of Colonsay Hotel
Isle of Colonsay
Argyll
PA61 7YP
Tel: 09512 316

Ferry via Oban (2½ hours), Mon/Wed/Fri only. Additional sailings via Islay in high season.

Probably the most isolated hotel in Great Britain, this 18th century inn is run by Kevin and Christa Byrne on a beautiful Hebridean island which is uniquely rich in wildlife and scenery. Fishing, golf, sailing. Bicycles gratis. Full central heating.

Open all year, except Christmas Day
Rooms: 11, 8 with private facilities
Breakfast 8.30 - 9.30 am
Lunch 12.30 - 1.30 pm (a)
Dinner 7.30 pm (d)
Yacht suppers 7 - 8.30 pm May to Sep
No smoking area in restaurant
Bed & breakfast from £37
Dinner B & B rates on application.

In season: oysters, mussels, scallops, prawns, trout, salmon. Home-made soups, jam, marmalade and bread. Emphasis on fresh local produce with many vegetables from hotel's own garden.

STB   3 Crown Commended
AA   1 Star HBL
BTA   Commended

Credit cards: 1, 2, 3, 5

Proprietors: Kevin & Christa Byrne

COLVEND
47   I6

Clonyard House Hotel
Colvend
Dalbeattie
Dumfriesshire
DG5 4QW
Tel: 055 663 372

4½ miles south of Dalbeattie on A710 Solway coast road. 18 miles west of Dumfries.

Victorian country house hotel in six acres wooded grounds. Typical 19th century dining room overlooking lawns. Also pleasant large cocktail bar for informal meals. Ground-floor bedroom wing with full facilities. One room fitted for disabled guests. Safe grounds for children.

Open all year
Rooms: 12, 7 with private facilities
Breakfast 8.30 - 9.30 am
Bar Lunch 12 -2 pm (a)
Dinner 7 - 9 pm (c)
Facilities for the disabled
Bed & breakfast from £20
Dinner B & B from £30

Solway salmon, Kirkcudbrightshire scallops, Galloway beef and lamb, venison.

STB   4 Crown Commended
RAC   2 Star
AA   2 Star

Credit cards: 1, 3

Proprietor: N M Thompson

COMRIE
48   F5

The Deil's Cauldron Lounge Bar & Restaurant
27 Dundas Street
Comrie
Perthshire
PH6 2LN
Tel: 0764 70352

On A85 west end of Comrie.

The Deil's Cauldron created from a 200 year old Listed building takes its name from a well known local beauty spot. The attractive black and white exterior leads to comfortable lounge featuring original stone walls, a good selection of malt whisky and decorated with fine watercolours, old photographs and prints.

Open all year
Bar Lunch 12 - 2 pm (b)
Lunch 12 - 2 pm (d)
Bar Supper 5.30 - 9 pm (b)
Dinner 6.30 - 8.30 pm (d)
Closed Tuesdays

Fresh local beef, lamb and home grown vegetables, fish and game in season. 'Auld Alliance' cooking.

Credit cards: 1, 3

Proprietors: Robert & Judith Shepherd

CONNEL FERRY
49   F4

Falls of Lora Hotel
Connel Ferry
by Oban
Argyll
PA37 1PB
Tel: 0631 71 483

On A85 (Crianlarich-Oban) at Connel Ferry, 5 miles before Oban.

This fine owner-run Victorian hotel with a modern extension is set back from the A85 overlooking Loch Etive. Two and a half hours' drive from Glasgow/Edinburgh and only five miles from Oban makes it an ideal centre for touring. During summer — superb presentation buffet on Sundays and a seven-course traditional Scottish dinner on Thursdays.

Open all year except Christmas and New Year's Day
Rooms: 30 with private facilities
Breakfast 8 - 9.30 am
Bar Lunch 12.30 - 2 pm (a)
Lunch 12.30 - 2 pm (a)
High Tea on request. Dinner 7 - 8 pm (c)
Lunch served in bar/bistro unless pre-booked. No smoking area in bar/bistro.
Bed & breakfast £15.50 - £44.50
Dinner B & B from £23.50 - £52.50.

Locally caught salmon and trout, prime Scottish lamb and beef, venison and pheasant.

STB   3 Crown Commended
RAC   2 Star
AA   2 Star

Credit cards: 1, 2, 3, 5, 6

Proprietor: C Webster

CONTIN
BY STRATHPEFFER
50   D5

Coul House Hotel
Contin
by Strathpeffer
Ross-shire
IV14 9EY
Tel: 0997 21487
Fax: 0997 21945

On A835 to Ullapool, 17 miles north-west of Inverness.

The ancient Mackenzies of Coul picked an incomparable setting for their secluded Highland country mansion, with fine views over forest and mountain. There are log fires, elegant public rooms and, of course, candlelit "Mackenzie's Taste of Scotland Restaurant". All bedrooms ▶

are en suite, equipped with colour teletext TV, radio, direct-dial telephone, hospitality tray, hair-dryer and trouser-press.

Open all year

Rooms: 21 with private facilities
Breakfast 7.45 - 9.30 am
Bar Lunch 12 - 2 pm (a)
Bar Supper 5.30 - 9 pm
Dinner 7 - 9 pm (d)
Bed & breakfast £23.50 - £29
Dinner B & B £41 - £46.50

Saute of Summer Isles scallops, venison saddle chops, smoked Conon salmon, prawns in Highland garlic butter, escalope of salmon in wine, cream and chive sauce, fillet steaks. Scottish Maiden's Kiss.

STB 4 Crown Commended
RAC Highly Acclaimed

Credit cards: 2, 5

Proprietor: Martyn Hill

CORSEMALZIE
51   **I4**

Corsemalzie House Hotel
Corsemalzie, Port William
Newton Stewart
Wigtownshire
DG8 9RL
Tel: 098 886 254

Off A714 Newton Stewart to Port William; take B7005 Wigtown to Glenluce road.

Sporting country house hotel set in 40 acres of woodland and gardens. Extensive game, fishing and shooting rights. Dogs accepted (small charge).

Open Mar to mid Jan

Rooms: 15, 14 with private facilities
Breakfast 8.30 - 10 am
Lunch 12.30 - 2 pm (a)
Dinner 7.30 - 9 pm (d)
Bed & breakfast from £24.50
Dinner B & B rates on application.

Fresh and smoked Bladnoch salmon and trout. Game in season, steaks and roasts a speciality; home-grown vegetables. Scottish sweet table and cheese board with oatcakes (Friday and Saturday evenings).

STB 4 Crown Commended
AA 3 Star

Credit cards: 1, 2, 3, 6

Proprietor: Peter McDougall

COUPAR ANGUS
52   **F7**

Enverdale Hotel
Pleasance Road
Coupar Angus
Perthshire
PH13 9JB
Tel: 0828 27606

Off 2 tourist routes – A94 Perth - Aberdeen, and A923 Dundee - Blairgowrie.

Pleasing 19th century hotel which prides itself on a personal service and a warm and friendly atmosphere. Ideally situated for touring the heart of Scotland – Glamis Castle, Scone Palace, Edinburgh and Glasgow, all within easy driving distance. For the sportsman – skiing, curling, shooting, fishing and golf – 40 courses within one hour's drive including Gleneagles, St Andrews and Carnoustie.

Open mid Jan to Dec

Rooms: 5, 2 with private facilities
Breakfast 7.30 - 9.15 am
Bar Meals 12 noon - 9.15 pm (a).
High Tea 5 - 6.30 pm (Booking essential Sat).
Dinner 7.15 - 9 pm except Sun, Mon (d)
Bed & breakfast from £17.50
Dinner B & B from £25

Fillet steak with cream sauce, mushrooms and Drambuie. Fresh Tay salmon. Home-made soups, pâté, haggis, cakes and pastries. Locally grown raspberries.

STB 2 Crown Commended

Credit cards: 1, 3

Proprietors: Martin & Rosemary Price

CRAIGELLACHIE
53   **D7**

Craigellachie Hotel
Craigellachie
Banffshire
AB3 9SS
Tel: 03404 204

On A941 12 miles south of Elgin.

One of Scotland's most famous and best loved fishing and shooting hotels. Overlooking the River Spey, the Craigellachie is family owned and run. Log fires, excellent cuisine and wine list, friendly service and home comforts give the Craigellachie a special atmosphere.

Open Mar to Dec

Rooms: 30 with private facilities
Breakfast 7.45 - 9.30 am
Bar Lunch 12 - 2.30 pm (a)
Lunch 12 - 2.30 pm (a)
High Tea 5.30 - 6.30 pm (b)
Dinner 7.30 - 9 pm (e)
Facilities for the disabled
Bed & breakfast from £35
Dinner B & B from £52.50

Game pâté, smoked haddock mousse with leek sauce, dill cured salmon, mussels with saffron and fennel, breast of pigeon with onion compote, grilled monkfish with apple and dry cider, chocolate whisky mousse.

STB 3 Crown Commended

Credit cards: 1, 3

Proprietors: Raymond & Ute Wyatt

CRAIL
54   **F7**

Caiplie Guest House
53 High Street
Crail
Fife
KY10 3RA
Tel: 0333 50564

High Street, Crail.

A comfortable and neatly maintained guest house in the historic and attractive fishing village of Crail. Small dining room. Guests' sittingroom with TV.

Open Mar to Oct

Rooms: 7
Breakfast 8 - 9 am
Dinner from 7 pm (b)
Residents only
No smoking area in restaurant
Bed & breakfast £10.50 - £13.50
Dinner B & B £19 - £22

Scottish and continental dishes prepared from fresh local produce. Cloutie dumpling, cranachan.

STB 2 Crown Commended
RAC Listed
AA Listed

No credit cards

Proprietor: Jayne Hudson

Allt-Chaorain Country House
Crianlarich
Perthshire
FK20 8RU
Tel: 08383 283

On A82 1 mile north of Crianlarich.

Roger McDonald bids "welcome to my home" which is situated in an elevated position 500 yards from the roadside, with commanding views of Benmore and Strathfinnan from the south-facing sun lounge. The traditional wood-panelled dining room caters for 18 people, while the lounge has a log fire burning throughout the year and considerable antique and reproduction furniture.

Open mid Mar to late Oct

Rooms: 9 with private facilities
Breakfast from 8.30 am - earlier by request
Dinner 7 pm (b) - later by arrangement
No smoking in restaurant and bedrooms.
Bed & breakfast £18 - £22
Dinner B & B £28 - £32

Wide range of traditional fresh fare. From game pie, pork fillets, braised steaks, breasts of chicken, beef olives stuffed with haggis. Clootie Dumpling.

STB 3 Crown Commended
BTA Commended

Credit cards: 1, 3

Proprietor: Roger McDonald

The Lodge House
Crianlarich
FK20 8RU
Tel: 08383 276

A82 one mile west of Crianlarich.

Unrivalled views of mountains, salmon river and glens from this the Young's home, which offers traditional Scottish hospitality and cooking. Relax in the malt whisky bar as you watch the birds and deer.

Open Mar to Oct.

Rooms: 6, 3 with private facilities
Breakfast 8 - 8.30 am - earlier by request
Dinner 7 - 8 pm (c) - à la carte (four course).
Residents only.
No dogs.
No smoking area in restaurant.
Bed & breakfast £13 -£16
Dinner B & B £22 - £26

STB 3 Crown Commended

No credit cards

Proprietors: Jean & Jimmy Young

Crieff Visitors Centre
Muthill Road
Crieff
Perthshire
PH7 4AZ
Tel: 0764 4014

On A822 leading out of Crieff to the south.

Quality self-service restaurant, showroom and audio-visual room complex alongside two rural factories producing thistle pattern Buchan pottery and high quality Perthshire paperweights. Within one hour of Glasgow, Edinburgh and St Andrews, close by Gleneagles amidst fine Highland scenery.

Open all year

Self-service open 9 am - 6 pm seven days a week. Closes earlier in the winter.
Facilities for the disabled.

Credit cards: 1, 2, 3, 4, 6

Proprietor: S Drysdale

Cultoquhey House Hotel
by Crieff
Perthshire
PH7 3NE
Tel: 0764 3253

On A85 2 miles east of Crieff.

Distant hills, log fires, wood panelling, loose covers, old gundog, croquet lawns, wild rhododendrons, ancient oaks, bumpy tracks, billiard room, vintage port, hot water bottles, stags' heads, four-poster beds, mountainous stairs, fresh sea trout, elderflower sorbet, family home, weathered sandstone, leaking roof, roe deer, bats at dusk.

Open Apr to Feb

Rooms: 12, 10 with private facilities
Breakfast 8.30 - 9.30 am
Bar Lunch 12 - 2.30 pm (a)
Lunch 12 - 2.30 pm (b)
Dinner 7.30 - 9 pm (d)
Bed & breakfast from £25
Dinner B & B from £37

Delicious soups. Fresh wild salmon. Grouse and blaeberry sauce. Perthshire venison terrine. Home-made hazelnut and Drambuie ice cream.

STB 4 Crown Commended
RAC 2 Star H
AA 2 Star H

Credit cards: 1, 2, 3, 5

Proprietors: David & Anna Cooke

Murraypark Hotel
Connaught Terrace
Crieff
Perthshire
PH7 3DJ
Tel: 0764 3731

A85 to residential part of town.

Pink-stoned large Victorian house standing in its own grounds in the residential part of town. A comfortable restaurant with uncrowded atmosphere overlooks a pleasant garden. Based on established Scottish foods with many interesting variations.

Open all year

Rooms: 14 with private facilities
Breakfast 8 - 9.30 am, 8.30 - 10 am Sun
Bar Lunch 12 - 2 pm (a)
Lunch 12.30 - 2 pm (b)
Dinner 7.30 - 9.30 pm (d)
Bed & breakfast from £25
Dinner B & B from £37.50

STB 4 Crown Commended
RAC 2 Star
AA 2 Star H
BTA Commended

Credit cards: 1, 2, 3, 5

Proprietors: Ann & Noel Scott

Pagoda Room
Glenturret Distillery
Crieff
Perthshire
PH7 4HA
Tel: 0764 2424
Fax: 0764 4366

A85 north-west of Crieff towards Comrie.

Fascinating unique 'Pagoda' shaped roof (ventilation chimney of a maltings kiln) overlooking the Glenturret Distillery, Scotland's oldest working Highland malt distillery. Over 150,000 visit the distillery and its 18th, 19th and 20th century buildings. The Pagoda Room is a new addition and is a must on the visitors' calendar.

Open Mar to Dec

Lunch 12 - 2.30 pm except Sun (d)
Dinner (f) group reservations only.
Reservations essential. Closed Sunday.
No smoking restaurant.

Smoked salmon, fresh salmon, venison and Hosh haggis.

Credit cards: 1, 2, 3

Smugglers Restaurant

Glenturret Distillery
The Hosh
Crieff
Perthshire
PH7 4HA
Tel: 0764 2424

On A85 north-west of Crieff.

Self-service restaurant (130 seats) situated in an 18th century converted whisky warehouse within Scotland's oldest highland malt distillery. Award-winning visitors centre. Audio visual presentation and 3-D exhibition. Whisky tasting bar – taste different ages of Glenturret, 12, 15, 18, 21 years old, and The Glenturret Malt Liqueur.

Open Mar to Dec

Bar Lunch 12 - 2.30 pm (b)
Lunch 12 - 2.30 pm (b)
High Tea 4 - 5 pm
Dinner – group bookings only
Lunch/dinner not served Sun, nor Sat in Mar, Nov and Dec.
No smoking in restaurant.

Glenturret-flavoured pâté, smoked salmon, venison steak, cranachan, gâteaux.

Credit cards: 1, 2, 3
Best Bar Lunch 1989
Proprietor: Peter Fairlie

CRINAN

57   G3

Crinan Hotel

Crinan
Lochgilphead
Argyll
PA31 8SR
Tel: 054 683 261
Fax: 054 683 292

A82 Glasgow-Inveraray. A83 to Lochgilphead. Follow road to Oban – 5 miles out of Lochgilphead.

Magnificent views over Loch Crinan, the sea and islands. Exclusive seafood restaurant enjoys breathtaking sunsets and stunning views.

Open all year

Rooms: 22 with private facilities
Breakfast 8.30 - 10 am
Bar Lunch 12.30 - 2 pm (a)

Dinner 7 - 9 pm (f)
Bed & breakfast £37 - £45
Dinner B & B rates on application.

Jumbo Prawns Corryvreckan, Scottish beef, local wild salmon.

STB   4 Crown Commended
RAC   3 Star
AA   3 Star + Rosette
BTA   Commended

Credit cards: 1, 3

Proprietors: Nick & Frances Ryan

CROMARTY

58   D5

Royal Hotel

Marine Terrace
Cromarty
Ross-shire
IV11 8YN
Tel: 03817 217

On A832 20 miles north-east of Inverness.

The hotel is situated overlooking the beach and harbour in the ancient and historic village of Cromarty. All the well-appointed bedrooms have views of the sea and Ross-shire mountains. The reputation for excellent food and value for money plus traditional Scottish hospitality is guarded with pride by the staff.

Open all year

Rooms: 10 with private facilities
Breakfast 8 - 9.30 am
Bar Lunch 12 - 2 pm (a)
Lunch 12 - 2 pm (b)
High Tea 5 - 6 pm
Bar Supper 5.30 - 9 pm
Dinner 7 - 8.30 pm (c)
No smoking area in restaurant.
Bed & breakfast from £20
Dinner B & B from £30

Wide range of traditional Scottish fare. Farmhouse crepe. T-bone steak. Crab salads.

STB   3 Crown Commended
RAC   2 Star
AA   2 Star

Credit cards: 2, 3

Proprietors: Stewart & Betty Morrison

CULLODEN MOOR

59   D6

Leanach Farm

Culloden Moor
by Inverness
IV1 2EJ
Tel: 0463 791027

5 miles south of Inverness off B851 to Culloden/Croy.

This attractive farmhouse run by Iain and Rosanne MacKay is beautifully situated in historic surroundings within easy distance of Inverness. Emphasis is placed on a warm welcome combined with good well-cooked food and comfortable accommodation.

Open all year

Rooms: 3
Breakfast 7 - 8.30 am
Dinner 6.30 pm except Sun, Sat (b)
No smoking in the dining room.
Residents only. Unlicensed.
Bed & breakfast from £12
Dinner B & B from £18

Home-made soups and puddings. Fresh trout and salmon. Scottish meats and fresh vegetables.

STB   Listed Commended
No credit cards
Proprietors: Iain & Rosanne MacKay

CUPAR

60   F7

Ostlers Close

Bonnygate
Cupar
Fife KY15 4BU
Tel: 0334 55574

A92, Cupar town centre.

A small, intimate restaurant, situated up a small lane off the main street of Cupar. The emphasis is to serve the best of local produce in season imaginatively, with a relaxed, welcoming atmosphere to complement the food.

Open all year except 1 wk in Oct and 1 wk in Jun.

Lunch 12.15 - 2 pm (c)
Dinner 7 - 9.30 pm (e)
Closed Sun and Mon

Cream of Tay salmon soup, Pittenweem seafood, e.g. prawns with garlic and fresh herb butter. Selection of game in season with home-made jellies.

AA   Rosette
Credit cards: 1, 3
Best Informal Restaurant 1989
Proprietors: Jimmy & Amanda Graham

DALBEATTIE
61   **I6**

Auchenskeoch Lodge
by Dalbeattie
Kirkcudbrightshire DG5 4PG
Tel: 038 778 277

5 miles south-east Dalbeattie on B793.

Former Victorian shooting lodge personally run by the proprietors. Period furnishings throughout ensure a genuine country house atmosphere, whilst woodlands, formal gardens and rhododendron walks provide privacy and tranquillity. Facilities include fishing on own loch, billiard room and croquet lawn.

Open Mar to Dec

Rooms: 5 with private facilities
Breakfast 8.15 - 9 am
Dinner 7.30 - 8 pm (c) - booking essential for non-residents
Bed & breakfast £18 - £20
Dinner B & B £28 - £30

Small menu, changing daily. Emphasis on fresh local produce. Wherever possible soft fruit and vegetables from own garden.

STB 3 Crown Commended

Credit cards: 1, 3

Proprietors: Christopher & Mary
                Broom-Smith

The Granary Restaurant
Barend, Sandyhills
Dalbeattie
Kirkcudbrightshire DG9 4NU
Tel: 038 778 663

Turn off A710 in Sandyhills, 7 miles south-east of Dalbeattie and follow signpost to Barend (½ mile).

The white-washed walls of this converted cow byre, with the printed curtains and tablecloths, offers an attractive and friendly atmosphere to the diner. The Restaurant and Bars surround a Spanish style courtyard where one may eat and drink. This is the focal point of the chalet village of Barend.

Open Apr to Jan

Bar Lunch 12 - 2 pm (a)
Dinner 7.30 - 9 pm (c)

Solway queen scallops with garlic mayonnaise. Ayrshire baked ham with apricot sauce. Wild Solway salmon en croute with hollandaise sauce.

Credit cards: 1, 3

Proprietors: Frank & Susan Gourlay

DAVIOT
62   NEAR INVERNESS   **D5**

Daviot Mains Farm
Daviot
Inverness
IV1 2ER
Tel: 046 385 215

On B851 (B9006) to Culloden/Croy, 6 miles south of Inverness.

Comfortable early 19th century Listed farmhouse in quiet situation six miles from Inverness, under the personal supervision of Margaret and Alex Hutcheson. Relax in the warm atmosphere of this friendly home where delicious meals are thoughtfully prepared for you and where log fires burn in both sittingroom and dining room.

Open all year

Rooms: 4
Breakfast 7.30 - 8.30 am
Dinner 6.30 pm
No smoking in dining -room.
Unlicensed. Guests welcome to take own wine.
Bed & breakfast from £12
Dinner B & B from £17

According to season – home-made soups, fresh local salmon and trout, Scottish meats, vegetables and cheeses. Local fruit and home-made puddings.

STB 2 Crown Commended

No credit cards

Proprietors: Margaret & Alex Hutcheson

DINGWALL
63   **D5**

The National Hotel
High Street
Dingwall
Ross-shire
IV15 9HA
Tel: 0349 62166

On A835, 12 miles north of Inverness.

Built of sandstone and dating from 1859, the National Hotel retains gracious period features such as a panelled dining room and lounge with interior leaded light windows. Contemporary menus mix with old world surroundings. The hotel is in the centre of town but offers plenty of free parking.

Open all year

Rooms: 40 with private facilities

Breakfast 7.30 - 9.30 am
Bar Lunch 12 - 5 pm (a)
Lunch 12 - 2.30 pm (a)
High Tea 5 - 7 pm (a)
Bar Supper 5 - 9 pm (a)
Dinner 7 - 10 pm (c)
Facilities for the disabled.
Bed & breakfast from £20
Dinner B & B from £28.50

Saddle of venison with wild mushrooms and red wine sauce. Grilled salmon served with a light tarragon cream.

STB 3 Crown Approved
RAC 2 Star

Credit cards: 1, 2, 3

DIRLETON
64   **G7**

Open Arms Hotel
Dirleton
East Lothian
EH39 5BG
Tel: 0620 85 241

A198 between Gullane and North Berwick.

An up-market inn set in one of Scotland's prettiest villages overlooking the 13th century castle village green. In the same family's hands for 40 years, the well-known restaurant specialises in a warm welcome complemented by log fires and fresh foods.

Open all year

Rooms: 7 with private facilities
Breakfast 7.30 - 10 am
Bar Lunch 12.30 - 2.30 pm (a)
Lunch 12.30 - 2.30 pm (b)
Dinner 7 - 10 pm (d)
Bed & breakfast £36 - £50
Dinner B & B £50 - £60

Mussel and onion stew. Supreme of chicken de Vaux. Cranachan with blackcurrants.

STB 4 Crown Commended
RAC 3 Star
AA 3 Star
BTA Commended

Credit cards: 1, 2, 3, 5

Proprietor: Arthur Neil

DOLPHINTON
65   G6

Dolphinton House Hotel
Dolphinton
nr West Linton
Peeblesshire EH46 7AB
Tel: 0968 82286

*On A702 7 miles east of Biggar and 3
miles west of West Linton.*

Imagine the finest natural fare served in a
Victorian dining room overlooking the
Border hills. Consider the skills of a master
chef preparing gourmet food for a limited
number. Deliberate over some 125 of the
world's best wines – reasonably priced.
You've discovered Dolphinton – a 19th
century manor in 186 acres of woodland –
idyllic!

Open all year

Rooms: 12 with private facilities
Breakfast 8 - 9.30 am
Bar Lunch 12 - 2 pm (a)
Lunch 12.30 - 2 pm (c)
Dinner 7 - 9 pm (e)
No smoking area in restaurant.
Bed & breakfast from £72
Dinner B & B from £102.50

*All Scottish produce – venison, sea trout,
grouse, lamb, beef, soft fruits. 'The
Scottish Gourmet' food.*

STB 4 Crown Highly Commended
RAC 3 Star.

Credit cards: 1, 2, 3, 5, 6.

DORNOCH
66   D6

Dornoch Castle Hotel

Castle Street
Dornoch
IV25 3SD
Tel: 0862 810216

*In the centre of the cathedral town of
Dornoch, 2 miles off A9.*

Former Bishop's Palace opposite 13th
century cathedral, offering comfortable
bedrooms, most of which overlook the
sheltered garden. The elegant coffee
lounge opens onto the terrace. The
panelled bar is welcoming for a pre-dinner
drink or guests may simply enjoy relaxing
in the comfortable TV lounge. The
Bishop's Room Restaurant – once the
palace kitchen – is one of the finest in the
area, with a wine list to match.

Open Apr to Oct

Rooms: 19, 17 with private facilities
Breakfast 8 - 9.30 am
Bar Lunch 12.30 - 2 pm (a)
Lunch 12.30 - 2 pm (b)
Dinner 7.30 - 8.30 pm except Sun (d)
No smoking in restaurant.
Bed & breakfast £22.50 - £32
Dinner B & B rates on application.

*Local venison, salmon, trout and lobster.
Aberdeen Angus steaks. Game birds.
Home-made soups, e.g. Brochan Buidhe,
and chef's pâtés.*

STB 3 Crown Commended
RAC 2 Star
AA 2 Star

Credit cards: 1, 2, 3, 6

Proprietor: Michael Ketchin

DUFFTOWN
67   D6

A Taste of Speyside
Balvenie Street
Dufftown
AB5 4AB
Tel: 0340 20860

*50 yards from Tourist Information Centre
on Elgin road.*

Situated in Dufftown, the malt whisky
capital of the world, this small
independent restaurant and whisky
tasting centre aims to promote the best of
Speyside food and fine Speyside malts, of
which there is an unrivalled selection.
Proprietors Joe Thompson and Ann
McLean are on hand to assure a warm
welcome. Caithness Glass/Taste of
Scotland Best Bar Lunch Award 1988.

Open early Mar to early Jan

Bar lunch (a)
Lunch (b)
Dinner (c)

*Taste of Speyside Platter, roast loin of
Scottish lamb, venison and red wine pie,
home-made pâtés, soups, bread.*

Credit cards: 1, 3

Best Bar Lunch 1988

Proprietors: Joe Thompson &
Ann McLean

DULNAIN BRIDGE
68   E6

Auchendean Lodge Hotel
Dulnain Bridge
Grantown-on-Spey
Morayshire
PH26 3LU
Tel: 047 985 347

On A95 1 mile south of Dulnain Bridge.

An Edwardian hunting lodge, now a
comfortable country hotel, which retains
its homeliness with elegant antique
furnishings. Relax informally with
Highland hospitality and log fires while
marvelling at the views across the River
Spey and Abernethy Forest to the
Cairngorm mountains. Then enjoy the
award-winning home-cooked dinners and
outstanding cellar.

Open all year except Nov and early Dec

Rooms: 7, 5 with private facilities
Breakfast 8 - 9 am
Dinner 7.30 - 10.30 pm (d)
Bed & breakfast £15 - £25
Dinner B & B £30.50 - £40.50

*Arbroath smokies in ale and cream,
smoked haddock tartare, Spey salmon,
venison with juniper berries, pork with
chanterelles, mallard with blaeberries,
orange pancakes with Strathspey malt
whisky.*

STB 3 Crown Commended

No credit cards

Proprietor: Ian Kirk

Muckrach Lodge Hotel
Dulnain Bridge
Grantown-on-Spey
Morayshire
PH26 3LY
Tel: 047 985 257

On A938 ½ mile west of Dulnain Bridge.

Former shooting lodge located in ten
secluded acres in the beautiful Dulnain
valley. The Dulnain River is adjacent to the
hotel. This tributary of the Spey is famous
for salmon and sea trout. Frequent visitors
to the hotel grounds are the timid roe deer
and the capricious red squirrel along with
the numerous bird life of the area. Log
fires, fully centrally heated. All rooms have
colour TV, telephones and tea/coffee
makers. Table d'hôte dinners and
extensive wine cellar.

Open all year.   ►

Rooms: 10 with private facilities
Breakfast 8 - 9.30 am
Bar lunch 12 - 2 pm (b)
Dinner 7.30 - 8.45 pm (e)
Bed & breakfast from £26.25
Dinner B & B from £44

Aberdeen Angus beef, Morayshire lamb, Spey salmon and sea trout. Kinlochbervie shellfish, Aberdeen fresh fish. Scottish cheeseboard. Muckrach substantial sandwiches - lunchtime. Home-made soups, pâté.

STB   4 Crown Commended
RAC   2 Star
AA   2 Star

Credit cards: 1, 2, 3, 5
Proprietors: Roy & Pat Watson

---

69   DUMFRIES   H6

Cairndale Hotel
English Street
Dumfries
Dumfriesshire DG1 2DF
Tel: 0387 54111
Telex: 777530
Fax: 0387 50555

Situated close to centre of town, on A75 Dumfries to Carlisle route.

Originally three Victorian town houses, the Cairndale Hotel is the largest hotel in Dumfries. Recent refurbishment and improvements to the hotel have resulted in a grand hotel with a total of 60 letting bedrooms. Executive rooms and suites boast queen size double beds, jacuzzi spa baths, trouser presses and minibars.

Open all year
Rooms: 60 with private facilities
Breakfast 7.15 - 10 am: 8 - 10 am Sun
Bar Lunch 12 - 2 pm (b)
Lunch 12 - 2 pm (b)
High Tea 5 - 6.30 pm (b)
Dinner 7 - 9.30 pm (d)
Bed & breakfast rates on application.
Dinner B & B rates on application.

Clam chowder, fresh scallops, scampi in the chef's own style, Border lamb, Galloway beef, hot butterscotch pancakes.

STB   4 Crown Commended
RAC   3 Star
AA   3 Star

Credit cards: 1, 2, 3, 5

Station Hotel
Lovers Walk
Dumfries
Dumfriesshire DG1 1LT
Tel: 0387 54316
Telex: 778654

Just outside town centre opposite railway station.

The hotel offers a delightful combination of modern guest comfort and facilities within the maintained character of a Listed building. It is conveniently situated close to the commercial and shopping centre of this charming historic town, yet is only one mile from the attractive Borders countryside and Burns Heritage trail.

Open all year
Rooms: 32 with private facilities
Breakfast 7.30 - 9.30 am
Bar Lunch 12 - 2 pm (a)
Lunch 12 - 2 pm (b)
Bar Supper 5 - 10.30 pm
Dinner 7 - 9.30 pm (c)
No smoking area in restaurant.
Bed & breakfast from £36
Dinner B & B from £25

STB   4 Crown Commended
RAC   3 Star
AA   3 Star

Credit cards: 1, 2, 3, 5, 6

---

70   DUNBLANE   F5

Cromlix House
Kinbuck
Dunblane
Perthshire
FK15 9JT
Tel: 0786 822125

A9 to Dunblane then B8033 to Kinbuck.

Now a superb country house hotel, Cromlix House, built in 1880, stands in 5,000 acres and has four private lochs. Log fires burn in public rooms which still contain original furnishings and fine porcelain and silver. Rooms available for exclusive conferences and private dinner parties. Sports include fishing, shooting, croquet, riding and tennis. A recent addition is a magnificently recreated Victorian conservatory where non-residents are served lunch, full afternoon tea and dinner.

Open all year
Rooms: 14 with private facilities

Breakfast – on request
Lunch 12 - 2 pm (b-d)
Full afternoon tea (b)
Dinner 7 - 10 pm (f) - 6 course fully inclusive of canape, petit fours and coffee.
No smoking area in restaurant.
Bed & breakfast from £75
Dinner B & B from £105

Sauted partridge breast with sorrel on braised cabbage in a port wine sauce. Sauted medallions of monkfish on aubergine fondue in rosemary butter sauce. White coffee mousse with toasted hazelnut sauce.

STB   5 Crown Highly Commended
AA   3 Star + Rosette
BTA   Commended

Credit cards: 1, 2, 3
Best Country House Hotel 1989

Stakis Dunblane Hydro Resort
Perth Road
Dunblane
Perthshire FK15 0HG
Tel: 0786 822551
Telex: 776284
Fax: 0786 825403

The Stakis Dunblane Hydro is situated on the fringe of the rural town, from which it takes its name. Set in 44 acres of private mature grounds and commanding a magnificent view; the splendid Victorian façade of this famed hotel is just a foretaste of the luxury to follow. Extensive leisure facilities both indoors and outdoors. Regular entertainment.

Open all year
Rooms: 223 with private facilities
Breakfast 7.30 - 9.30 am: 8 - 10 am Sun
Lunch 12.30 - 1.45 pm (b)
Afternoon Tea 3 - 5.30 pm
Dinner 6.30 - 9.30 pm (c)
No smoking area in restaurant.
Room rate from £60
Dinner B & B from £31 (min. 2 nights stay).

Terrine of Perthshire pheasant, pigeon and pistachio. Steamed fillet of Tay salmon with fresh spinach and pine kernels.

AA   3 Star
Credit cards: 1, 2, 3, 5, 6

CREDIT/CHARGE CARDS

1 Access/Mastercard/Eurocard
2 American Express
3 Visa
4 Carte Bleu
5 Diners Club
6 Mastercharge

The Old Mansion House Hotel
Auchterhouse
by Dundee
DD3 0QN
Tel: 082 626 366

On A923 west of Dundee, then B954 past Muirhead.

A small luxury hotel converted by the present owners from a 16th century baronial home, within 10 acres of beautiful gardens and woodlands. The lands around the house steeped in Scottish history have been in the ownership of several noted families, namely the Ogilvies, Strathmores, and the Earls of Buchan. Superb dining and excellent wine cellar.

Open all year except Christmas/New Year period

Rooms: 6 with private facilities
Breakfast 7 - 10 am
Bar Lunch 12 - 2 pm (b)
Lunch 12 - 2 pm (c)
Dinner 7 - 9.30 pm (e)
Bed & breakfast from £35
Dinner B & B from £50

Cullen Skink, collops in the pan, venison terrine.

STB   4 Crown Commended
AA   3 Star + Rosette
BTA   Commended

Credit cards: 1, 2, 3, 5

Proprietors: Nigel & Eva Bell

Stakis Earl Grey Hotel
Earl Grey Place
Dundee
DD1 4DE
Tel: 0382 29271
Telex: 76569
Fax: 0382 200072

City location on the waterfront.

Situated on Dundee's waterfront, commanding magnificent views over the River Tay. Only minutes from the City Centre, this luxurious hotel promotes the very highest standards of service and accommodation. Leisure interests are well catered for too – the hotel's own leisure suite incorporates a pool, exercise area, whirlpool and sauna.

Open all year

Rooms: 103 with private facilities
Lunch 12.30 - 2.30 pm (b-c)
Dinner 6.30 - 10 pm (d)

Bed & breakfast from £72.25
Dinner B & B from £29 (min. 2 nights stay).

Highland venison in honey and Drambuie sauce, breast of pheasant in whisky sauce. Cranachan, Atholl brose, Drambuie cream.

STB   5 Crown Commended

Credit cards: 1, 2, 3, 5

Dundonnell Hotel
Dundonnell
by Garve
Ross-shire
IV23 2QR
Tel: 085 483 204

On A832 south of Ullapool.

Set by the shores of Little Loch Broom in the spectacular wilderness of Wester Ross this three star hotel renowned for its quality and comfort has been in the ownership of the Florence family for the past 27 years. Mid-way between Ullapool and Gairloch this is the ideal place from which to explore the surrounding hills and glens as well as the better known attraction of Inverewe Gardens.

Open Easter to Oct

Rooms: 24 with private facilities
Breakfast 8 - 9.15 am
Bar Lunch 12.30 - 2.30 pm (a)
Lunch by arrangement only (c)
Dinner 7 - 8.30 pm (d)
Bed & breakfast £24.50 - £29.50
Dinner B & B £33 - £42.50

Home-made soups, scallops Moniack, Drambuie prawn, seafood chicken, salmon in dill, cranachan, Scottish flummery, Caledonian cream.

STB   4 Crown Commended
RAC   3 Star
AA   3 Star L

Credit cards: 1, 3, 6

Proprietors: Mr & Mrs S W Florence

Pitfirrane Arms Hotel
Main Street
Crossford
Dunfermline
Fife
KY12 8NJ
Tel: 0383 736132

A994 west of Dunfermline i.e. Glasgow road.

The Pitfirrane Arms Hotel is one of the few original coaching inns left in the country which has been restored and extended to meet the modern demand for excellent cuisine and high standards. Situated in the pleasant residential village of Crossford, on the main Dunfermline-Glasgow road (A994), the hotel is within easy access of the M90.

Open all year

Rooms: 38 with private facilities
Breakfast 7 - 9.30 am
Bar Lunch 12 - 2 pm (a)
Lunch 12 - 2 pm (b)
Dinner 6 - 10.15 pm (c)
Bed & breakfast from £33
Dinner B & B from £40

Locally available fresh produce.

STB   4 Crown Commended
RAC   3 Star
AA   3 Star

Credit cards: 1, 2, 3

Proprietor: M McVicars

Stakis Dunkeld House Hotel
Dunkeld
Perthshire
PH8 0HX
Tel: 03502 771
Telex: 76657
Fax: 03502 8294

Dunkeld House stands on the bank of the River Tay, one of Scotland's finest salmon rivers and is set in over 200 acres of gardens and grounds in the magnificent Perthshire countryside. The addition of modern leisure and sporting facilities enhance the attraction of this elegant country house.

Open all year   ▶

Rooms: 91 with private facilities
Breakfast 8 - 10 am
Lunch 12.30 - 2.30 pm (c)
Dinner 7 - 10 pm (f)
Bed & breakfast from £50
Dinner B & B from £48 (min. 2 nights stay)
STB   5 Crown Commended
AA   4 Star
Credit cards: 1, 2, 3, 4, 5, 6

DUNLOP
75   **G5**

Struther Farmhouse
Newmill Road
Dunlop
Ayrshire
KA3 4BA
Tel: 0560 84946

North Ayrshire – 12 miles Glasgow –
8 miles Kilmarnock.

Struther is set in a beautiful well
established garden on the edge of a rural
village. Large comfortable rooms, great
food and hospitality combine to make
Struther the perfect place for a home from
home stay or a private dinner party.
Guests welcome to take own wine.

Open all year but booking essential.

Rooms: 5
Breakfast as required
Dinner 6.30 - 8.30 pm (c)
Unlicensed
Bed & breakfast from £12.50
Dinner B & B from £25

Roast meats, fresh fruit and vegetables,
poached salmon. Sweets always a
speciality.

No credit cards

Proprietors: Bob & Peggy Wilson

DUNOON
76   **G4**

Ardenslate Hotel
James Street
Hunters Quay
Dunoon
Argyll
PA23 8JS
Tel: 0369 2068

On A815 400 yards past Western Ferries
Terminal.

The dining room at Ardenslate Hotel must
have one of the finest views of the Firth of
Clyde. The hotel is set in about an acre

of garden with ample parking facilities.
Two comfortable lounges, one with a
small bar, the other with television. Eight
bedrooms, most with private facilities,
three of which are on the ground floor.

Open Mar to Oct

Breakfast 8.15 - 9.15 am
Lunch 12.15 - 1.45 pm (b)
Dinner 6.30 - 8.30 pm (c); 6.30 - 9 pm Sat
Sun dinner residents only

Credit cards: 1, 3

Ardfillayne Hotel
Beverley's Restaurant
Bullwood Road
Dunoon
Argyll
PA23 7QJ
Tel: 0369 2267
Fax: 0369 2501

West end of Dunoon (A815).

Country house hotel set in six acres of
grounds overlooking Clyde estuary.
Beverley's Restaurant is designed in the
style of Charles Rennie Mackintosh,
featuring lace, silver, crystal and fine
furnishings. A top class restaurant
specialising in local seafood, beef, pork
and venison. Vegetarians catered for.
Extensive wine cellar.

Open all year
Rooms: 8 with private facilities
Breakfast 7.30 - 9.30 am
Lunch by prior arrangement, à la carte
only.
Dinner 7 - 10 pm (d)
Restaurant closed Sun evening in winter.
No smoking area in restaurant.
Bed & breakfast rates on application
Dinner B & B rates on application

Steak Glengoyne, Pork Loin Argyll,
Venison Lady Mary de Guise, Scampi
Prince Charlie, Halibut Jean Ecosse, Loch
Fyne Crab Mornay, Scallops Saint
Veronique.

STB   4 Crown Highly Commended
BTA   Commended

Credit cards: 1, 2, 3, 5

Proprietors: Bill & Beverley McCaffrey

Enmore Hotel
Marine Parade
Dunoon
Argyll
PA23 8HH
Tel: 0369 2230

Seafront between Dunoon and Hunters
Quay.

Charming Georgian country house hotel
situated on the seafront between Dunoon
and Hunters Quay. Lovingly tended and
cared for by the resident proprietors. Local
and own garden produce to provide
superb Scottish fare. Scottish delicacies
from Loch Fyne and Argyll.

Open Mar to Nov
Rooms: 12 with private facilities
Breakfast 8 - 9 am
Bar Lunch 12 - 3 pm (a)
High Tea 4 - 6 pm
Dinner 7 - 9 pm (d)
Bed & breakfast from £32.50
Dinner B & B from £48.50

Loch Fyne fish dishes, local venison and
salmon.

STB   4 Crown Commended
AA   2 Star H
BTA   Commended

Credit cards: 1, 3, 5

Proprietors: David & Angela Wilson

DUNS
77   **G8**

Whitchester Christian Guest House
& Conference Centre
Duns
Berwickshire
TD11 3SF
Tel: 036 17 271

One mile off B6355 Gifford-Duns road,
between Ellemford and Longformacus.

A country house set amongst rare trees,
plants and rhododendrons. David and
Doreen Maybury welcome guests in an
atmosphere of peace and beauty where
care and attention to detail are paramount.
All food is cooked on the premises, the
majority is grown locally. Full board
includes a traditional Scottish afternoon
tea.

Open all year
Rooms: 10,1 with private facilities
Breakfast 8.30 - 9.30 am
Lunch 12.45 - 1.15 pm except Sun (a)
Tea 4 - 4.30 pm
Dinner 7 - 8.30 pm except Sun (c)   ▶

Sun – light meal only, available in the evening.
Unlicensed
Bed & breakfast from £12.65
Dinner B & B from £21.45

Rowan poached trout, Border beef steak in black pepper sauce, blackcurrant nut meringue gâteau. cranachan, syllabubs, home-made soups and bread.

STB 2 Crown Commended

No credit cards

Proprietors: David & Doreen Maybury

Abbotsford Restaurant & Bar
3 Rose Street
Edinburgh
EH2 2PR
Tel: 031 225 5276

Rose Street, behind Jenners.

Victorian surroundings in both restaurant and bar with ornate ceiling, good pub food, convenient city centre just off St Andrew Square.

Open all year

Bar Lunch 12 - 2 pm (a)
Lunch 12 - 2.15 pm (b)
Dinner 6.30 - 10 pm (c)
Closed Sun

Credit cards: 1, 3

Proprietor: Colin Grant

Caledonian Hotel
Princes Street
Edinburgh
EH1 2AB
Tel: 031 225 2433
Telex: 72179
Fax: 031 225 6632

The 'Grande Dame' of Edinburgh dominating the west end of Princes Street, this magnficent deluxe hotel offers gracious accommodation and a range of superb food. The elegant Pompadour Restaurant with its subtle colours and delicate murals features Scottish specialities, while the Gazebo Restaurant offers a more informal luncheon buffet and an à la carte or table d'hôte dinner menu with many Scottish dishes.

Open all year

Rooms: 237 with private facilities
Breakfast 7 - 10 am
Bar Lunch 12 - 2 pm (b)
Lunch (Pompadour) 12.30 - 2 pm except Sun, Sat (d)
Lunch (Gazebo) 12 - 2.30 pm (c)
Afternoon Tea 3 - 5.30 pm
Dinner (Pompadour) 7.30 - 10.30 pm (f)
Dinner (Gazebo) 6 - 10 pm (d)
No smoking area in restaurants.
Bed & breakfast from £81
Dinner B & B rates on application

Fresh baked bread, Achiltibuie smoked chicken, Tobermory smoked trout, trout in oatmeal, cranachan.

STB 5 Crown Highly Commended
RAC 5 Star
AA 5 Star H

Credit cards: 1, 2, 3, 5, 6

Best Hotel 1988

Dubh Prais Restaurant
123B High Street
Edinburgh
EH1 1SG
Tel: 031 557 5732

Edinburgh Royal Mile.

Tucked away in a cavern on the High Street below the Royal Mile – Dubh Prais (pronounced 'Doo Prash') is an interesting new restaurant on this famous Edinburgh street. James McWilliams, the chef/proprietor, has created a delightful cosy atmosphere which offers fine Scottish cuisine with an interesting international touch.

Open all year

Lunch 12 - 2.30 pm except Sat (b)
Dinner 6.30 - 10.30 pm (e)

Closed Sun

Saddle of hare with chestnut stuffing – served with raspberry barquets (Gold Medal winning dish). Game, seafood, salmon and Aberdeen Angus steak.

Credit cards: 1, 3

Proprietor: James McWilliams

Edinburgh Sheraton
1 Festival Square
Edinburgh
EH3 9SR
Tel: 031 229 9131
Telex: 72398

Lothian Road opposite Usher Hall and only 5 minutes from Princes Street.

A superb luxury hotel in the city centre within easy walking distance of theatres and concert halls. It has every amenity to be expected from the Sheraton chain. The elegant restaurant overlooks Festival Square and is noted for the excellence of its food and service. An extensive range of 'Taste of Scotland' dishes is offered. Sunday lunch is a speciality and there is also a 'Taste of Scotland' banqueting menu.

Open all year

Rooms: 263 with private facilities
Breakfast 7 - 10 am
Lunch 12 - 2.30 pm (d)
Dinner 7 - 10.30 pm (e)
Banqueting for up to 485. Coffee, light lunch and afternoon tea served in Lobby Lounge (no smoking area available).
No smoking area in restaurant.
Bed & breakfast rates on application.

Seafood in season a speciality, using the best of local produce. Home-made terrines and gravlax are particularly good.

STB 5 Crown Highly Commended
RAC 5 Star

Credit cards: 2, 3, 4, 5, 6

George Hotel
George Street
Edinburgh
EH3 2PB
Tel: 031 225 1251

City centre of Edinburgh.

Listed amongst Edinburgh's premier hotels, the George enjoy a fine reputation. There are 195 comfortable bedrooms, with superb views over the city. Le Chambertin Restaurant offers the finest cuisine and the Carvers Table offers traditional roasts. The Clans Bar has a Scottish theme, decorated with artifacts and curios of the whisky trade. ▶

Open all year
Rooms: 195 with private facilities
Breakfast 7.30 - 10 am
Lunch 12.30 - 2 pm (d)
High Tea 3 - 5.30 pm
Dinner 7 - 10 pm (d)
No smoking area in restaurant.
Bed & breakfast £94 - £138
Dinner B & B rates on application.
STB   5 Crown Commended
RAC   4 Star
AA   4 Star
Credit cards: 1, 2, 3, 4, 5, 6

Henderson's Salad Table
94 Hanover Street
Edinburgh
EH2 1DR
Tel: 031 225 2131

2 minutes from Princes Street under Henderson's wholefood shop.

Established for 25 years, Henderson is a well known and popular rendezvous for healthy eaters. It offers a continuous buffet of fresh salads and savouries and sweets prepared with care and served in an informal cosmopolitan atmosphere. Seating for up to 200. Live music in the evenings. Innovators of healthy eating.

Open all year. Closed Sun except during Festival.
Open Mon to Sat 8 am - 10 pm
No smoking area in restaurant.

Wide selection of herb teas, freshly squeezed juice, wines from growers using organic methods, hand-made bakery items made with stoneground flour, free-range eggs.

Credit cards: 1, 2, 3
Proprietors: Henderson Family

Jackson's Restaurant
2 Jackson Close
209 High Street, Royal Mile
Edinburgh
EH1 1PL
Tel: 031 225 1793

A small interesting restaurant tucked away down the historic Jackson Close. Popular amongst both Scots and visitors. Jackson's offers excellent Scottish cuisine with a subtle French flair. Friendly service and a relaxing ambience make dinner in Jackson's a night to remember.

Open all year
Lunch 12 - 2 pm (b)

Dinner 6 - 10.30 pm (c-d).
Extended hours during Edinburgh Festival.

Haggis balls served in a whisky cream sauce, smoked salmon, Aberdeen Angus steaks with speciality sauces, fresh salmon, game and seafoods.

Credit cards: 1, 2, 3, 4, 6
Proprietor: Lynn MacKinnon

Keepers Restaurant
13B Dundas Street
Edinburgh
EH3 6QG
Tel: 031 556 5707

Dundas Street is to north of Princes Street and the continuation of Hanover Street.

Set in a delightful Georgian basement on the site of Scotland's first wine bar, this restaurant comprises three cellar rooms and a wine/coffee bar. The cellar rooms, with their original stone walls and floors, provide a warm, relaxing atmosphere and may be reserved for business meetings and private functions.

Open all year
Bar Lunch 12 - 2.30 pm (a)
Lunch 12 - 2.30 pm (a)
Dinner from 6 pm (c)
Coffee bar upstairs open from 10.30 am all day.
Closed Sun except during Festival or on request.
No smoking area in restaurant.

Imaginative game and poultry dishes – duck in wine and honey sauce garnished with grapefruit; roast venison haunch with red wine and cranberry sauce. Extensive range – fish, steak, vegetarian dishes.

Credit cards: 1, 2, 3, 5
Proprietor: Sheena Marshall

Kelly's Restaurant
46 West Richmond Street
Edinburgh
EH6 9DZ
Tel: 031 668 3847

West Richmond Street is off Clerk Street – the continuation of North Bridge from the east end of Princes Street.

Situated in an old bakehouse in an atmosphere which is warm and comfortable. Sociable candlelight dinners are enjoyed amongst old pine, linen napery and antique lace. Patronised by a wide variety of diners – Kelly's aims to give value for money, friendly service and the best of Scottish food, and has earned a

fine reputation. Booking essential.

Open all year except 2 weeks in Jan
Dinner 6.45 - 9.45 pm (d)
Closed Sun + Mon.

Smoked Scottish salmon with mushrooms in Pernod sauce. Border lamb cutlets with an orange Grand Marnier and rosemary glaze. Scallops poached in cream, spring onion and whisky sauce. Chocolate box surprise.

Credit cards: 1, 2, 3
Proprietor: Jacque Kelly

King James Thistle Hotel
Leith Street
Edinburgh
EH1 3SW
Tel: 031 556 0111

East end of Princes Street.

The Restaurant St Jacques is an authentic brasserie serving traditional Scottish food in a distinctly French manner. The limed oak, gleaming marble and glistening brass make it impressive for business lunches or intimate for a special occasion.

Open all year
Rooms: 147 with private facilities
Breakfast 7.30 - 10 am
Bar Lunch 11.30 am - 2 pm (a)
Lunch 12.30 - 2 pm (b)
Dinner 6.30 - 10.30 pm (d)
Bar Lunch (Boston Bean Co). Lunch and Dinner (Restaurant St Jacques).
Bed & breakfast from £40
Dinner B & B from £52

Both the à la carte and cafe menu feature Scottish dishes including west coast oysters, saddle of hare with game sauce, medallions of venison with wild mushrooms and chocolate Glayva pot.

STB   5 Crown Highly Commended
Credit cards: 1, 2, 3, 5, 6 + Trumpcard

Lightbody's Restaurant & Bar
23 Glasgow Road
Edinburgh
EH12 8HW
Tel: 031 334 2300

On the main Corstorphine road out of Edinburgh towards the airport and Glasgow.

Family-run business with friendly, warm atmosphere and consistent standards. A popular business rendezvous at lunchtime and light bar meals are also available for lunch and evening (week days only). More leisurely meals chosen from à la   ►

carte menu which changes regularly using the best of fresh, Scottish produce.

Open all year
Lunch 12 - 2.30 pm (b)
Dinner 6 - 10.30 pm (d)
Bar meals available. Closed Sun.

Fresh soups made with Scottish seafoods. Salmon, mussels and lobsters (when available), Scotch beef, venison in a variety of sauces. Duck, freshwater trout, and white fish bought locally.

Credit cards: 1, 2, 3

Proprietors: Malcolm & Norman Lightbody

Martins Restaurant
70 Rose Street North Lane
Edinburgh
EH2 3DX
Tel: 031 225 3106

In the north lane off the pedestrianised precinct of Rose Street between Frederick Street and Castle Street.

Not easy to find, but persist. This is a gem of a restaurant run personally by Martin and Gay Irons. They are superb hosts and are justifiably proud of this delightful intimate restaurant. The table linen is always spotless, the flowers are fresh and the food exceptionally well prepared and imaginatively presented. Chef David McCrae's fine cooking has made this one of Edinburgh's best. Caithness Glass/Taste of Scotland Hospitality Award 1988.

Open all year except from 25 Dec to 3 Jan (incl)

Lunch 12 - 2 pm except Sat (b)
Dinner 7 - 10 pm; 7 - 10.30 pm Fri, Sat (d-e)
Closed Sun + Mon.
No smoking in restaurant.

Menus are based on the availability of fresh local produce, are regularly changed and specialise in fresh Scottish seafish, shellfish and game.

Credit cards: 1, 2, 3, 5

Best Welcome 1988

Proprietors: Martin & Gay Irons

The Royal Over-Seas League
Over-Seas House
100 Princes Street
Edinburgh
EH2 3AB
Tel: 031 225 1501
Telex: 721654
Fax: 031 226 3936

Over-Seas House Edinburgh is one of the few remaining of the original Princes Street buildings. The bedrooms, however, have all been refurbished in keeping with today's standards. The restaurant, with its spectacular view of Edinburgh Castle, is in the more modern part of the building and has been recently redecorated.

Open all year

Rooms: 15, 5 with private facilities
Breakfast 8 - 9.30 am
Bar Lunch 12 - 2 pm (a)
Lunch 12.30 - 2 pm (a-b)
High Tea 5.30 - 6 pm
Dinner 7.30 - 9.30 pm (a-b)
Bed & breakfast from £32
Dinner B & B rates on application.

Loch Tay salmon supreme, collops of pork 'Auld Reekie', fillet of beef medallion Cockpen.

STB 3 Crown Commended

Credit cards: 1, 2, 3, 5

Skippers Bistro
1A Dock Place
Leith
Edinburgh
EH6 6UY
Tel: 031 554 1018

Leith, Edinburgh.

Situated as it is, in the centre of the rejuvenated Leith waterfront, 'Skippers' is proud of its justified reputation as a leading fresh seafood restaurant, where local and Scottish produce is handled with care and imagination.

Open all year
Lunch 12.30 - 2 pm (b)
Dinner 7.30 - 10 pm (d)

Specialises in fresh seafood.

Credit cards: 1, 2, 3, 4, 6

Proprietors: Allan & Jennifer Corbett

Stakis Grosvenor Hotel
7-21 Grosvenor Street
Edinburgh
EH12 5EF
Tel: 031 226 6001
Telex: 72445.
Fax: 031 220 2387

Opposite Haymarket Station in the West End.

Ideally situated in Edinburgh's elegant West End, the Stakis Grosvenor Hotel's style goes beyond its fashionable façade. From the comfortable chesterfields in the hotel's public areas to the fine furnishings you'll find in the private bedrooms, the hotel has a unique ambience.

Open all year

Rooms: 134 with private facilities
Breakfast 7 - 10 am; 7.30 - 10 am Sun
Bar Lunch 12 - 3 pm except Sun (a)
Dinner 5 - 9.30 pm (c)
Bed & breakfast from £49
Dinner B & B from £27 (min. 2 nights stay)

Specialities include game and shellfish (some locally caught), Beef Balmoral, Trout Rob Roy, cranachan, peach Highland cream, haggis.

STB 4 Crown Commended
RAC 3 Star
AA 3 Star

Credit cards: 1, 2, 3, 4, 5, 6

The Tattler
23 Commercial Street
Leith
Edinburgh
EH6 6JA
Tel: 031 554 9999

On main road in Leith port area (North Edinburgh).

Cosy Victorian-style pub and restaurant in the historic port of Leith, which won the National Pub Caterer of the Year 1985 — first in Scotland, runner-up in Britain. In keeping with its situation, The Tattler offers a wide range of seafoods in addition to an imaginative selection of meat, poultry and vegetarian dishes.

Open all year

Bar Lunch 12 -2 pm (a)
Lunch 12 - 2 pm (b)
High Tea
Bar Supper 6 - 10 pm (a)
Dinner 6 - 10 pm (d)

Some dishes unique to the Tattler, on extensive restaurant menu with emphasis on use of first class local produce. Bar menu is particularly interesting.

Credit cards: 1, 2, 3, 5, 6

Proprietors: Alan & Linda Thomson

The Witchery by the Castle
Castlehill
Royal Mile
Edinburgh
EH1 1NE
Tel: 031 225 5613

Situated at the entrance to Edinburgh Castle.

The Witchery survives the tourist crush to remain intimate. friendly and quite unique. Already steeped in eight centuries of history, The Witchery, once the very centre of witchcraft in the Old Town, now offers excellent food prepared under ▶

the personal supervision of James Thomson. Seafood specialities change daily – oysters, mussels, meat, fish, sole, etc.

Open all year

Meals served from 12 noon - 11 pm (b-c)

Steak 'Auld Reekie' – in a whisky and smoked cheese sauce, Venison 'Marie Stuart', noisette of lamb, Duck Nor'loch, Scotch salmon and lobster sauce, burn trout, scallops, langoustines.

Credit cards: 1, 2, 3, 5, 6

Proprietor: James Thomson

ELGIN
79   **D7**

The Mansion House Hotel
The Haugh
Elgin
Morayshire
IV30 1AN
Tel: 0343 48811

The charm of the past with the up to date comfort you deserve – all the facilities you would expect in this 19th century old mansion house. The hotel is situated in a quiet location surrounded by mature trees and parkland by the riverside, and yet only minutes walk from Elgin town centre, capital of the whisky trail and heart of Scotland's castle trail.

Open all year

Rooms: 15, 12 with private facilities
Breakfast 7.30 - 9.30 am
Bar Lunch 12.15 - 1.45 pm (a)
Lunch 12.15 - 1.45 pm (b)
High Tea available for residents on request.
Dinner 7.30 - 9 pm (c-d)
Bed & breakfast from £30
Dinner B & B from £40

Fresh local produce – fish, game, fruit and vegetables, talented presentation and natural flavours of the cuisine match the most demanding expectations.

STB 4 Crown Highly Commended
AA 3 Star HB
BTA Commended

Credit cards: 1, 2, 3, 5

Proprietor: Fernando de Oliveira

EDINBURGH
See late entry p95: **The Magnum**

ELIE
See late entry p95: **Bouquet Garni**
Ref 79A on main map

Park House Hotel & Restaurant
South Street
Elgin
IV30 1JB
Tel: 0343 7695

Situated to the west end of Elgin just off A98 and 5 minutes walk from the town centre.

Park House is well placed locally as a base for touring or business. The architecturally Listed building is of classical Georgian design. There is an atmosphere of gracious and practical hospitality within a compact, intimate setting.

Open all year

Rooms: 6 with private facilities
Breakfast 7.30 - 9 am
Lunch 12 - 2 pm (b)
High Tea 5.15 - 6.15 pm
Dinner 7 - 10 pm (c)
Bed & breakfast from £30
Dinner B & B from £45

Scottish fare is the produce of sea, lochs, rivers and countryside. Try perhaps smoked salmon and avocado souffle, venison casserole, cranachan.

STB 3 Crown Commended
RAC Highly Acclaimed
AA 2 Star

Credit cards: 1, 2, 3, 5, 6

Proprietor: Ken Asher

FALKIRK
80   **G6**

Inchyra Grange Hotel
Grange Road
Polmont
Falkirk
FK2 0YB
Tel: 0324 711911
Telex: 777693
Fax: 0324 716134

Junction 4 of M9 motorway. Situated on border of Polmont/Grangemouth.

A fine example of a Scottish country house set in eight acres of private grounds and offering every modern amenity. In the restaurant you can choose from the varied à la carte or table d'hôte menus, carefully prepared dishes featuring local favourites.

Open all year

Rooms: 33 with private facilities
Breakfast 7 - 10 am; 8 - 10 am Sun
Bar Lunch 12 - 2 pm; 12.30 - 2 pm Sun (a)
Lunch 12.30 - 2 pm except Sat (b)
High Tea 5 - 6.30 pm Sun only

Bar Supper 6 - 10 pm
Dinner 7 - 9.30 pm (c)
À la carte only, Sat dinner.
Bed & breakfast from £57
Dinner B & B from £70

STB 4 Crown Commended
RAC 3 Star
AA 3 Star

Credit cards: 1, 2, 3, 5

Proprietor: K Marwick

Stakis Park Hotel
Camelon Road
Falkirk
FK1 5RY
Tel: 0324 28331
Telex: 776502.
Fax: 0324 611593

On A803 central Falkirk.

The Stakis Park Hotel is ideally located less than one hour from Glasgow and Edinburgh. Its 55 highly appointed bedrooms all include private facilities, radio, TV, telephone and hospitality tray. For the business user, function facilities from 5 to 200. The hotel restaurant boasts à la carte menus specialising in 'Taste of Scotland' dishes.

Open all year

Rooms: 55 with private facilities
Breakfast 7.30 - 9.30 am
Bar Lunch 12.30 - 2.30 pm (a)
Lunch 12.30 - 2.30 pm (b)
Dinner 7 - 10 pm (c)
Bed & breakfast from £40
Dinner B & B from £34 (min. 2 nights stay)

STB 4 Crown Commended

Credit cards: 1, 2, 3, 4, 5, 6

FALKLAND
81   **F7**

Covenanter Hotel
The Square
Falkland
Fife
KY7 7BU
Tel: 0337 57224
Fax: 0337 57272

Centre of Falkland.

17th century coaching inn run for the past ten years by George and Margaret Menzies. A warm welcome awaits you at the Covenanter Hotel, long famous for good food and hospitality. There is a ▶

choice of the traditional restaurant or informal bistro.

Open all year

Rooms: 4 with private facilities
Breakfast 7.30 - 9.30 am
Bar Lunch 12 - 2 pm (a)
Lunch 12 - 2 pm (b)
Bar Supper 6 - 9.30 pm (a)
Dinner 7 - 9 pm (d)
Table d'hôte dinner available as well as à la carte.
Closed Mon.
No dogs.
Bed & breakfast £20 - £32.50
Dinner B & B rates on application

A selection of made to order dishes with emphasis on home produce. Scampi Falkland, Tay salmon, and Scottish beef dishes.

STB   Award Pending
RAC   Acclaimed
Credit cards: 1, 2, 3, 5, 6
Proprietor: George Menzies

Kind Kyttock's Kitchen
Cross Wynd
Falkland
Fife KY7 7BE
Tel: 0337 57477

Off main street in village.

Situated in the heart of the historic village of Falkland, three minutes' walk from Falkland Palace, this very popular and charming restaurant offers the visitor a chance to sample good wholesome fare.

Open Feb to Dec

Meals available all day (a). Separate tearoom for non-smokers.

Home-baked pancakes, scones, fruit squares, shortbread, wholemeal bread, stovies, clootie dumpling. Locally grown vegetables used in Scotch broth and at salad table. Selection of teas available.

No credit cards
Proprietor: Bert Dalrymple

Templelands Farm
Falkland
Fife KY7 7DE
Tel: 0337 57383

On A912 south of Falkland village.

Comfortable modernised farmhouse on small working farm with panoramic views all around. Ideal touring centre. Twenty golf courses within 20 miles including St Andrews. National Trust properties nearby. Swimming pools, tennis, bowling

in the area. Abundance of home-made food with soups and sweets a speciality. Coffee/tea facilities in bedrooms. Guests welcome to take own wine.

Open Easter to Oct

Rooms: 2
Breakfast 8.30 am
Dinner 7 pm
Advanced booking preferred. No smoking in dining room. Residents only.
Unlicensed.
Bed & breakfast from £12
Dinner B & B from £18

STB   2 Crown Commended
Scottish Farmhouse Holidays

No credit cards
Proprietor: Sarah McGregor

Idvies House
Letham
by Forfar
Angus
DD8 2QJ
Tel: 0307 81787

4 miles east of Forfar.

Fine Victorian country house standing in spacious wooded grounds surrounded by lovely Angus countryside. Tastefully furnished public rooms and well appointed bedrooms offer a high standard of comfort. The hotel is personally run by the resident owners.

Open all year

Rooms: 7, 6 with private facilities
Breakfast 7.30 - 10 am
Bar Lunch 12 - 2 pm (a)
Lunch 12 - 2 pm (b)
High Tea 5 - 7 pm; 5 - 6 pm Sat
Dinner 7 - 9.30 pm (c-e); 7 - 8 pm Sun residents only. Special terms available for weekends/3 nights.
Bed & breakfast from £30
Dinner B & B rates on application

Home-smoked salmon and Arbroath smokie mousse. Angus beefsteak dishes with Scottish liqueur and whisky sauces. Isle of Mull mussels. Local crab and lobster. Orkney oysters. Local game.

STB   4 Crown Commended
AA   3 Star
Credit cards: 1, 2, 3, 5, 6
Proprietors: Pat & Fay Slingsby, Judy Hill

Knockomie Hotel
Grantown Road
Forres
Moray
IV36 0SG
Tel: 0309 73146

On A940 just south of Forres on Grantown Road.

Knockomie Hotel stands overlooking the Royal Burgh of Forres which has an outstanding reputation for its gardens. Moray is beautiful and interesting with castles, distilleries, fishing, sailing, golfing, activities to suit everyone. The Restaurant endeavours to provide the best of Scottish produce while the bar has an enviable selection of malts.

Open all year

Rooms: 7 with private facilities
Breakfast 8 - 9.30 am - earlier by request.
Bar Lunch 12 - 2.30 pm (a)
Lunch 12 - 2 pm by arrangement.
Dinner 7 - 9 pm (c)
Bed & breakfast from £25
Dinner B & B from £34.25

Scottish produce – scallops, salmon, rib of Aberdeen Angus beef, venison.

STB   4 Crown Commended
Credit cards: 1, 3
Proprietor: Gavin Ellis

Parkmount House Hotel
St Leonards Road
Forres
Morayshire
IV36 0DW
Tel: 0309 73312

On B9010 Forres to Dallas road, 400 yards from town centre.

Delightful Victorian town house in its own walled flower garden within easy walking distance of town centre, golf course and award-winning floral displays. Family-run hotel providing value for money fresh Scottish fare and very comfortably furnished bedrooms. Low cost self-drive car hire available for guests.

Open all year except Christmas week

Rooms: 6 with private facilities
Breakfast 8 - 9 am - earlier by arrangement.
Dinner from 7 pm (c)

▶

Special diets and non-residents by prior arrangement.

No smoking area in restaurant.

Bed & breakfast from £16.50

Dinner B & B from £29.50

Specialising in good, fresh food including Findhorn salmon, Aberdeen Angus beef and local vegetables.

STB   4 Crown Commended

Credit cards: 1

Proprietors: David & Angela Steer

FORT AUGUSTUS
84   E5

Lovat Arms Hotel

Fort Augustus

Inverness-shire

PH32 2BE

Tel: 0320 6206

On A82 in middle of the village.

A large country house hotel of the Victorian era set in own grounds of 2½ acres with large lawns to the front overlooking Loch Ness and the Benedictine Abbey and Monastery. Amidst beautiful Highland scenery yet centrally located in the village. All bedrooms are centrally heated with colour TVs, direct dial telephones, tea making facilities, trouser presses etc. Relax after your meal with coffee by the open fires.

Open all year

Rooms: 19 with private facilities

Breakfast 8 - 9.30 am

Bar Lunch 12.30 - 2 pm (a)

Lunch 12.30 - 2 pm (b)

Bar Supper 6.30 - 8 pm (b)

Dinner 7 - 8.30 pm (d)

Bed & breakfast from £25.50

Dinner B & B from £37

Highland game terrine with cranberries, roast prime Aberdeen Angus beef traditional style, fillet of wild Scottish salmon with Hollandaise and watercress. Cranachan.

STB   4 Crown Commended

RAC   2 Star

AA   2 Star H

Credit cards: 1, 3, 6

Proprietor: Alan F Lees

FORT WILLIAM
85   E4

Crannog Seafood Restaurant
Town Pier

Fort William

Inverness-shire

PH33 7NG

Tel: 0397 5589/3919

Fax: 0397 5026

Fort William town pier – off A82 Fort William town centre by-pass.

Crannog is run by fishermen who have built a self-contained community based on the fruits of the sea. The fishing boats, smokehouse and processing base market directly to discerning customers. The marketing ideal was brought to fruition when their fishing store on Fort William town pier was tastefully converted to a restaurant where you can enjoy the freshest seafood in a delightful waterfront location.

Open Feb to Dec

Lunch 12 - 3 pm (b)

Dinner 6 - 9.30 pm (d)

Langoustine, crab, lobster and finfish direct from own boats. Salmon, trout, mussels etc fresh or smoked in own smokehouse.

Credit cards: 1

Glen Nevis Restaurant
Glen Nevis

Fort William

Inverness-shire

PH33 6SX

Tel: 0397 5459

2½ miles along Glen Nevis from Fort William.

The restaurant is set amidst the scenic splendour of one of Scotland's loveliest glens, at the foot of mighty Ben Nevis. It is situated just outside Fort William and has ample parking. Large windows give every table a view of river and mountains.

Open mid Mar to mid Oct

Lunch from 12 noon (a-b)

High Tea from 2.30 pm

Dinner 5.30 pm (a-c)

Speciality menu changed each week – always features local produce.

Credit cards: 1, 3

The Moorings Hotel
Banavie

Fort William

Inverness-shire

PH33 7LY

Tel: 03977 797/550

3 miles from Fort William.

The Moorings stands beside the Caledonian Canal at Neptune's Staircase, with splendid views towards Ben Nevis and Aonach Mor. The Jacobean-styled restaurant is renowned for its Scottish cuisine using indigenous Scottish produce, complemented by its gracious surroundings.

Open all year except Christmas

Rooms: 24 with private facilities

Breakfast 7.45 - 9.15 am

Dinner 7 - 9 pm (d)

Taste of Scotland applies to main restaurant.

Bed & breakfast £24 - £30

Dinner B & B £39 - £49

Lochy salmon parcel, Loch Linnhe prawns, Fassock quail. Fresh salmon, halibut, monkfish, scampi, veal, venison.

STB   4 Crown Commended

RAC   2 Star

AA   2 Star

Credit cards: 1, 2, 3, 5, 6

Proprietor: Norman Sinclair

CREDIT/CHARGE CARDS
1   Access/Mastercard/Eurocard

2   American Express

3   Visa

4   Carte Bleu

5   Diners Club

6   Mastercharge

The Steading Restaurant
Achtercairn
Gairloch
Ross-shire
IV21 2BP
Tel: 0445 2449

On A832 at junction with B802 in Gairloch.

Coffee shop/restaurant located in converted 19th century farm buildings retaining their old world peace and charm and adjoining the prize-winning Gairloch Museum of West Highland life.

Open Easter to Sept

Meals available all day 8.30 am - 9 pm (5 pm in Apr and May) (a-c).
Closed Sun.

Local seafoods; salmon, lobster, crab, prawns, marinated herring, smoked mackerel. Also steaks, venison casserole, haggis, home-baking.

No credit cards

Murray Arms Hotel
High Street/Ann Street
Gatehouse-of-Fleet
DG7 2HY
Tel: 055 74 207

Off A75 66 miles west of Carlisle between Dumfries and Stranraer.

Warmth, welcome and good food – where you'll enjoy a drink with the locals. In this inn in July 1793 Robert Burns wrote 'Scots Wha Hae'. In one of Scotland's scenic heritage areas rich historically and with a wide variety of birds and wild flowers. Free golf, fishing and tennis.

Open all year

Rooms: 13 with private facilities
Breakfast 8 - 9.30 am; 9 - 10 pm Sun
Bar meals served all day.
Lunch from 12 noon (b)
Dinner 7.30 - 9 pm (c)
Bed & breakfast from £32
Dinner B & B from £42

Galloway beef, locally caught fish including salmon and smoked salmon.

STB   4 Crown Commended
RAC   3 Star
AA   3 Star

Credit cards: 1, 2, 3, 5, 6
Proprietor: R Raphael

Gigha Hotel
Isle of Gigha
Argyll
PA41 7AD
Tel: 05835 254

Isle of Gigha, Kintyre.

The only hotel on the lovely unspoilt Isle of Gigha, tastefully restored to provide great comfort along with a warm welcome and superb traditional Scottish fare with local specialities. Discover the beauty of Achamore Gardens or simply enjoy the peace and quiet, superb views, sandy beaches or nine holes of golf.

Open all year

Rooms: 9, 3 with private facilities
Breakfast 8 - 9 am
Bar Lunch 11.30 am - 2 pm (a)
Lunch 11.30 am - 2 pm (b)
Dinner 7 - 8.30 pm (c)
Bed & breakfast £24 - £27
Dinner B & B £39 - £42

Popular buffet lunch every day with extensive cold table including local salmon and king prawns as available.

STB   3 Crown Commended
AA   2 Star HL

Credit cards: 1, 3

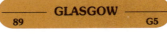

The Albany Hotel
Bothwell Street
Glasgow
G2 7EN
Tel: 041 248 2656

M8 inner ring road, exit at junction 18 at Charing Cross.

One of Glasgow's premier hotels, situated in the heart of the city. Modern amenities, courteous service and attention to the smallest detail, a first class international hotel where guests can enjoy unequalled comfort and luxury. Voted 'Hotel of the Year 1986' by the travel trade.

Open all year

Rooms: 253, 250 with private facilities
Breakfast 7 - 10 am
Bar Lunch (a)
Lunch (Club House) 12.30 - 2.30 pm except Sat (c)
Lunch (Original Carvery) 12 - 2.30 pm
Dinner (Club House) 7 - 11 pm (c) - dinner/dance Sat; 7 - 10 pm Sun

Dinner (Original Carvery) 5.30 - 10 pm.
Bed & breakfast rates on application.
Dinner B & B rates on application.

Lounge service - 24 hours. Scottish afternoon tea. Menus include a selection of traditional Scottish and continental specialities, seafood and meats.

AA   4 Star
Credit cards: 1, 2, 3, 4, 5, 6

The Buttery
652 Argyle Street
Glasgow
G3 8UF
Tel: 041 221 8188

Exit 19 from A8 motorway.

One of Glasgow's finest – a genuine Victorian restaurant renowned for its game dishes and extensive wine list. From the first, as you enter the elegant panelled interior, with its marble Oyster bar, the tone is set to transport you back to a more leisurely age.

Open all year except public holidays

Bar lunch 12 - 2.30 pm except Sat (a)
Lunch 12 - 2.30 pm except Sat (d)
Dinner 7 - 10 pm (f)
Closed Sun

Cheese choux pastries on cranberry puree. Supreme of guinea fowl with almonds and caramelised pears. Drambuie and oatmeal creme brulee.

AA Rosette
Credit cards: 1, 2, 3, 5

The Colonial Restaurant
25 High Street
Glasgow
G1 1LR
Tel: 041 552 1923

City centre.

Set in the merchant centre of the city, the Colonial has an outstanding reputation and offers only the finest and freshest of Scottish ingredients cooked in a modern style. One of Glasgow's finest restaurants.

Open all year

Lunch 12 - 2.30 pm except Sat (b)
Dinner 6 - 10.30 pm except Mon (e)
Closed Sun

Warm pigeon salad with lentils and apricots, summer fruit soup with a banana mousse, fisherman's soup, seafood ravioli with basil.

AA   Rosette
Credit cards: 1, 2, 3, 5, 6
Proprietor: Peter Jackson

The Dalmeny Park Hotel

Lochlibo Road
Barrhead
Glasgow
G78 1LG
Tel: 041 881 9211

On A736 heading south from Glasgow.

The Dalmeny Park Hotel – an attractive 19th century house – stands in its own beautiful grounds and is situated only 20 minutes from Glasgow city centre and 15 minutes from Glasgow Airport. It features both a la carte in its Garden Restaurant and less formal meals in the Tudor Gallery lounge.

Open all year except Boxing Day, 1 and 2 Jan.

Rooms: 20,15 with private facilities
Breakfast 7.30 - 9.30 am
Bar Lunch 12 - 2 pm (a-b)
Lunch 12 - 2 pm except Sat; 12 - 3 pm Sun (b)
Bar Supper 6 - 9.30 pm (a-b)
Dinner 7 - 9.30 pm except Sun (c)
Dinner - Sun residents only. À la carte available lunch and dinner.
Bed & breakfast £23 - £39.50
Dinner B & B rates on application

Taste of Scotland and vegetarian.

STB 3 Crown Commended
RAC 2 Star
AA 2 Star

Credit cards: 1, 2, 3, 5, 6

Forum Hotel Glasgow

Congress Road
Glasgow
G3 8QT
Tel: 041 204 0733
Telex: 776244
Fax: 041 221 2022

Situated on the banks of the River Clyde next to the SECC.

The Forum Glasgow has 300 guest rooms including 15 suites, each one offering panoramic views, each one a delightful home away from home, luxuriously equipped for your comfort. Everything you need to unwind at the end of the day is provided, complemented by the superb dining and leisure facilities.

Open all year

Rooms: 300 with private facilities
Breakfast 6.30 am - 12 noon
Lunch 12 - 3 pm (c-f)
High Tea 3 - 6 pm (a)
Dinner 6.30 - 11 pm (c-f)
All day dining 12 noon - 11 pm.
24 hour room service.
No dogs.
Facilities for the disabled.

No smoking area in restaurant.
Bed & breakfast from £58.59
Dinner B & B from £69.84
STB Award Pending
Credit cards: 1, 2, 3, 4, 5, 6

Holiday Inn

Argyle Street
Glasgow
G3 8RR
Tel: 041 226 5577
Fax: 041 221 9202

Junction 19, M8.

The Holiday Inn, Glasgow, is a splendid city centre hotel, offering all the facilities expected of Holiday Inns and within easy walking distance of the main shopping and entertainment areas. Access to the hotel is offered by motorway (M8), the main railway station which is just five minutes' walk away, and Glasgow Airport is a mere ten minutes' drive. Courtesy coach service can be provided.

Open all year

Rooms: 298 with private facilities
Breakfast 7 - 11 am
High Tea 2.30 - 6.30 pm
Meals 11 am - 10.30 pm
(Patio Restaurant) (c)
Dinner 7 - 10.30pm (L'Academie and Patio) (d).
L'Academie closed all day Sun.
No smoking area in restaurant.
Bed & breakfast rates on application.
Dinner B & B rates on application.

The buffet table offers a new selection of dishes every day. Specialities are served in L'Academie Restaurant.

RAC 4 Star M

Credit cards: 1, 2, 3, 4, 5, 6

Hospitality Inn & Convention Centre

36 Cambridge Street
Glasgow
G2 3HN
Tel: 041 332 3311

¼ mile from Exit 16 Cowcaddens/Exit 17 Dumbarton Road on M8 motorway.

The Hospitality Inn is a modern four star luxury hotel set in the heart of the entertainment and shopping centre of Glasgow. It offers 306 spacious bedrooms, a choice of two bars, two restaurants and hairdressing salon.

Open all year

Rooms: 306 with private facilities
Breakfast 7 - 10.30 am
Bar Lunch 12.30 -2.30 pm (a)
Lunch 12.30 - 2.30 pm (a-c)

Dinner 7 - 10.30 pm (b-c)
Lunch: Captain's Table (a), Garden Cafe (b), Prince of Wales (c). Dinner: Garden Cafe (b), Prince of Wales (c).
Garden Cafe menu available all day.
Bed & breakfast rates on application.
Dinner B & B rates on application.
STB 5 Crown Commended
AA 4 Star

Credit cards: 1, 2, 3, 5, 6

Kensington's Restaurant

164 Darnley Street
Glasgow
G41 2LL
Tel: 041 424 3662

On the south side of the city.

Tucked away in a quiet backwater on the south side of the city – but worth looking for -- and only minutes from the centre of town. The restaurant is small, intimate and luxuriously appointed with delightful oil paintings and interesting antiques.

Open all year.

Lunch 12 - 2 pm except Sat (b)
Dinner 6.30 - 9.30 pm (e)
Closed Sun

Scottish seafood, game, beef and lamb are featured on all menus.

Credit cards: 1, 2, 3, 5, 6
Proprietor: Denise Drummond

Killermont House Restaurant

2022 Maryhill Road
Glasgow
G20 0AB
Tel: 041 946 5412

North-west Glasgow.

Killermont House Restaurant is the country house restaurant in the city. The house was built in the 19th century as a manse and was tastefully converted in 1987 into a 50 cover restaurant of distinction using the finest Scottish and continental produce handled with care.

Open all year except 1st wk in Jan and 2 wks in Jul.

Lunch 12 - 2.30 pm (c)
Dinner 6.30 - 10.30 pm (e)
Facilities for the disabled.

Scottish game in season, west coast shellfish, Tay salmon, unusual Scottish cheeses and home-made bread.

AA 2 Knives & Forks

Credit cards: 1, 2, 3
Proprietors: Paul & Christine Abrami

Rogano

11 Exchange Place
Glasgow
G1 3AN
Tel: 041 248 4055

Glasgow city centre.

Since 1876, Rogano has been famed worldwide for its seafood and ambience. Remodelled in 1935 in similar 'art deco' style to the 'Queen Mary' which was at the time being built on the Clyde. Rogano today maintains the same ambience and high standards on which its reputation was founded. Elegant restaurant on ground floor. Bistro style downstairs.

Open all year
Bar lunch 12 - 2.30 pm
Lunch 12 - 2.30 pm   } Restaurant
Dinner 7 - 10 pm (f)
Lunch/Dinner 12 noon - 11 pm in downstairs restaurant (c).

Specialist fish restaurant.

Credit cards: 1, 2, 3, 5

Stakis Grosvenor Hotel

Great Western Road
Glasgow
G12 0TA
Tel: 041 339 8811.
Telex: 776247
Fax: 041 334 0710

On A82 Great Western Road.

Discreetly elegant, the Stakis Grosvenor Hotel is without question one of the most impressive buildings in Glasgow's fashionable West End. Directly opposite the City's Botanical Gardens. The Stakis Grosvenor Hotel is one mile from the motorway network, and two miles from the City Centre.

Open all year
Rooms: 95 with private facilities
Breakfast 7 - 9.30 am
Bar Lunch 12 - 2.30 pm (a)
Lunch 12 - 2.30 pm (b-c)
Dinner 5 - 11 pm (b-f)
Bed & breakfast from £51.50
Dinner B & B from £38 (min 2 nights stay).

Arbroath smokie salad. Roast haunch of venison and game sauce.

STB   5 Crown Commended
AA   4 Star

Credit cards: 1, 2, 3, 5, 6

The Triangle

37 Queen Street
Glasgow
G1 3EF
Tel: 041 221 8758
Fax: 041 204 3189

Halfway down Queen Street, above Tam Shepherd's (joke shop).

The Triangle is the most cosmopolitan restaurant in the very heart of Glasgow. Famous for its exciting decor by Glasgow's leading artists, it is friendly and stylish, formal or informal. Fine restaurant and brasserie. The Triangle is open from early morning till late evening. The dining room is available for private parties.

Open all year
No Parking
Breakfast 9 - 11.30 am
Bar Lunch 12 - 3 pm (a)
Lunch 12 - 3 pm (c)
High Tea 5 - 7 pm (b)
Bar Supper 5 - 12 pm (c)
Dinner 6 - 12 pm (e-f)

Favourite recipes from Scotland and Europe. The best of Scotland's fish, game and farmed produce (Pentland lamb, wild salmon, Islay scallops, Loch Fyne oysters, Highland venison etc).

Credit cards: 1, 2, 3, 4, 5, 6

Proprietor: Suzanne Ritchie

The Ubiquitous Chip

12 Ashton Lane
Glasgow
G12 8SJ
Tel: 041 334 5007

A secluded lane in the heart of Glasgow's west end.

A white-washed Victorian mews stable is the setting for one of Glasgow's most renowned restaurants. The wealth of local Scottish produce is polished by traditional and original recipes, to make this restaurant "a wee gem".

Open all year
Bar meals available 12 noon - 11 pm.
Lunch 12 - 2.30 pm (e)
Dinner 5.30 - 11 pm (e)
Closed Sun.

One of the UK's most celebrated, extensive and modestly priced wine lists.

Credit cards: 1, 2, 3, 5

Proprietor: Ron Clydesdale

Newton House Hotel

Glencarse
by Perth
PH2 7LX
Tel: 073 886 250
Fax: 073 886 717

A85 between Perth and Dundee.

A former Victorian dower house set in its own mature grounds. The ten en-suite bedrooms are tastefully decorated and the elegant public rooms and restaurant feature open fires. Fresh local produce is used when planning menus which are complemented by a fine wine list.

Open all year
Rooms: 10 with private facilities
Breakfast 7.30 - 9.30 am
Bar Lunch 12 - 2 pm (a)
Lunch 12 - 2 pm (b)
Dinner 7 - 9.30 pm (d)
Bed & breakfast from £26
Dinner B & B from £38

Cream of Arbroath Smokie soup, entrecote Isla, venison in bramble sauce, Islay prawns.

STB   4 Crown Commended
RAC   3 Star
AA   3 Star

Credit cards: 1, 3, 5, 6

Proprietors: Geoffrey & Carol Tallis

Minmore House

Glenlivet
Ballindalloch
Banffshire
AB3 9DB
Tel: 08073 378

Adjacent to The Glenlivet Distillery.

Minmore House was the home of the founder of The Glenlivet Distillery. Situated amidst four acres of gardens with glorious views. Ten en suite bedrooms. Log and peat fires. Specialises in the best of Scottish produce, the menu changing daily. Marvellous walking, bird watching, ideally situated for whisky and castle trails.

Open Easter to Nov
Rooms: 10 with private facilities
Breakfast by arrangement
Bar Lunch 12 - 2 pm Sun + Sat only (a) ▶

Lunch 12 - 3 pm (by arrangment – prior booking).
High Tea by arrangement.
Dinner from 8 pm (d)
No smoking area in restaurant.
Bed & breakfast from £22
Dinner B & B £37 - £40

Fresh Lossiemouth langoustine, roast Highland rack of lamb with fresh mint and honey glaze, Cullen skink, venison and game, Lochin Ora burnt cream.

STB 3 Crown Commended
Credit cards: 1, 3
Proprietor: Belinda Luxmoore

GLENROTHES
92   **F7**

Balgeddie House Hotel
Balgeddie Way
Glenrothes
Fife KY6 3ET
Tel: 0592 742511
Fax: 0592 621702

Just off A911 (North) Glenrothes.

Balgeddie House Hotel is set in acres of manicured gardens with a panoramic view over Glenrothes. Guests may relax in the elegant cocktail bar before sampling the culinary delights of the head chef in the well appointed restaurant.

Open all year. Closed 1 and 2 Jan.

Rooms: 18 with private facilities
Breakfast 7 - 9.30 am
Bar Lunch 12 - 2 pm (a)
Lunch 12 - 2 pm (c)
Bar Supper 7 - 10 pm (b)
Dinner 7 - 9.30 pm (d)
No dogs.
Bed & breakfast from £47.85
Dinner B & B from £58.85

A wide variety of fresh local produce is used.

STB 4 Crown Commended
RAC 3 Star
AA   3 Star
BTA Commended
Credit cards: 1, 2, 3
Proprietor: J Crombie

Rescobie Hotel & Restaurant
Valley Drive
Leslie
Fife KY6 3BQ
Tel: 0592 742143

Just off A911 – 8 miles from M90 motorway, in Leslie.

Rescobie is a small family-run hotel of elegance and charm. The style is that of an old country house; the service and hospitality match. The food is fresh and varied. The table d'hôte menu changes daily and there is an extensive à la carte menu featuring international and Scottish dishes.

Open all year

Rooms: 8 with private facilities
Breakfast 7 - 9 am
Dinner 7 - 9 pm (d)
Bed & breakfast from £27.50
Dinner B & B from £35

Scallops and bacon with vinaigrette, pheasant breast with haggis and juniper berries, home-made shortbread with raspberries and cream sauce.

STB 4 Crown Commended
Credit cards: 1, 2, 3, 5
Proprietors: Tony & Wendy
                    Hughes-Lewis

GOUROCK
93   **G4**

Stakis Gantock Hotel
Cloch Road
Gourock
PA19 1AR
Tel: 0475 34671
Telex: 778584
Fax: 0475 32490

2 miles west of Gourock.

The hotel, which has been recently modernised and considerably extended, has 101 bedrooms, a full leisure complex including indoor pool, two all-weather floodlit tennis courts, and three conference and banqueting suites set against a breathtaking woodland backdrop on the outskirts of Gourock. The Stakis Gantock Hotel has a magnificent view over the Firth of Clyde to the hills of Argyll.

Open all year

Rooms: 101 with private facilities
Breakfast 7 - 9.30 am; 8 - 10 am Sun
Bar Lunch 12.30 - 2.30 pm (a)
Lunch 12.30 - 2 pm (b)
Dinner 6.30 - 9.30 pm (d)
Bed & breakfast rates on application
Dinner B & B from £25 (min. 2 nights stay).

Venison 'Auld Reekie'; Tay salmon.

STB 5 Crown Commended
RAC 3 Star M
AA   3 Star
Credit cards: 1, 2, 3, 5, 6

GRANTOWN ON SPEY
94   **D6**

The Ardlarig
Woodlands Terrace
Grantown-on-Spey
Moray
PH26 3JU
Tel: 0479 3245

On A95 as it enters Grantown-on-Spey.

Spoil yourself in an elegantly presented Victorian home set amidst its own gardens. Enjoy high standards of accommodation, service and cuisine complemented with fine wines and spirits. Leisure programme includes residential cookery courses, champagne breaks in the four-poster bedroom and exclusive packages for private parties. Deutsch. Francais.

Open all year

Rooms: 7, 4 with private facilities
Breakfast 8.15 - 9 am
Lunches/Picnic Lunches by arrangement.
Dinner 7 - 8 pm (c) - later by arrangement.
No smoking throughout.
Bed & breakfast from £13
Dinner B & B from £22

Imaginative and carefully presented fare based mainly on traditional Scottish, as well as vegetarian, recipes using fresh local produce daily.

STB 2 Crown Commended
No credit cards
Proprietors: Kevin W Gee &
                    Andrew Hunter

Garth Hotel
The Square
Grantown-on-Spey
PH26 3HN
Tel: 0479 2836/2162

On the Square of Grantown-on-Spey

Set amidst four acres of landscaped garden, the Garth Hotel commands a view of the picturesque Square of Grantown-on-Spey. The hotel dates from the 17th century, offers old world charm with every modern comfort and convenience. 14 individually furnished bedrooms – all en suite – with direct-dial telephone, colour TV and tea/coffee making facilities.

Open all year

Rooms: 14 with private facilities ▶

Breakfast 8.30 - 9.30 am
Bar Lunch 12 - 2 pm (a)
Lunch 12 - 2 pm (b)
Dinner 7.30 - 8.30 pm (c)
No smoking area in restaurant.
Bed & breakfast from £26
Dinner B & B from £39.50

Extensive and selective menu specialising in Taste of Scotland dishes with an accent on fresh local produce, e.g. salmon, trout, venison, game.

STB   4 Crown Commended
RAC   3 Star
AA   3 Star

Credit cards: 1, 3, 4, 5, 6
Proprietor: Gordon McLaughlan

HADDINGTON
95   G7

Barney Mains Farmhouse
Barney Mains
Haddington
East Lothian
EH41 3SA
Tel: 062 088 310

¾ mile off A1 to the right (Dunbar to Haddington), council road sign for Barney Mains, ½ mile before Haddington.

This attractive farmhouse is situated on the top of a hill and has spectacular views of the surrounding countryside and Forth estuary. The atmosphere is comfortable and homely. An ideal place for touring, many fine beaches and golf courses close by. Edinburgh only 30 minutes drive.

Open Mar to mid Nov
Rooms: 3
Breakfast 7.30 - 9 am
Dinner 6.30 - 8 pm (b)
Residents only.
Unlicensed.
No dogs.
No smoking area in dining room.
Bed & breakfast from £10 - £14
Dinner B & B £16 - £22

Good home cooking using home produced lamb and beef, vegetables and fruit in season.

STB   Listed Commended
AA   Listed

No credit cards
Proprietor: Katie Kerr

HARRIS
96   ISLE OF   C2

Ardvourlie Castle
Aird A Mhulaidh
Isle of Harris
Western Isles
PA85 3AB
Tel: 0859 2307

On A859 10 miles north of Tarbert.

Ardvourlie Castle is a Victorian hunting lodge built by the Earl of Dunmore in a beautiful setting on the shores of Loch Seaforth in the mountains of North Harris. Carefully restored, it is now a guest house of unusual elegance and charm.

Open all year
Rooms: 4
Breakfast, Lunch and Dinner (e) by arrangement.
Unlicensed.
Bed & breakfast £19.55 - £25.30
Dinner B & B £34.50 - £43.70

Food based on blend of traditional Scottish and innovation, using local and free-range ingredients when available.

No credit cards
Proprietors: Paul & Derek Martin

HAWICK
97   H7

Kirklands Hotel
West Stewart Place
Hawick
Roxburghshire
TD9 8BH
Tel: 0450 72263

200 yards off A7, ½ mile north of Hawick High Street.

Charming Victorian house hotel with a fine outlook across the town and surrounding hills. Impressive public rooms and spacious, well-furnished bedrooms all with radio, colour TV, tea-making facilities and telephone. Excellent cuisine and friendly, efficient service under the personal supervision of the proprietor. Very large garden, children's play area. Ideal place for touring the beautiful Scottish Borders.

Open all year except Christmas, Boxing and New Year's Days.
Rooms: 13, 10 with private facilities
Breakfast 8 - 9 am
Bar Lunch 12 - 2 pm (a)

Lunch 12 - 2 pm (a)
Dinner 7 - 9.30 pm (c)
Bed & breakfast from £24
Dinner B & B from £35

Tournedos 'Queen o' Scots', Salmon Teviotdale, Trout Belle Meuniere.

STB   4 Crown Commended
RAC   2 Star
AA   2 Star

Credit cards: 1, 2, 3, 5, 6
Proprietor: Barrie Newland

Mansfield House Hotel
Weensland Road
Hawick
Roxburghshire
TD9 9EL
Tel: 0450 73988

On the A698 approximately 1 mile from centre of Hawick.

The Mackinnon family own and run this Victorian country house hotel in 10 acres. Large public rooms with high ornately plastered ceilings, magnificent fireplaces of Italian marble and elegant brass chandeliers.

Open all year except Boxing Day to first Mon in Jan.
Rooms: 11, 8 with private facilities
Breakfast 7.30 - 9 am; 8.30 - 9.30 Sun + Sat
Bar Lunch 12 - 2 pm (a)
Lunch 12 - 2 pm except Sun, Sat (b)
Dinner 7.15 - 9.30 pm except Sun (c)
Sun dinner residents only.
Bed & breakfast £24.50 - £34
Dinner B & B £33.50 - £45

All meals individually prepared by prize-winning chef using the best local produce. Home-made desserts a speciality along with extensive range of Scottish cheeses, malt whiskies and liqueurs.

RAC   2 Star

Credit cards: 1, 2, 3, 5
Proprietor: Ian MacKinnon

The Old Forge Restaurant
Newmill on Teviot
by Hawick
TD9 0JU
Tel: 0450 85298

4 miles south of Hawick on A7.

The Old Forge was formerly the village Smiddy which retains the original forge, bellows, stone walls and beamed   ▶

ceiling. There is always a warm welcome at this small informal restaurant in the lovely Border country. Imaginative candelit dinners are personally prepared and served by proprietors Bill and Margaret Irving.

Open all year except 2 wks in May and 2 wks in Nov.

Rooms: 1 with private facilities
Dinner 7 - 9.30 pm except Sun, Mon (c)
Bed & breakfast rates on application.
Dinner B & B rates on application.

Haggis flamed with Teviotdale whisky, quail with cherries, aubergine stuffed with apricots and nuts, Dornoch Dreams, Scottish farmhouse cheeses. Guinea pig menu Tue to Fri.

AA   1 Knife & Fork

Credit cards: 1, 2, 3

Proprietors: Bill & Margaret Irving.

---

98   HELMSDALE   C6

Bunillidh Restaurant

2-4 Dunrobin Street
Helmsdale
Sutherland
KW8 6JX
Tel: 043 12 457

Just off A9 in centre of Helmsdale, next to Timespan Heritage Centre.

Bunillidh – pronounced "Buneely" – is a family-run restaurant situated in a modern building forming a corner of an attractive square, looking over the Strath of Kildonan and near the River Helmsdale. In the spacious dining area guests may enjoy a coffee, home-made sweets from the trolley, or partake in one of the many seafood specialities.

Open Mar to Nov

Menu available all day 10 am - 9 pm (a-d).
Open 7 days Jun to end Sep; closed Mon rest of year.

Chef/patron's harbour kettle, local lobster and salmon, langoustines in garlic butter. Ocean symphony – a platter of local cold fish.

Credit cards: 1, 3

Proprietors: Malcolm & Linda Holden

Navidale House Hotel

Helmsdale
Sutherland
KW8 6JS
Tel: 04312 258

On A9 road ½ mile north of Helmsdale.

John and Zena Gorrod maintain a high standard in this former hunting lodge of the Dukes of Sutherland which is set in five acres of woodland and gardens located on a cliff top position with panoramic views over the Moray Firth. Most bedrooms benefit from these views. Comfortable public rooms with open fires. Clay pigeon shooting in hotel grounds – pets welcome.

Open Feb to Nov

Rooms: 18, 12 with private facilities
Breakfast 8 - 9 am
Bar Lunch 12.30 - 2 pm (a)
Lunch 12.30 - 2 pm Sun only (b)
High Tea 5 - 6 pm
Dinner 7.30 - 8.30 pm (d)
Bed & breakfast £18.50 - £27.50
Dinner B & B £32 - £41

Menus prepared with imagination and care using Helmsdale salmon, lobster, king prawns, Moray Firth sole, Sutherland venison, grouse, wild duck, Orkney oysters, local lamb and Scotch beef.

RAC 2 Star
AA   2 Star

Credit cards: 1, 3

Proprietors: John & Zena Gorrod

---

99   HUMBIE   G7

Johnstounburn House Hotel

Humbie
East Lothian
EH36 5PL
Tel: 087533 696

On B6137, 2 miles from A68 to Jedburgh.

A 17th century country house hotel, 15 miles from Edinburgh, nestling at the foot of the Lammermuir Hills and surrounded by 40 acres of elegant park and gardens. 20 bedroomed house, modern bathrooms, colour televisions, and the wood-panelled public rooms have log fires and antiques.

Open all year

Rooms: 20 with private facilities
Breakfast 8 - 9 am: 8.30 - 9.30 am Sun
Bar Lunch 12.30 - 2 pm (a)
Lunch 12.30 - 2 pm (c)
Dinner 7.30 - 9 pm (e)
Bed & breakfast from £41.25
Dinner B & B rates on application

Fresh crayfish with smoked salmon. Roast rack of border lamb.

STB 4 Crown Commended
AA   3 Star HL
BTA Commended

Credit cards: 1, 2, 3, 5, 6

---

100   HUNTLY   D7

The Old Manse of Marnoch

Bridge of Marnoch
Huntly
AB5 5RS
Tel: 04665 873

On B9117, one mile off Huntly/Banff A97 route.

Georgian country house on the River Deveron. Five acres, mature grounds, including herb garden, combine with well-appointed bedrooms, elegant lounge and dining room to provide an example of the true character of Scotland. Residential courses January to June with the accent on Scottish cookery and culinary herbs. AA "Best in Britain" 1989 – Guesthouses, Farmhouses and Inns.

Open all year

Rooms: 4, 2 with private facilities
Breakfast 8 - 9 am
Lunch & Packed Lunch - as requested (a)
Dinner 7 - 10 pm (c)
Unlicensed
No smoking area in restaurant.
Bed & breakfast from £14.50
Dinner B & B from £23

Fine Scots cooking, traditional and contemporary. Breakfast menu includes spiced beef, devilled ham, home-baked breads, own jams and marmalades.

No credit cards

Proprietors: Patrick & Keren Carter

Glenmoriston Arms Hotel
Invermoriston
Glenmoriston
Inverness-shire
IV3 6YA
Tel: 0320 51206

At the junction of the A82 and A887 in Invermoriston.

A warm welcome awaits you at this 200 year old coaching inn nestling at the foot of Glenmoriston. One of Scotland's loveliest glens. A few minutes from world famous Loch Ness. Local game and wild salmon available in season. A unique selection of malt whiskies to complement your meal.

Open all year

Rooms: 8 with private facilities
Breakfast 8.15 - 9.15 am
Bar Lunch 12 - 2 pm (a)
Lunch 12 - 2 pm Sun only (b)
Bar Supper 5.30 - 8.30 pm (a)
Dinner 6.30 - 8.30 pm (d)
Bed & breakfast from £22.50
Dinner B & B from £36.50

Noisettes of local venison in cointreau and orange sauce. Loch Ness salmon parcelled in lemon sole fillets with wine sauce.

STB   4 Crown Commended
RAC   2 Star
AA   2 Star

Credit cards: 1, 3

Proprietor: Alan Draper

Culloden House Hotel
Culloden
nr Inverness
IV1 2NZ
Tel: 0463 790461

3 miles from Inverness, 5 miles from Inverness Airport.

Culloden House is an architectural gem with an historic and romantic association with Bonnie Prince Charlie and the Battle of Culloden which was fought nearby. It has acres of parkland, fine lawns and trees, and is an oasis of exceptional quiet. Magnificent public rooms and very well equipped bedrooms.

Open all year

Rooms: 20 with private facilities
Breakfast 7 - 10 am
Lunch 12.30 - 2 pm (d)
Dinner 7 - 9 pm (f)
Bed & breakfast from £52.50

Aberdeen Angus steaks and salmon specialities, game in season.

STB   5 Crown Highly Commended
AA   4 Star B
BTA   Commended

Credit cards: 1, 2, 3, 5, 6

Proprietors: Ian & Marjorie McKenzie

Dunain Park Hotel
Dunain Park
Inverness
IV3 6JN
Tel: 0463 230512

A82 one mile from Inverness.

Ann and Edward Nicoll give a warm welcome and offer fine food in this beautiful small hotel, secluded in six acres of gardens and woodland. They maintain high standards of cuisine, comfort and service while retaining the aura of a country house. An atmosphere enhanced by log fires, antiques and oil paintings. Centrally heated throughout. Two acres vegetable garden. Indoor heated swimming pool and sauna. Egon Ronay recommended. Macallan Scottish Restaurant of the Year 1989.

Open all year except 3rd wk Nov, Christmas Day and 2 wks Jan/Feb.

Rooms: 8 with private facilities
Breakfast 8 - 9.30 am
Light Lunch 12.30 - 2 pm (b)
Dinner 7 - 9 pm (e)
No smoking area in restaurant.
Bed & breakfast £35 - £45
Dinner B & B £54 - £64

Saddle of venison, lamb, Highland Cattle steaks, guinea fowl, duck, quail, salmon, seafood and extensive sweet buffet.

STB   4 Crown Highly Commended
AA   2 Star HBL
BTA   Commended

Credit cards: 1, 2, 3, 5

Proprietors: Ann & Edward Nicoll

Glen Mhor Hotel & Restaurant
Ness Bank
Inverness
IV2 4SG
Tel: 0463 234308

On river bank below castle.

Superbly situated on the south bank of the River Ness near the town centre. Most bedrooms have en suite facilities. Freshly-prepared local produce in both the up-market riverview restaurant (open for dinner only) and Nico's Bistro Bar, an interesting alternative for snacks and meals, day or night.

Open all year except 31 Dec to 3 Jan

Rooms: 30, 27 with private facilities
Breakfast 7 - 9.30 am; 8 - 9.30 am Sun + Sat
Bar Lunch 12 - 2.15 pm (a)
High Tea 5 - 7 pm
Dinner 6.30 - 9.30 pm (b)
Bed & breakfast from £31.50
Dinner B & B from £40

Salmon in various styles – langoustines, oysters, mussels, fresh fish, beef, lamb – all prepared to order. Game when available.

STB   4 Crown Commended
RAC   2 Star
AA   2 Star

Credit cards: 1, 2, 3, 5

Proprietor: Nicol Manson

Invermoy House Private Hotel & Carriages of Moy Restaurant
Moy
nr Tomatin
Inverness-shire
IV13 7YE
Tel: 080 82 271

On B9154, 11 miles south of Inverness.

Family-run hotel of unusual charm. Former Highland railway station. Ideally situated for touring Highlands. All rooms on ground level. Two restored railway carriages, furnished in Edwardian style form a separate unique restaurant (in addition to the hotel dining room) serving à la carte meals. Special diets by arrangement.

Open all year

Rooms: 7, 1 with private facilities
Breakfast 8.30 - 9.30 am
Dinner 7 - 9 pm (c-e)
No smoking area in restaurant
Bed & breakfast from £13
Dinner B & B from £23

Home-made soups and pâtés. Local salmon, trout and game in season. Scottish meats and vegetables with home-grown herbs. Scottish cheeses.

STB   2 Crown Approved
RAC   Listed
AA   Listed

Credit cards: 1, 3

Proprietors: D & V Simpson, H & T Pascoe

Kingsmills Hotel
Culcabock Road
Inverness
IV2 3LP
Tel: 0463 237166
Telex: 75566

Turn left off A9 at 'Crown and Kingsmills'. Follow sign to Kingsmills, bearing left at roundabout – just past the golf course.

A fine hotel in the Highlands. Kingsmills Hotel nestles in four acres of beautiful gardens, only one mile from town centre. Large garden rooms and luxury villas prove ideal for families – children free sharing parents' room. Also indoor heated swimming pool and leisure club.

Open all year

Rooms: 70 with private facilities
Breakfast 6.30 - 9.30 am; 8 - 10 am Sun
Bar Lunch 12.15 - 2 pm; 12.30 - 2 pm Sun (a-b)
Lunch 12.15 - 2 pm (c); 12.30 - 2 pm Sun (c)
Dinner 7 - 9 pm (d)
Bed & breakfast from £52
Dinner B & B £40 -£55
STB 4 Crown Commended
RAC 3 Star C

Credit cards: 1, 2, 3, 5, 6

Moniack Restaurant and Bar
Highland Wineries
Kirkhill
Inverness
IV5 7PQ
Tel: 046 383 336

Situated 7 miles from Inverness on the Beauly road.

The Castle Wine Bar Restaurant lies within 15 minutes of Loch Ness. The restaurant is an adjunct to the winery which makes an interesting range of Scottish wines. It is a traditional stone-built restaurant enhanced in the evening by candlelit tables and an open fire.

Open late May to mid Sep 11 am - 11 pm

Lunch 12 - 2.30 pm (a)
Dinner 7 - 9.30 pm except Sun, Mon (c)
In winter months, open Fri + Sat (dinner only) and Sun (lunch). Closed Jan.

Salmon en croute with dill cream sauce. Lobster in season; Fillet Rossini.

Credit cards: 1, 3

Proprietor: Kit Fraser

Station Hotel
Academy Street
Inverness
IV1 1LG
Tel: 0463 231926

The town centre of Inverness adjacent to the railway station.

This traditional town centre hotel has been at the hub of the business and social life of Inverness for over a century. The Victorian grandeur of the Strathconon Restaurant is matched by the excellence of cuisine and service which has been consistently acclaimed. Table d'hôte and à la carte menus.

Open all year

Rooms: 67, 53 with private facilities
Breakfast 7 - 10 am; 8 - 10 am Sun
Bar Lunch 11.30 am - 2.15 pm (a)
Lunch 11.30 am - 2.15 pm
Dinner 7 - 9.15 pm (d)
Bed & breakfast from £35
Dinner B & B from £48.50

Fresh local mussels with white wine and cream. Medallions of venison lightly cooked in honey and whisky with julienne of apricots.

STB 4 Crown Approved
RAC 3 Star
AA 3 Star

Credit cards: 1, 2, 3, 5, 6

Whinpark Hotel
17 Ardross Street
Inverness
IV3 5NS
Tel: 0463 232549

By Eden Court Theatre.

The restaurant with rooms. Within easy walking distance of the town centre and near to Eden Court Theatre on the River Ness. The restaurant offers 'something special' to the discerning diner. Using local produce such as Ness salmon, game and Aberdeen Angus steak. A relaxed house-party atmosphere with a truly Highland welcome.

Open all year

Rooms: 9, 4 with private facilities
Breakfast 8 - 9 am
Lunch 12 - 2 pm except Sun, Sat (a)
High Tea 5.30 - 7 pm
Dinner 6.30 - 9.30 pm (b)
Bed & breakfast from £20
Dinner B & B from £30

Collops of venison, finished in lemon thyme and whisky sauce, stuffed fillets of rock turbot with a smoked salmon and shrimp mousse.

STB 3 Crown Commended
Credit card: 3
Proprietor: Steven MacKenzie

INVERURIE
103   E8

Thainstone House Hotel
Thainstone Estate
Inverurie
Aberdeenshire
AB5 9NT
Tel: 0467 21643
Fax: 0467 25084

On A96 north of Aberdeen (8 miles from airport).

Mike and Edith Lovie extend a warm welcome from this palladian mansion house built in 1759. Set in 14 acres of pasture and woodlands, the hotel offers high standards of cuisine, comfort and service while retaining the charm of a country house enhanced by log fires, books and paintings.

Open all year

Rooms: 8 with private facilities
Breakfast 7 - 8.30 am; 8 - 9.30 am Sun + Sat
Bar Lunch 12 - 2 pm; 12.30 - 2.30 pm Sun (a)
Lunch 12 - 2 pm; 12.30 - 2.30 pm Sun (c)
High Tea 5 - 6.30 pm (b)
Bar Supper 6.30 - 9.30 pm (b)
Dinner 6.45 - 9.30 pm (e)
Bed & breakfast £25 - £37.50
Dinner B & B £40 - £50

Medallions of Scottish beef with strawberry coulis and Orkney cheese. Aberdeen Angus steaks, local salmon and game (seasonal).

STB 4 Crown Commended
Credit cards: 1, 2, 3, 5
Proprietor: Edith & Michael Lovie

CREDIT/CHARGE CARDS

1 Access/Mastercard/Eurocard
2 American Express
3 Visa
4 Carte Bleu
5 Diners Club
6 Mastercharge

Hospitality Inn, Irvine
46 Annick Road
Irvine
Ayrshire
KA11 4LD
Tel: 0294 74272
Telex: 777097 Fax: 0294 77287

On outskirts of Irvine on A71 to Kilmarnock.

The hotel is luxurious. The palm-festooned Hawaiian Lagoon is one of the most spectacular features with a myriad of tropical plants and rocks, an exquisitely-styled à la carte restaurant and a Moroccan-style bar. A conference and banqueting facility for up to 250.

Open all year

Rooms: 128 with private facilities
Breakfast 7 - 10 am; 7.30 - 10.30 am Sat + Sun
Lunch (La Mirage) 12.30 - 2 pm (c)
Lunch (Lagoon) 12.30 - 6 pm (b)
High Tea 6 - 11 pm
Dinner (La Mirage) 7.30 - 10 pm (e)
Dinner (Lagoon) 6 - 11 pm (c)
Bed & breakfast rates on application.
Dinner B & B rates on application.

The Chef prepares a new à la carte menu each season to offer the best of seasonal specialities.

STB 5 Crown Commended
RAC 4 Star
AA   4 Star

Credit cards: 1, 2, 3, 5, 6

Kilchoman House Cottages & Restaurant
by Bruichladdich
Isle of Islay
Argyll
PA49 7UY
Tel: 049 685 382

Off B8018 on the Atlantic coast.

Stuart and Lesley Taylor offer you magnificent crags, wild goats, historic site, peat fires, island hospitality, crack with mine host, great food from his missus, unspoilt island, 3 night off-season breaks at adjacent cottages. A real Taste of the Isles: Venison McHarrie, Tipsy Islay Prawns, Kilchoman Mist.
Open Dec to Oct

Dinner from 7.30 pm (d)
Reservations essential.
Dinner B & B £30.

Specialising in original and traditional recipes using seasonal island produce. Lobster, venison, rabbit, pheasant, beef, lamb. Changing menu.

5 Self Catering Cottages -
STB 4 Crown Commended to
        4 Crown Highly Commended
No credit cards
Proprietors: Stuart & Lesley Taylor

Jura Hotel
Isle of Jura
Argyll
PA60 7XU
Tel: 049682 243

Isle of Jura.

Originally an inn on the old drove road, the comfortable Jura Hotel provides an ideal base from which to explore this unspoilt and little known island of the Inner Hebrides. See the whirlpool of Corrievreckan, climb the Paps, explore the uninhabited west coast, watch the deer, otters and eagles and come back to warmth, comfort and good food.

Open all year

Rooms: 17, 5 with private facilities
Breakfast 8.30 - 9.15 am
Bar Lunch 12 - 2 pm (a)
Lunch by arrangement.
Bar Supper 8 - 9 pm
Dinner from 7.30 pm (c)
Bed & breakfast from £19.50
Dinner B & B from £33.25

Local shellfish, salmon, venison.

RAC 2 Star
AA   2 Star

Credit cards: 1, 2, 3, 5
Proprietor: F A Riley-Smith

Floors Castle
Kelso
Roxburghshire
TD5 7RW
Tel: 0573 23333

A699 west of Kelso.

A magnificent and imposing Border castle, the home of the Duke of Roxburghe. The restaurant is situated in the old stable courtyard overlooking the River Tweed and Kelso.

Open May to Sep except Fri + Sat
Lunch (a)
Also open Easter and on Fri Jul and Aug.

Floors Kitchen pheasant pâté, Tweed salmon, smoked Tweed salmon, home baking from Floors Castle kitchens.

No credit cards

The 1991 TASTE OF SCOTLAND GUIDE
is scheduled to be published in November 1990.

To reserve a copy at the 1990 price of £2.70 (including post & packaging), complete the coupon on page 141 and send it with your cheque or postal order, made payable to TASTE OF SCOTLAND, to

Taste of Scotland (Guide Sales),
33 Melville Street, Edinburgh EH3 7JF.

You will be placed on the priority list to receive the Guide as soon as it is published.

Sunlaws House Hotel

Heiton
Kelso
Roxburghshire
TD5 8JZ
Tel: 05735 331

On A698, Kelso to Jedburgh road in the village of Heiton.

The 18th century Scottish baronial gentleman's home, converted only five years ago and owned by the Duke and Duchess of Roxburghe. It offers the charm and comfort of a stylish period and luxurious country house, whether fishing, shooting, relaxing or enjoying the countryside.

Open all year

Rooms: 21 with private facilities
Breakfast 7.30 - 9.30 am
Bar Lunch 12.30 - 2 pm (b)
Lunch 12.30 - 2 pm except Sun, Sat (c)
High tea available on request
Dinner 7.30 - 9.30 pm (d)
Bed & breakfast from £62
Dinner B & B rates on application

Special children's menu.

STB   4 Crown Commended
AA   3 Star HBL
BTA   Commended
Credit cards: 1, 2, 3, 5

The Waggon Inn

10 Coalmarket
Kelso
Roxburghshire
TD5 7AH
Tel: 0573 24568

Town Centre.

A warm welcome awaits you from the Scott family and staff at this attractive stone-built inn situated in the romantic Borderland where Rivers Tweed and Teviot meet.

Open all year except Christmas Day

Lunch 12 - 2.30 pm (a)
Evening meals 5 - 9.45 pm;
6.30 - 9.45 pm Sun
No smoking area in restaurant.

Special dishes prepared daily using Eyemouth fish, locally produced beef, lamb and pork, fresh poultry and vegetables. Home-made soups served with crusty bread. Delicious sweets to tempt you.

Credit cards: 1, 3
Proprietor: Isabel H Scott

Ardsheal House

Kentallen of Appin
Argyll
PA38 4BX
Tel: 063 174 227

On A828 – 4 miles south of Ballachulish Bridge.

Set in 900 acres of woods and meadows overlooking Loch Linnhe, this 1760 house has oak panelling, open fires and is furnished with antiques. The relaxed, congenial atmosphere is conducive to enjoying the superb meals and fine wines, and offers a true taste of the best of Scotland.

Open Easter to Nov

Rooms: 13 with private facilities
Breakfast 8.30 - 9.30 am
Lunch 12 - 2 pm (b)
Dinner 8.30 pm (f)
No smoking in restaurant.
Bed & breakfast rates on application.
Dinner B & B £52 - £70

Ramekin of Loch Linnhe prawns and Colonsay oysters in rose jelly with garden herbs; razorfish stew; medallions of venison with blackcurrant vinegar. Rosette of beef with sage butter, chestnut puree and thyme.

BTA   Commended
Credit cards: 1, 2, 3
Proprietors: Bob & Jane Taylor

The Holly Tree Hotel

Kentallen
Appin
Argyll
PA38 4BY
Tel: 063 174 292

On A828 – 4 miles south of Ballachulish towards Oban.

This former Edwardian railway station has been enlarged and charmingly renovated. The platform is part of the new reception area and the waiting rooms form some of the bedrooms, which all have private facilities. The restaurant has spectacular views over Loch Linnhe towards the mountains of Ardgour. A log fire burns cheerfully in the centre of the restaurant where freshly caught shellfish are just some of the specialities.

Open mid Feb to Oct

Rooms: 12 with private facilities
Breakfast 8.30 am

Lunch 12.30 - 2 pm (b)
Dinner 7.30 - 9.30 pm (e)
Bed & breakfast rates on application.
Dinner B & B rates on application.

Salad of local quail, venison liver pâté with bramble jelly. Salmon cutlet with local chanterelles and cream. Beef, hare, rabbit, pigeon, sole, trout, scallops, prawns, etc.

Credit cards: 1, 3
Proprietors: Jane & Alasdair Robertson

Ardanaiseig Hotel

Kilchrenan
by Taynuilt
Argyll
PA35 1HE
Tel: 086 63 333
Fax: 086 63 222

3½ miles off B845 at Kilchrenan.

On the shores of Loch Awe beneath Ben Cruachan, Ardanaiseig is set in a renowned shrub and woodland garden. Unparalleled scenery, award winning cuisine and perfect peace. Special short and long stay breaks available throughout the season.

Open mid Apr to late Oct

Rooms: 14 with private facilities
Breakfast 8 - 9.30 am
Lunch 12.30 - 2 pm (c)
Dinner 7.30 - 9 pm (f)
Bed & breakfast rates on application.
Dinner B & B from £60 - £90

Warm home-smoked scallops with snow peas and chives. A symphony of west coast shellfish panfried and accompanied by a saffron butter sauce. Crisp brandy snap basket filled with fresh garden fruits.

STB   4 Crown Commended
BTA   Commended
Credit cards: 1, 2, 3, 5
Proprietors: Jonathan & Jane Brown

Taychreggan Hotel

Kilchrenan
by Taynuilt
Argyll
PA35 1HQ
Tel: 086 63 211

Leave A85 at Taynuilt on to B845 on loch side past Kilchrenan.

A charming old drovers' inn, recently modernised, on the shores of Loch Awe surrounded by beautiful scenery. The hotel offers a warm welcome and is an ▶

65

ideal place to relax in an away-from-it-all atmosphere. The restaurant makes much use of local produce which naturally includes superb fresh fish and shellfish.

Open all year

Rooms: 16 with private facilities
Breakfast 8 - 9.30 am
Bar Lunch 12.15 - 2.15 pm (a)
Lunch 12.15 - 2.15 pm (c)
Dinner 7.30 - 9.15 pm (e)
Bed & breakfast rates on application.
Dinner B & B from £54

Local fresh fish, prawns, turbot, halibut, salmon, venison, roast beef, etc. Served in an enterprising and interesting manner.

RAC 3 Star HR
AA 3 Star

Credit cards: 1, 2, 3, 5
Proprietors: John & Monika Tyrrell

KILDRUMMY
110   E7

Kildrummy Castle Hotel
Kildrummy
by Alford
Aberdeenshire
AB3 8RA
Tel: 09755 71288

On A97 Ballater/Huntly road, 35 miles west of Aberdeen.

A converted mansion house overlooking the ruins of the original 13th century castle amidst acres of planted gardens and woodland. The interior features the original turn-of-the-century wall tapestries and oak panelling. Full central heating and all modern facilities have not detracted from the original atmosphere or character of the house.

Open all year

Rooms: 16 with private facilities
Breakfast 8 - 9.30 am
Lunch 12.30 - 1.45 pm (c)
Dinner 7 - 9 pm (d)
No smoking in dining room.
No dogs.
Bed & breakfast £35 - £40
Dinner B & B £39 - £58

Fillet of Beef Kildrummy Castle, Scampi Glenlivet.

STB 4 Crown Highly Commended
RAC 3 Star HC
AA 3 Star HBL
BTA Commended

Credit cards: 1, 2, 3, 4, 6
Proprietor: Thomas Hanna

KILFINAN
111   G4

Kilfinan Hotel
Kilfinan
nr Tighnabruaich
Argyll
PA21 2AP
Tel: 070 082 201

On the eastern shores of Loch Fyne.

Ancient coaching inn, modernised to very high standards without losing any of its traditional character, set in breathtaking beautiful countryside on the eastern shores of Loch Fyne.

Open all year

Rooms: 11, 10 with private facilities
Breakfast 7.30 - 9.30 am
Lunch 12 - 2 pm (b)
Dinner 7.30 - 9.30 pm (e)
Bed & breakfast rates on application.
Dinner B & B rates on application.

Fresh local produce including scallops, mussels, prawns and salmon from Loch Fyne, pheasant, wild duck and venison from adjoining Otter Estate form the basis for a variety of memorable meals.

STB 2 Crown Commended
AA 2 Star HB
BTA Commended

Credit cards: 2, 3, 5
Proprietor: T Wignell

KILLIECRANKIE
112   E6

Killiecrankie Hotel
by Pitlochry
Perthshire
PH16 5LG
Tel: 0796 3220
Fax: 0796 2451

On old A9, 3 miles north of Pitlochry.

A converted dower house, set in four acres of well-kept gardens overlooking the historic Pass of Killiecrankie. Furnished to a high standard to reflect the expected small country house atmosphere and comfort requirements of the most fastidious guest.

Open late Feb to mid Nov

Rooms: 12 with private facilities
Breakfast from 8 am
Bar Lunch 12.30 - 2 pm (a)
Bar Supper 7 - 9.30 pm (b)
Dinner 7 - 8.30 pm (d)
No smoking in dining room.

Bed & breakfast £29 - £32.50
Dinner B & B £45 - £48.50

Traditional Scottish menu featuring speciality soups, smoked haddock flan, Tay salmon, fresh Buckie fish, Angus beef, Scotch lamb, venison, game and cheeses.

STB 2 Crown Commended
RAC 2 Star H
AA 2 Star HB

Credit cards: 1, 3
Proprietors: Colin & Carole Anderson

KILLIN
113   F5

The Ardeonaig Hotel
South Loch Tay
nr Killin
Perthshire
FK21 8SU
Tel: 05672 400

On the south side of Loch Tay (Edinburgh 1½ hours).

Set in 20 acres on the banks of Loch Tay, this 17th century coaching inn offers good food in an informal atmosphere, superb salmon and trout fishing on the loch, rough shooting over 5,000 acres and clay pigeon facility in grounds. Golf, riding, hill-walking and watersports available in area.

Open Mar to Nov

Rooms: 13 with private facilities
Breakfast 8.15 - 9.30 am
Bar Lunch 12 - 2 pm (b)
Dinner 7 - 8.30 pm (d)
Bed & breakfast from £22
Dinner B & B from £33

Fresh Tay salmon, local game, fresh brown trout, best of local fruits and vegetables and Scottish cheeses.

STB 3 Crown Approved
RAC 2 Star
AA 2 Star

Credit cards: 1, 2, 3, 5
Proprietors: Stephen & Sian Brown

Dall Lodge Hotel
Main Street
Killin
Perthshire
FK21 8TN
Tel: 056 72 217

Situated in its own grounds on the edge of Killin overlooking the River Lochay.

Friendly and relaxed country house hotel on the banks of the River Lochay with own boats. Specialising in providing ▶

delicious home-cooking and a warm personal atmosphere. An ideal centre for touring, walking, golf and water sports.

Open all year

Rooms: 9, 5 with private facilities
Breakfast 8 - 9.30 am
Lunch 12 - 2 pm (a)
Dinner 7 - 9.30 pm (d)
No smoking area in restaurant.
Bed & breakfast from £19.50
Dinner B & B from £30.50

Fresh local produce – salmon, venison, Angus beef. Home-made soups and desserts. Interesting vegetarian dishes.

STB Award Pending

Credit cards: 1, 3

Proprietors: Sally & Peter Stewart

KILMARNOCK
114   **G5**

The Coffee Club
30 Bank Street
Kilmarnock
Ayrshire
KA1 1HA
Tel: 0563 22048

On A77 between Glasgow and Ayr.

Situated in one of the oldest streets in Kilmarnock opposite the Laigh Kirk. Offering something for everyone – quick service, snack meals and large varied menu including grills and vegetarian dishes and dinner by candlelight. All food is produced to order using fresh produce where practicable and bakery items are a speciality. You may take your own wine.

Open all year

No Parking
All meals served from 10 am - 10 pm (a-c).
Closed Sun.
Unlicensed.
No smoking area in restaurant.

Hamburgers, baked potatoes. Salad bar and vegetarian dishes. Children's menu. Open sandwiches. Haggis.

Credit cards: 1, 3

Proprietors: Svend Kamming &
             William MacDonald

KINCLAVEN
115   **NEAR PERTH**   **F6**

Ballathie House Hotel
Kinclaven
by Stanley
Perthshire
PH1 4QN
Tel: 025 083 268
Telex: 76216

Off A9 north of Perth through Stanley or off A93 south of Blairgowrie to Kinclaven.

A superior country house within its own estate overlooking the River Tay (salmon). Totally refurbished to a high standard. Very comfortable, informal and relaxed. Attentive and friendly staff. Four-poster and canopied beds. Sportsman's lodge available.

Open Mar to Jan

Rooms: 22 with private facilities
Breakfast 7.30 - 9.30 am
Lunch 12.30 - 2 pm (a-c)
Dinner 7 - 8.30 pm (d-e)
Bed & breakfast £40 - £50
Dinner B & B £57 - £68

Local salmon and game. Soft fruits in season.

STB 4 Crown Commended
RAC 3 Star
AA 3 Star BL
BTA Commended

Credit cards: 1, 2, 3, 5

Proprietor: David Assenti

KINCRAIG
116   **E6**

Invereshie House
Kincraig
Kingussie
Inverness-shire
PH21 1NA
Tel: 05404 332
Fax: 05404 260

Off A9, 5 miles south of Aviemore.

Country house dating from 1680, furnished with the care and attention such a beautiful building deserves. Situated in 40 acres of parkland, Invereshie House is a haven of tranquillity.

Open all year

Rooms: 9 with private facilities
Breakfast 8.30 am - 12 noon
Lunch available on request to residents only
Dinner 7.15 - 10 pm (d)

Bed & breakfast from £24.50
Dinner B & B from £39.50

Start the day "18 choice" breakfast – finish it with prime halibut, turbot, lobsters, prawns, grouse, wigeon, mallard, venison or Aberdeen Angus beef.

BTA Commended

Credit cards: 1, 3

Proprietors: A & P Methven-Hamilton

March House
Lagganlia
Feshiebridge
Kincraig
Inverness-shire
PH21 1NG
Tel: 054 04 388

Off A9 at Kincraig – follow B970 for 2 miles to Feshiebridge. Turn right, ½ mile to Lagganlia.

Situated in the tranquillity of beautiful Glenfeshie with outstanding views of the Cairngorm mountains. Perfect location for the outdoor enthusiast and bird watcher. Easy access for Cairngorm ski area. Open Swedish log fire and friendly relaxed atmosphere. Most bedrooms have either private bath or shower.

Open Dec to Oct

Rooms: 6, 3 with private facilities
Breakfast 8 - 9 am
Dinner from 7 pm (b)
Residents only.
Unlicensed.
Bed & breakfast from £11
Dinner B & B from £18

Local Rothiemurchus trout, venison and salmon (in season). All soups, casseroles and desserts home-made from fresh local ingredients. Home-baking.

STB 1 Crown Commended
AA Listed

No credit cards

Proprietors: Caroline & Ernie Hayes

CREDIT/CHARGE CARDS
1 Access/Mastercard/Eurocard
2 American Express
3 Visa
4 Carte Bleu
5 Diners Club
6 Mastercharge

The Cross
High Street
Kingussie
Inverness-shire
PH21 1HX
Tel: 0540 661762

2 hours north of Edinburgh, in centre of Kingussie.

Relax in front of a blazing log fire; ponder over the delicious offerings on the menu; sip a glass of chilled dry sherry while perusing the award-winning wine list; take your seat at a candlelit table in the smoke-free dining room; then savour a meal "long to be cherished".

Open all year except 2 wks in May and 3 wks in Dec.

Rooms: 3 with private facilities
Breakfast by arrangement.
Private party luncheons by arrangement
Dinner 6.30 - 9.30 pm except Sun, Mon (e)
No smoking in restaurant.
Dinner B & B from £42

Hramsa mushrooms, mousseline of pike, chanterelle soup, fillet of wild roe deer "Francatelli", chocolate whisky laird or raspberry fantasy.

AA   Rosette

No credit cards

Best Formal Restaurant 1989

Proprietors: Tony & Ruth Hadley

The Osprey Hotel
Ruthven Road
Kingussie
Inverness-shire
PH21 1EN
Tel: 0540 661510

In Kingussie village.

Scottish Taste of Britain winner 1985. A gem of a small Highland hotel where only the best of everything is served. A warm, hospitable place where guests enjoy one another's company and the conversation flows. The proprietor was described by the Consumers Association in 1987 as one of life's great hosts. Great food and outstanding cellar.

Open Jan to Oct

Rooms: 8, 4 with private facilities
Breakfast 8.30 - 9.30 am
Dinner 7.30 - 8 pm (d)
No smoking area in restaurant
Bed & breakfast £16 - £28
Dinner B & B £30 - £44

Wild mushrooms, North Sea bake, peat-smoked salmon. Venison with chanterelles, noisettes of lamb, chicken with wild mushrooms. Highland casserole. Chocolate meringue gateau, blackcurrant pie.

STB   3 Crown Commended
AA   1 Star H
BTA   Commended

Credit cards: 1, 2, 3, 4, 5, 6

Proprietors: Duncan & Pauline Reeves

Kinlochbervie Hotel
Kinlochbervie
by Lairg
Sutherland
IV27 4RP
Tel: 097 182 275
Fax: 097 182 438

An imposing modern three star family hotel with superb views of Kinlochbervie harbour and Loch Clash. Recently refurbished to a high standard. Candlelit dining room. Personally supervised by David and Geraldine Gregory whose confidence in the service they provide leaves you free to enjoy Kinlochbervie and the surrounding area. Sutherland's only BTA commended hotel.

Open all year except restricted pre-booked service Nov to mid Mar

Rooms: 14 with private facilities
Breakfast 8.30 - 9.30 am
Bar Lunch 12 - 1.45 pm (b)
Dinner 7.30 - 8.30 pm (e)
No smoking area in restaurant.
Bed & breakfast £36 - £48
Dinner B & B from £41

Cordon bleu cuisine. Locally caught white fish, king prawns, salmon and lobster (when available and in season) are prepared and cooked with skill and pride.

STB   4 Crown Commended
RAC   3 Star
AA   3 Star
BTA   Commended

Credit cards: 1, 3, 6

Proprietor: David Gregory

Cuilmore Cottage
Kinloch Rannoch
Perthshire
PH16 5QB
Tel: 08822 218

100 yards from east corner of Loch Rannoch.

Cosy 18th century croft in secluded surroundings. Traditionally decorated and cheery log fires. The cooking covers high class Scottish fare, organically grown fruits and vegetables from the cottage garden. Breakfasts feature free-range eggs and freshly baked bread and pastries. Guests have the complimentary use of mountain bikes, dinghy and canoe to explore the splendid locality.

Open all year except Christmas and New Year.

Rooms: 3
Breakfast 7 - 9 am
Dinner 7 - 8.30 pm (d-e)
Prior booking essential for dinner for non-residents. Take your own wine.
Unlicensed.
No smoking area in restaurant.
Bed & breakfast £12 - £15
Dinner B & B from £22

The seasons dictate the selection of game and seafood. Every meal is home-made and prepared fresh daily, in imaginative dishes.

STB   Listed Commended

No credit cards

Proprietor: Anita Steffen

The Lomond Country Inn & Restaurant
Main Street
Kinnesswood
nr Kinross
KY13 7HN
Tel: 0592 84 317

4 miles from Kinross. From south M90 junc 5, B9097 via Scotlandwell. From north, M90 junc 7, A911 via Milnathort.

The historical hotel, which overlooks Loch Leven, has long since been the focal point of the area and now with the addition of the modest annexe provides accommodation for visitors in 12 en suite rooms. Thus adding to the attraction of the well established and renowned ▶

restaurant, where game dishes, local caught fish and Scottish produce adorn the à la carte menu. Bar lunches and suppers are served. Open fires and friendly atmosphere.

Open all year

Rooms: 12 with private facilities
Breakfast 7.30 - 9.30 am
Bar Lunch 12 - 2 pm (a)
Lunch 12 - 2 pm (a)
Bar Supper 6.30 - 9 pm; 6.30 - 9.30 pm Fri + Sat (a)
Dinner 6.30 - 9 pm; 6.30 - 9.30 pm Fri + Sat (c-d)
Light snacks (scones, sandwiches and tea) served on request all day.
Bed & breakfast from £16
Dinner B & B from £25

Loch Leven trout – this distinctive local trout is simply grilled in butter to retain its special flavour and served with fresh local vegetables.
Credit cards: 3

KINROSS
121   **F6**

Croftbank House Hotel
30 Station Road
Kinross
Fife
KY13 7TG
Tel: 0577 63819

Junction 6 M90 on approach to Kinross.

Chef/patron Bill Kerr and his wife Diane run this old Victorian house as a small and friendly hotel and restaurant, serving creative and imaginative food. Ideally situated for shooting, fishing and golf – surrounded by world famous golf courses – and with good access to Edinburgh, Perth, Stirling and St Andrews. Chef appointed to Master Chef Institute of UK.

Open all year

Rooms: 4 with private facilities
Breakfast 8 - 9.30 am
Bar Lunch 12 - 2 pm (b)
Lunch by arrangement.
Dinner 7 - 9 pm (e)
Closed Mon lunchtime Oct to Mar.
Bed & breakfast rates on application.
Dinner B & B rates on application.

Seafood parcel, beef and oyster pie, mignons of beef and veal fillets with a duo sauce.
Credit cards: 1, 3
Proprietors: Bill & Diane Kerr

KIPPEN
122   **G5**

Cross Keys Hotel
Main Street
Kippen
by Stirling
FK8 3DN
Tel: 078 687 293

On B822 Callander-Fintry road and just off A811 Stirling-Erskine Bridge road, only 8 miles west of Stirling.

A small family-run 18th century hotel set in the peaceful and picturesque village of Kippen (near Stirling). The hotel has old world character augmented by log fires in the bars during winter, a cosy stone-walled restaurant and family room.

Open all year except evening December 25 and New Year's Day.

Rooms: 3
Breakfast 8.30 - 10 am
Bar Lunch 12 - 2.15 pm (a)
Lunch 12 - 2.15 pm (b)
High Tea 5.30 - 6 pm
Dinner 7.30 - 9 pm (c)
Bed & breakfast £14 - £17

Home-made soups and pâtés. Roast venison and fresh raspberry and red wine sauce.
Credit cards: 1
Proprietors: Angus & Sandra Watt

KIRKCUDBRIGHT
123   **I5**

Selkirk Arms Hotel
High Street
Kirkcudbright
Kirkcudbrightshire
DG6 4JG
Tel: 0557 30402
Fax: 0557 31639

Off A75, 27 miles west of Dumfries.

Historic 18th century hotel with Burns connection in picturesque harbour town. Newly refurbished but still retaining the character of the hotel. Extensive à la carte and daily changing table d'hôte menus. Marvellous walking, fishing, birdwatching. Nearby beaches. Large secluded garden.

Open all year

Rooms: 15 with private facilities
Breakfast 7.30 - 9.30 am
Bar Lunch 12 - 2 pm (a)
Lunch 12 - 2 pm (c)

Bar Supper 6.30 - 9 pm (a)
Dinner 7 - 9.30 pm (d)
Bed & breakfast £26.50 - £33
Dinner B & B £38.50 - £45

Seafood, scallops, salmon, Dover sole, plaice, lobster. Galloway beef and lamb. Wide selection of fresh vegetables or salads.
STB 3 Crown Commended
RAC 2 Star
AA 2 Star
Credit cards: 1, 2, 3, 5
Proprietor: John Morris

KIRKINTILLOCH
124   **G5**

The Lady Margaret Canalboat
Glasgow Road Bridge
Kirkintilloch
Tel: 041 776 6996

Glasgow Road Bridge jetty, on A803 between Bishopbriggs and Kirkintilloch.

Calm water canal cruises on the northern outskirts of Glasgow, in country scenery, with floodlights and central heating for year-round operation. The purpose-built canalboat is tastefully appointed. Crystal glasses and Wedgwood crockery enhance attractive table settings, with pink linen and fresh flowers. A relaxing experience, unrivalled in Scotland. Available for group bookings at any time, any day.

Open all year
Lunch 1 pm Sunday (d)
Dinner 7.30 pm Thurs, Fri, Sat (e)
Dinner cruises sail at 7.30 pm. Sunday lunch cruises sail at 1 pm from Cadder Jetty. Advance booking essential.

Imaginative set menus incorporating the best in fresh Scottish produce and dishes with an emphasis on quality and presentation.
Credit cards: 1, 2, 3, 5
Proprietor: Patrick Le Pla

KIRKMICHAEL
125   **E6**

The Log Cabin Hotel
Kirkmichael
by Blairgowrie
Perthshire
PH10 7NB
Tel: 025 081 288

Signposted off A924 in Kirkmichael.

Uniquely built of whole Norwegian pine logs, nestles high in Glen Derby with ▶

panoramic views. The hotel is centrally heated and double glazed so you are assured of a warm welcome and a memorable meal in the restaurant. An ideal centre for touring Perthshire and for ski-ing in Glenshee.

Open all year

Rooms: 13 with private facilities
Breakfast 8.45 - 9.30 am
Bar Lunch 12 - 2 pm (a)
Dinner 7.30 - 9 pm (d)
Bed & breakfast from £18.15
Dinner B & B from £30.95

Home-produced dishes including Edinburgh club special, game dishes, collops, lamb Lady Lucy, and delicious sweets – chocolate whisky gâteau, hazelnut and cinnamon tart with Blair raspberries.

RAC   2 Star.
AA   2 Star.

Credit cards: 1, 3, 5

Proprietor: A F Finch

KYLE OF LOCHALSH
126   E3

The Lochalsh Hotel
Kyle of Lochalsh
Ross-shire
IV40 8AF
Tel: 0599 4202

At the ferry terminal for Skye.

A fine Highland hotel with uninterrupted views of the Isle of Skye. A haven of comfort and hospitality. The popular restaurant faces the picturesque island and makes good use of the wide range of fresh local produce.

Open all year except Christmas week.

Rooms: 38 with private facilities
Breakfast 8 - 9.45 am
Dinner 7.30 - 9 pm (d)
Bed & breakfast from £40.
Dinner B & B rates on application.

Local game, seafood, collops of beef with wild mushrooms, Scottish salmon in many different dishes.

Credit cards: 2, 3, 5, 6

Wholefood Cafe, Highland Designworks
Plockton Road
Kyle of Lochalsh
IV40 8DA
Tel: 0599 4388

On Kyle/Plockton road.

Situated on the outskirts of Kyle, in the old village school. Snacks or complete meals served from 12 noon till closing time. All food cooked on the premises using only fresh and natural ingredients. No smoking.

Open Easter to Oct 10 am - 9.30 pm
Morning coffee 10 - 12 noon.
Lunch 12 - 6 pm
Dinner 6 - 9.30 pm (a-b)
Also open during winter and early spring. Please telephone to check opening times.

Home-made soups: potato and chive; celery and cashew nut; herring in oatmeal, walnut and celery quiche, wild Loch Duich salmon, fresh spinach and cashew bake, buckwheat pancakes with broccoli and cream cheese.

Credit cards: 1, 3

Proprietor: Fiona Begg

KYLESKU
127   C4

Linne Mhuirich
Unapool Croft Road
Kylesku, by Lairg
Sutherland
IV27 4HW
Tel: 0971 2227

¾ of a mile south of the new Kylesku Bridge on A894.

Fiona and Diarmid MacAulay welcome non-smokers to their modern crofthouse. Panoramic views of hills and lochs, quietly situated overlooking Loch Glencoul. RSPB Handa Island, and lovely, lonely sandy beaches nearby. Dinner menus discussed with guests after breakfast. Vegetarian food available. Listed in "Complete Healthy Holiday Guide". Guests welcome to take their own wine. Non-smoking residents only.

Open May to Oct and by arrangement.

Rooms: 3, 1 with private facilities
Breakfast 8.30 - 9 am; 9 - 9.30 am Sun
Dinner 7.30 pm
No smoking throughout.
Residents only.
Unlicensed.
Bed & breakfast £12 - £15
Dinner B & B £18.50 - £21.50

Freshly prepared local fish and seafood; venison; home-made quiches, pâtés, soups, casseroles, tempting desserts and home-baking. Filter coffee, Scottish honey and cheeses.

STB 2 Crown Commended

No credit cards

Proprietors: Fiona & Diarmid MacAulay

LAGGAN
128   NEAR NEWTONMORE   E5

Gaskmore House Hotel
Laggan
nr Newtonmore
Inverness-shire
PH10 1BS
Tel: 052 84 250

On A86 Newtonmore - Fort William road.

This award-winning restaurant commands spectacular views over the Upper Spey Valley. All bedrooms with private facilities – an ideal choice to stay in comfort and enjoy excellent food.

Open all year

Rooms: 11 with private facilities
Breakfast 8 - 9.30 am
Bar Lunch 12 - 2 pm (a)
Dinner 7 - 9 pm (d)
Bed & breakfast from £25
Dinner B & B from £36

Specialising in freshness of food with an emphasis on local game, fish, meat and vegetables.

STB 4 Crown Commended
RAC   3 Star
AA   3 Star

Credit cards: 1, 2, 3

Proprietors: James & Jacqueline Glendinning

LANGBANK
129   G5

Gleddoch House
Langbank
Renfrewshire
PA14 6YE
Tel: 0475 54 711
Telex: 779801

Off M8 Glasgow-Greenock at Langbank.

Beautifully situated in 250 acres overlooking the River Clyde and Loch Lomond hills the hotel offers all the advantages of gracious living and distinctive cuisine. Amenities include free use of the 18-hole golf course within the grounds and Clubhouse facilities of squash, sauna, snooker and horse-riding. Formerly a family residence the hotel has been tastefully converted, yet retains the features of a private home with service and accommodation of the highest standard.

Open all year   ▶

Rooms: 33 with private facilities
Breakfast 7 - 9.30 am
Bar Lunch (Clubhouse) 12.30 - 2.30 pm
Lunch 12.30 - 2.30 pm except Sat (c)
High Tea - residents only by request
Dinner 7.30 - 9 pm (f)
Bed & breakfast from £54
Dinner B & B from £55 (weekend break)

*West coast seafood; scallops etc.
Seasonal game dishes. Regional Scottish
traditional dishes.*

STB 4 Crown Commended
RAC 3 Star R
AA   3 Star B + Rosette
BTA Commended
Credit cards: 1, 2, 3, 5, 6

130 LARGS G4

Elderslie Hotel
Broomfields
Largs
Ayrshire
KA30 8DR
Tel: 0475 686460

Largs seafront on A78 north of Ardrossan.

Picturesque Listed building with many
interesting architectural features.
Overlooking the Firth of Clyde with views
to Cumbrae and Arran. Extensive use of
fresh local Ayrshire meats, poultry and fish
according to season. Menu changes daily.
Bedrooms equipped to a very high
standard. Traditional comfort and service.

Open all year

Rooms: 25, 13 with private facilities
Breakfast 8 - 9.30 am
Bar Lunch 12.30 - 2 pm (a)
Lunch 12.30 - 2 pm (b)
High Teas available only to parties booked
in advance.
Dinner 7 - 8.30 pm (c)
Bed & breakfast from £27
Dinner B & B rates on application.

STB 3 Crown Commended
RAC 2 Star
AA   2 Star
Credit cards: 1, 2, 3, 5

Wham's & The Platter
80 Main Street
Largs
KA30 8DH
Tel: 0475 672074

*A78 west coast route between Ardrossan
and Greenock.*

Situated in a building dating from 1887,
these two restaurants operate similar self-
service menus over lunchtime, but in the
evening the style changes to a more
relaxed table service – Wham's offering
seafood as its speciality while The Platter
specialises in steaks. Dine in the
conservatory-style Wham's, or in The
Platter's Victorian ambience.

Open all year

Lunch 11.45 am - 2.45 pm
High Tea 5 - 6.30 pm
Dinner 5 - 8.45 pm (c)
Closed Sunday

*Menu and seasonal daily specials
including Cullen skink, Arbroath smokies,
Loch Fyne kippers, mussels, oysters,
crayfish, lobster. Platter fillet of beef,
Scottish lamb chops, home-made steak
pie.*

Credit cards: 1

131 LETHAM F7

Fernie Castle Hotel
Letham
Cupar
Fife
KY7 7RU
Tel: 033 781 381

On A914, 1 mile north of A91 intersection.

Fernie Castle, built as a 16th century
fortified hunting tower and set in 30 acres
of secluded grounds, is now a beautifully
refurbished country house hotel. Situated
in Central Fife, it is an ideal base for
golfing, shooting and fishing or those
wishing to explore the considerable
historic attractions of this ancient county.

Open all year

Rooms: 16 with private facilities
Breakfast 7.30 - 10 am
Bar Lunch 12.30 - 2 pm (a)
Lunch 12.30 - 2 pm (d)
Dinner 7.30 - 9.30 pm (e)
Bed & breakfast £50 - £90
Dinner B & B rates on application.

Pastry case of game liver souffle, breast of
guinea fowl on corn bannock, venison
saddle and juniper berries. Marinated
fruits whipkull.
RAC 3 Star
AA   3 Star L
Credit cards: 1, 2, 3, 5
Proprietors: Norman & Sheila Cinnamond

132 LIVINGSTON VILLAGE G6

The Post Office Bistro
15/17 Main Street
Livingston Village
West Lothian
EH54 7AF
Tel: 0506 411226

Original village of Livingston New Town.

The Postmistress, Ally, and Chef/Patron
Peter, invite you to stay in Britain's only
residential licensed Post Office. Formerly
a 17th century coaching inn and a Post
Office since Queen Victoria's reign (see
the Victorian post box) and set in a
conservation village in the heart of
Livingston New Town on the banks of the
River Almond. Equidistant from Glasgow
and Edinburgh, just off the M8.

Open all year

Rooms: 3 with private facilities
Meals served all day from 7 am - 11 pm
(a-c)
No dogs.
Facilities for the disabled.
No smoking area in restaurant.
Bed & breakfast from £30
Dinner B & B rates on application.
Aberdeen Angus beef.
Credit cards: 1, 2, 3, 5
Proprietors: Peter & Ally Fildes

133 LOCH EARN ST FILLANS F5

Achray House Hotel
Loch Earn, St Fillans
Perthshire
PH6 2NF
Tel: 076485 231

Loch Earn, St Fillans.

Beautifully situated overlooking Loch Earn
and mountains beyond. 12 miles west of
Crieff (A85). Richly furnished, small hotel
owned and run by husband and wife.

Open Mar to Nov

Rooms: 6, 3 with private facilities
Breakfast 8 - 9 am ▶

Bar Lunch 12 - 2 pm (a)
Bar Supper 6.30 - 9.30 pm
Dinner 6.30 - 9.30 pm (c)
Bed & breakfast from £17.50
Dinner B & B from £26
Game, steaks, seafood and outstanding sweet menu.
STB 3 Crown Commended
Credit cards: 1, 2, 3
Proprietors: Tony & Jane Ross

Golden Larches Restaurant
Balquhidder Station
Lochearnhead
Perthshire FK19 8NX
Tel: 05673 262
Situated on A84, 2 miles south of Lochearnhead.
Family-run restaurant featuring Georgian style bow windows. Tea garden. All meals freshly cooked. Traditionally Scottish soups. Aberdeen Angus steaks and steak pies. Loch Tay trout, local vegetables. Speciality home-made fruit pies, scones, shortbread and cakes.
Open Easter to Oct
Breakfast from 10 am
Meals and snacks served all day. Low season 7 pm closing (a); high season 9.30 pm closing (a-b).
Home baking of sweets and cakes. Scottish high tea.
No credit cards
Proprietors: James & Loraine Telfer

Lochearnhead Hotel
Lochearnhead
Perthshire FK19 8HP
Tel: 056 73 229
On A84 at the side of Loch Earn.
Small friendly-run hotel and restaurant at the west end of Loch Earn and with lovely views across the loch in a popular water ski-ing and windsurfing area.
Open Mar to Nov
Rooms: 14, 5 with private facilities
Breakfast 8.30 - 9.30 am
Bar meals served all day 11 am - 9.30 pm
Lunch 12 - 2.30 pm (a)
Dinner 7.30 - 9.30 pm (b)
Bed & breakfast from £14
Dinner B & B rates on application.
Venison and salmon in season. Special vegetarian menu.
STB 2 Crown Approved
AA 1 Star
Credit cards: 1, 2, 3, 5
Proprietor: Angus Cameron

Stag Hotel
Argyll Street
Lochgilphead
Argyll PA31 8NE
Tel: 0546 2496
On A83 between Oban and Inveraray.
Central for Oban, Inveraray and Mull of Kintyre. Family-run hotel – furnished to the highest standard throughout. All rooms with colour TV, telephone, tea/coffee making facilities. Residents' lounge, sauna and solarium available. Free golf available for guests at the local nine-hole course.
Open all year
Rooms: 23, 17 with private facilities
Breakfast 7.30 - 9 am
Bar Lunch 12 - 2 pm (a-b)
Bar Supper 6 - 8.30 pm
Dinner 7 - 9 pm (c)
Bed & breakfast £18 - £23
Dinner B & B from £32
Loch Fyne salmon, venison steak, Sound of Jura clams, Islay malt whisky syllabub.
STB 4 Crown Commended
RAC 2 Star
Credit cards: 1, 3

Cruachan Guest House
Stoer
by Lochinver
Sutherland IV27 4JE
Tel: 05715 303
B869, 7 miles north of Lochinver.
Cruachan is a small family run licensed guest house. There are five letting bedrooms with hot and cold water including one with a private shower. All bedrooms have electric blankets and tea/coffee making facilities. There are two public bath/shower rooms, a comfortable visitors lounge and spacious dining room, central heating and fitted carpets throughout. TV available.
Open all year
Rooms: 5, 1 with private facilities
Breakfast 7.45 - 8.45 am
Dinner 7.30 pm (c)
Bed & breakfast from £11
Dinner B & B from £21
Fresh local food including venison, wild salmon and shellfish.
STB 2 Crown Commended
No credit cards
Proprietor: Rosemarie Shairp

Somerton House Hotel
Carlisle Road
Lockerbie
Dumfriesshire
DG11 2DR
Tel: 05762 2583
Outskirts of Lockerbie approx 300 yards from main A74.
A robust Victorian mansion standing in its own grounds, with interesting architectural aspects especially the unusual Kauri timber panelling and plaster cornices. All bedrooms en suite, TV, central heating, etc.
Open all year except 1 Jan
Rooms: 7 with private facilities
Breakfast 8 - 9 am
Bar Lunch 12 - 2 pm (a)
Bar Supper 6 - 9.30 pm
Dinner 7 - 9 pm (c)
Bar Lunch and Dinner à la carte. No smoking in restaurant.
Bed & breakfast from £25
Dinner B & B rates on application.
Whole grilled sardines and garlic bread. Devil's Beeftub soup. Local lamb cooked in yoghurt with apricots. Collops in the pan. Galloway pork and beef. Local salmon and trout (in season).
RAC 2 Star
AA 2 Star
Credit cards: 1, 2, 3
Proprietors: Mr & Mrs S J Ferguson

Portland Arms Hotel
Lybster
Caithness
KW3 6BS
Tel: 059 32 208
On A9 – 12 miles south of Wick.
The Portland was built to serve as a staging post early last century. There have been many changes, but the quality of personal service established then has been maintained. Fully central heated and double glazed. All rooms have private facilities including colour TV, telephone, tea-making facilities. Four-poster beds available. Executive rooms with jacuzzi baths also available.　▶

Open all year.

Rooms: 20 with private facilities
Breakfast 6.30 - 9 am
Bar Lunch 12 - 2.30 pm (a)
Lunch 12 - 2.30 pm (a)
High Tea 4.30 - 6.30 pm
Dinner 7 - 9.30 pm (c)
Bed & breakfast from £25
Dinner B & B from £36.90

Succulent Aberdeen Angus steaks, seafood platters, game dishes, fresh cream sweets.

Credit cards: 1, 2, 3, 5, 6

MACDUFF
139   D8

The Highland Haven
Shore Street
Macduff
AB4 1UB
Tel: 0261 32408

Situated on A98 overlooking Macduff harbour entrance and Deveron Bay.

Situated amidst quaint harbours and picturesque coastline. This area is rich in fishing and agricultural heritage. The panoramic outlook and relaxing atmosphere combine with the hotel's excellent leisure facilities (spa, sauna, steam room, snooker, etc.) to make your stay memorable. Golfing, fishing, angling and conference packages available.

Open all year

Rooms: 18, 16 with private facilities
Breakfast 7.45 - 9.15 am
Bar Lunch 12 - 2 pm (a)
Lunch 12 - 2 pm (a)
High Tea 5 - 6.30 pm
Bar Supper 5 - 10 pm
Dinner 7 - 9 pm (c)
Bed & breakfast £19.50 - £24.75
Dinner B & B from £30.25 - £35.25

Cullen skink, Moray Firth seafood platter, poached salmon Brig O' Banff, baked haddock St William, steaks – Bonnie Prince Charlie (sirloin), Highlander, Cassanova (fillet).

STB   4 Crown Commended
RAC   2 Star
AA   3 Star

Credit cards: 1, 2, 3, 5, 6

Proprietor: William Alcock

MACHRIHANISH
140   H3

Ardell House
Machrihanish
by Campbeltown
Argyll
PA28 6PT
Tel: 0586 81 235

Situated on the south-west coast of Kintyre.

Ardell house is a stone-built Victorian villa overlooking Machrihanish Golf Course and miles of sandy beaches with magnificent views over Islay, Jura and Gigha. There are three golf courses in the area and pony-trekking, windsurfing and angling can be arranged nearby. All rooms en suite with tea/coffee making facilities and colour TV. AA award winner – Guest House of the Year for Scotland.

Open Apr to Oct except for advance bookings in Winter.

Rooms: 10, 9 with private facilities
Breakfast 8 - 9.15 am
Dinner from 7 pm (c)
Residents only.
Bed & breakfast from £16
Dinner B & B £24 - £30

Local seafood, Scottish beef and cheeses (including Campbeltown Cheddar), home-made soups using fresh vegetables, home-grown herbs, delicious sweet dishes using fresh fruit in season – pavlovas, syllabubs.

STB   3 Crown Commended

No credit cards

Proprietors: David & Jill Baxter

MELROSE
141   G7

Burts Hotel
Market Square
Melrose
Roxburghshire
TD6 9PN
Tel: 089 682 2285
Fax: 089 682 2870

B6361 2 miles from A68 – 38 miles south of Edinburgh.

A delightful hotel situated in this historic town in the heart of the Border country. Ideally situated for walking, horse-riding, golf, game shooting and salmon fishing. Much of the hotel has recently been refurbished to a high standard. The elegant restaurant offers a choice of Scottish and international cuisine. An extensive lunch and supper menu is also available in the popular lounge bar. Mini-break terms available from November to May.

Open all year

Rooms: 21 with private facilities
Breakfast 8 - 9.30 am
Bar Lunch 12 - 2 pm (a)
Lunch 12.30 - 2 pm (c)
Bar Supper 6 - 9.30 pm: 6 - 10.30 pm Fri + Sat
Dinner 7 - 9.30 pm (d)
Bed & breakfast from £28
Dinner B & B from £38

Specialities include Tweed salmon, chicken Howtowdie, venison and Scottish beef, complemented by an excellent wine list.

STB   4 Crown Commended
RAC   2 Star
AA   2 Star

Credit cards: 1, 2, 3, 5, 6

Proprietors: Graham & Anne Henderson

Melrose Station Restaurant
Palma Place
Melrose
Roxburghshire
TD6 9PR
Tel: 089 682 2546

On A6091, 3 miles from A68 at Newton St Boswells. 2 miles from A7 by Galashiels.

Melrose Station has been described as "the handsomest provincial station in Scotland". The restaurant is part of the award winning conversion of this Grade A Listed building which has retained its original ambience whilst adding comfort and style. Friendly restaurant serving traditional home-cooking and Scottish fare throughout the day. Vegetarians catered for. À la carte menu in the evening. Children most welcome daytime and evenings.

Open all year except Christmas, Boxing and New Year's Days.

Lunch 12 - 3.30 pm (b)
Afternoon tea 2 - 4 pm (a)
High Tea 4 - 6 pm (b)
Dinner 7 - 11 pm Thurs, Fri, Sat only (c)

Local fish, game and Scottish sirloin steaks. Home-made soup. Fresh local vegetables and fruit (in season). High teas a speciality.

Credit cards: 1, 2, 3

Proprietor: Dennis G Rodwell

Corehead Farm
Annanwater
Moffat
Dumfriesshire
DG10 9LT
Tel: 0683 20973

"Devil's Beef Tub".

Picturesque farmhouse on 2,500 acre hill farm set in the "Devil's Beef Tub", amidst beautiful Moffat hills. Scottish Farmhouse Award winner. Traditional farmhouse cookery using beef, pork and lamb from own farm. Home-produced vegetables/fruit (in season) and freshly laid eggs. Home-made soups and sweets a speciality.

Open May to Oct

Rooms: 3
Breakfast 8.30 - 9 am
Dinner 6.30 - 7 pm (b)
Bed & breakfast from £11
Dinner B & B from £18

STB   2 Crown Commended

No credit cards

Proprietor: Berenice Williams

Hartfell House
Moffat
Dumfriesshire
DG10 9AL
Tel: 0683 20153

One mile off A74.

A delightful, small family-run hotel. 19th century Listed building in rural setting overlooking the surrounding hills and only a few minutes from the town centre. Beautiful woodwork and spacious rooms. Very comfortable homely atmosphere. Ideal for visiting Borders and south-west. Large garden to relax in with putting green.

Open Mar to Nov

Rooms: 9
Breakfast 8.15 - 9 am
Dinner 6 - 7 pm (c)
Non-residents by prior booking.
Bed & breakfast from £12.50
Dinner B & B from £21.50

Home-made soups. Gigot lamb in ginger sauce, Scotch beef braised in local beer. Gaelic pudding with Heather Cream sauce.

STB   2 Crown Commended

RAC   Listed
AA   Listed

Credit cards: 1, 3

Proprietors: Andrea & Alan Daniel

Well View Hotel
Ballplay Road
Moffat
Dumfriesshire
DG10 9JU
Tel: 0683 20184

Set in half an acre of garden overlooking hills and town, this 19th century country house has been extensively converted and refurbished to make this a small comfortable privately run hotel. An extensive wine list complements the creative table d'hôte menus.

Open all year

Rooms: 7, 5 with private facilities
Breakfast 8 - 9 am
Lunch 12 - 2 pm (b)
Dinner 7 - 8.30 pm (c)
Lunch and Dinner – by prior reservation.
Facilities for the disabled.
No smoking area in restaurant.
Bed & breakfast £17.50 - £33
Dinner B & B £28 - £44

Freshly cooked local produce including fish and game – subject to availability. Home-made soups and pâtés a speciality; fresh fruit and vegetables in season.

STB   3 Crown Highly Commended
RAC   Acclaimed
AA   Selected

Credit card: 3

Proprietors: Janet & John Schuckardt

Park Hotel
61 John Street
Montrose
Angus
DD10 8RJ
Tel: 0674 73415

Midway between town centre and beach.

A very comfortable privately-owned hotel, managed by the resident proprietors, Nigel and Norma Henderson. The main building dates from Victorian times. Tasteful alterations and additions have been effected during recent years, so the hotel now offers over 50 bedrooms with private facilities, conference and function suites for up to 200 people and a very attractive cedar-arched restaurant. Set in two acres of well-tended, landscaped gardens overlooking the town's mid links.

Open all year

Rooms: 59, 53 with private facilities
Breakfast 7.30 - 9.30 am
Bar Lunch 12 - 2 pm (a)
Lunch 12 - 2 pm (c)
Dinner 7 - 9.30 pm (c)
Bed & breakfast from £44
Dinner B & B rates on application.

Ham and haddie for breakfast, Musselburgh kail, fillets of sole, prime Aberdeen Angus beef and Highland coffee.

STB   4 Crown Commended
AA   3 Star

Credit cards: 1, 2, 3, 5, 6

Proprietors: Nigel & Norma Henderson

Gilchrist Farm
Muir of Ord
Ross-shire
IV6 7RS
Tel: 0463 870243

From Tore Roundabout on A9 take A832 for 4½ miles. Left turn to B862 (Beauly) and Gilchrist signposted first left.

Ann Fraser assures you of a warm welcome to this comfortable farmhouse set in an attractive garden. This working farm is ideally situated for touring the Highlands. 18-hole golf course less than a mile away. Inverness 20 minutes away by car.

Open Apr to Oct – advance booking preferred

Rooms: 2
Breakfast 8 - 9.30 am
Dinner 6.30 - 7.30 pm (b)
Residents only.
No smoking area in restaurant.
Bed & breakfast from £12
Dinner B & B from £18

Good home cooking from fresh local produce. Home-made soups and desserts a speciality. Salmon, trout, venison, Scottish beef, lamb, etc in season.

STB   Listed Commended
Scottish Farmhouse Holidays

No credit cards

Proprietor: Ann Fraser

Ord House Hotel
Muir of Ord
Ross-shire
IV6 7UH
Tel: 0463 870492

½ mile west of Muir of Ord on A832 Ullapool road.

John and Eliza Allen offer you at Ord House a stay which will be comfortable, relaxed and enjoyable. Table d'hôte and à la carte menus are made up from their own garden produce and local meat, game and fish. Beautiful formal gardens and woodland, combined with a 17th century laird's house, make Ord something very special.

Open May to mid Oct

Rooms: 12 with private facilities
Breakfast 8 - 9.30 am
Bar Lunch 12.30 - 2 pm (a)
Dinner 7.30 - 9 pm (d)
Bed & breakfast £23 - £26
Dinner B & B £37 - £40

Ord pigeon pâté; west coast scallops in the shell; chargrilled quail with hazelnut and basil dressing. Fillet of fresh wild salmon en papillote with cepes and cream. Baked ham, heather honey glazed crust.

STB 3 Crown Commended
Credit cards: 1, 2, 3
Proprietors: John & Eliza Allen

MULL
145   ISLE OF   F3

Ardrioch
Ardrioch Farm
Dervaig
Isle of Mull
PA75 6QR
Tel: 06884 264

1 mile from Dervaig on Calgary road.

Ardrioch – a comfortable cedar-wood farmhouse, traditionally furnished, with relaxing atmosphere. Peat fires, book shelves, views of sea loch and hills. Short stroll to the loch side, two miles from coast, own sea sailing available. Ideal for walking, bird-watching and fishing. Working farm – sheep, cows, friendly collies, lambs and calves, enjoyed by children. Guests welcome to take own wine.

Open May to Oct

Rooms: 4
Breakfast 7 - 9 am

Dinner 6.30 - 8 pm (b)
No smoking throughout
Unlicensed
Bed & breakfast from £14
Dinner B & B from £20

Tobermory smoked trout, home-made crab and smoked mackerel pâté, Orkney marinated herring. Fresh Mull salmon, venison, mutton from the farm, Tobermory trout.

STB 2 Crown Commended
No credit cards
Proprietors: Jenny & Jeremy Matthew

Craig Hotel
Tobermory Road
Salen
Isle of Mull
PA72 6JG
Tel: 0680 300347

In Salen Village – on Tobermory to Craignure Road.

More home than hotel and situated by the Sound of Mull – ideal for exploring the beauties of Mull, Iona and Staffa – the Craig is a typical 19th century Scottish family house with 20th century comforts, including attractive lounge with log fire, magazines and board games.

Open mid Mar to mid Oct

Rooms: 7
Breakfast 8.30 - 9 am
Dinner from 7.15 pm
Residents only.
No smoking area in restaurant.
Bed & breakfast £17 - £20
Dinner B & B £23 - £28

Local seafood and Scottish meats cooked with fresh garden herbs. Home-made soups, pâtés, puddings and conserves. Interesting cheese board, cafetiere coffee.

STB 2 Crown Commended
AA Listed
Credit cards: 3
Proprietors: James & Lorna McIntyre

Druimard Country House & Theatre Restaurant
Dervaig
Isle of Mull
Argyll
PA75 6QW
Tel: 06884 345

On B8073 8 miles west of Tobermory.

Peaceful family-run small country house hotel just outside village overlooking glen, river and sea loch. Well situated for touring, boat trips, fishing, walking, with

sandy beaches nearby. Elegant restaurant with well balanced menu specialising in fresh local produce, well appointed bedrooms (colour TVs etc), and Britain's smallest professional theatre.

Open Feb to Dec except Christmas

Rooms: 5, 3 with private facilities
Breakfast 8.45 - 9.15 am
Dinner 6 - 9 pm; 7 - 8 pm Sun (c)
Bed & breakfast £20 - £30
Dinner B & B rates on application.

Freshly cooked local produce, wild salmon, scallops, crab, venison. Scottish roasts and vegetarian dishes. Home-made soups, individual starters and sweets. Menu changed daily according to availability.

STB 3 Crown Highly Commended
RAC Highly acclaimed
Credit cards: 1, 3
Proprietors: Clive & Jenny Murray

Druimnacroish
Dervaig
Isle of Mull
Argyll
PA75 6QW
Tel: 06884 274

Via ferry from Oban to Craignure. On Salen-Dervaig road, 1½ miles south of Dervaig.

Druimnacroish is an exclusive country house hotel providing accommodation of the highest calibre and a cuisine based largely upon local foods. Vegetables and fruit are culled from the hotel's own six-acre garden and the cellar houses carefully selected wines. To discover the subtle values of tranquillity and, perhaps, a new slant on life, it is a most rewarding experience to join Donald and Wendy McLean in this delightful spot.

Open May to Oct

Rooms: 6 with private facilities
Breakfast from 9 am
Dinner from 8 pm (d)
Packed lunches to order.
No smoking area in restaurant.
Bed & breakfast from £38
Dinner B & B from £50

Specialities include scampi marinated in malt whisky, rib of Aberdeen Angus beef carved at table off the bone.

STB 4 Crown
BTA Commended
Credit cards: 1, 2, 3, 5
Proprietors: Donald & Wendy McLean

Linndhu House

Tobermory
Isle of Mull
PA75 6QB
Tel: 0688 2425

On A848 south of Tobermory.

A most comfortable, traditional Highland hotel set in 35 acres of glorious woodland two miles south of Tobermory and offering superb cuisine, spacious accommodation and outstanding views, with a trout stream in the grounds. Fishing, walking, bird-watching, golf, deerstalking and pony-trekking can be arranged.

Open all year

Rooms: 8, 2 with private facilities
Breakfast 8.30 - 9.30 am
Light Luncheon 12.30 - 2.30 pm (a-b)
High Tea for children by arrangement
Dinner 8 - 10 pm (d)
Bed & breakfast £25 - £50
Dinner B & B £43 - £65

Scallops in saffron sauce, carbonade venison, cranachan.

STB 2 Crown Commended

No credit cards

Proprietors: Ian & Jennifer McLean

The Puffer Aground

Main Road
Salen, Aros
Isle of Mull
Argyll
PA72 6JB
Tel: 068 03 389

On Craignure-Tobermory road.

The quaint name of this restaurant derives from the old days when the 'puffer' – the local steamboat – ran right on to the shore to unload its cargo and went off on the next high tide. The restaurant has a maritime theme and usually features an exhibition of oil paintings during July and August.

Open mid Apr to mid Oct

Lunch 12 - 2.30 pm (a-b)
Dinner 7 - 9 pm (b-d)
Closed Sun.

Scottish and Mull produce used whenever possible to create 'home-type' cooking in a friendly atmosphere.

No credit cards

Proprietors: Graham & Elizabeth Ellis

Tiroran House

Tiroran
Isle of Mull
Argyll
PA69 6ES
Tel: 06815 232

From Craignure, A849 towards Iona, turn right onto B8035 at head of Loch Scridain until signposted to Tiroran.

A remote and enchanting country house hotel, beautifully situated on Loch Scridain, offering the highest standards of comfort for those seeking to explore the lovely islands of Mull, Iona and Staffa. Set in over 50 acres of grounds, the lovely gardens include lawns, shrubberies and woodlands which slope down to the loch. Dinners are elegantly served by candlelight in the dining room overlooking gardens and sea loch. Caithness Glass/Taste of Scotland Best Picnic Lunch Award 1988.

Open May to early Oct

Rooms: 9 with private facilities
Breakfast and Lunch as required, for residents only.
Dinner from 7.45 pm (e)
No smoking in dining room.
Bed & breakfast £48 - £66
Dinner B & B £70 - £88

Fresh seafood, including scallops and crab, Hebridean smoked trout and own gravadlax are regular starters. Main courses using lamb and beef from the estate and island venison, with fresh vegetables.

BTA Commended

No credit cards

Best Picnic Lunch 1988

Proprietors: Robin & Susan Blockey

Western Isles Hotel

Tobermory
Isle of Mull
PA75 6PR
Tel: 0688 2012

40 minute drive from Oban-Craignure ferry.

A magnificent Gothic style building enjoying a truly remarkable situation on the cliff overlooking Tobermory Bay. The views from the dining room, terrace lounge and many of the bedrooms are breathtaking and must surely be regarded as some of the best in Scotland.

Open Mar to Jan

Rooms: 24 with private facilities
Breakfast 8 - 9 am

Bar Lunch 12.45 - 1 pm (a)
Dinner 7 - 8.30 pm (d)
No smoking area in restaurant.
Bed & breakfast £30 - £35
Dinner B & B £45 - £50

Home-made soups – menu features many specialities using local products including trout, venison, salmon, prawns, scallops and lobster.

STB 4 Crown Commended
RAC 3 Star

Credit cards: 1, 3

Proprietors: Sue & Michael Fink

Golf View Hotel

Seabank Road
Nairn
IV12 4HD
Tel: 0667 52301
Telex: 75134

An imposing Victorian hotel overlooking the sea and the Black Isle hills. A full range of leisure centre facilities and a heated outdoor pool. Near to the championship golf course. The chef has earned renown for the standard of preparation and presentation of food.

Open all year

Rooms: 40 with private facilities
Breakfast 7.30 - 10 am
Lunch 12.30 - 2 pm (b)
High Tea 2 - 5 pm
Dinner 7 - 9.30 pm (d)
Bed & breakfast rates on application.
Dinner B & B rates on application.

Locally smoked or chef's dill-cured salmon, carved from trolley, served with wholemeal toast. Highland game terrine – rich terrine of pheasant, duck and hare flavoured with whisky and berries in jelly.

STB 4 Crown Commended
AA 4 Star

Credit cards: 2, 3, 5, 6

Taste Bud Restaurant & Bar

44 Harbour Street
Nairn
IV12 4HU
Tel: 0667 52743

A traditional restaurant-bar of high reputation with pine and stone walls, the main theme of the premises, with log fires and comfortable seating. This ▶

restaurant is in easy walking distance of Nairn's harbour and fine beaches.

Open all year

Bar Lunch 12 - 2 pm (a)
Bar Snacks 2 - 6 pm (a)
Afternoon Tea 3 - 5 pm (a)
Bar Supper 5 - 10 pm (b)
Dinner 7 - 10 pm (c)

Prime Scottish meat. Local seafood speciality. Selection of game in season and traditional Scottish fare.

Credit cards: 1, 2, 3, 5, 6

Proprietors: William MacLeod & Karen Charman

NEWTONMORE
147　　　　　　　　　**E5**

Ard-na-Coille Hotel
Kingussie Road
Newtonmore
Inverness-shire
PH20 1AY
Tel: 054 03 214

At northern end of Newtonmore Village.

Built early this century as a millionaire's shooting lodge, now a comfortable country house hotel commanding superb views from all rooms over the Spey Valley and surrounding mountains. Comfortably furnished with masses of pictures and interesting books everywhere.

Open Jan to Oct except one wk Apr.

Rooms: 7 with private facilities
Breakfast 8.30 - 9.15 am
Dinner from 7.45 pm (d)
No smoking in dining room
Bed & breakfast £18.50 - £37.50
Dinner B & B £35 - £55

Smoked pheasant terrine, Arbroath smokie soup with spinach cream, wild duck with cranberry and orange sauce, butterscotch pudding with butterscotch sauce.

No credit cards

Proprietors: Nancy Ferrier & Barry Cottam

The Tea Cosy
Main Street
Newtonmore
Inverness-shire
PH20 1DD
Tel: 054 03 315

Within the book and craft shop on the Main Street of Newtonmore village.

Daintily set tables with a co-ordinating colour scheme of pretty china and tablecloths and posies of fresh flowers overlook a small patio ablaze with summer flowers where meals are served on fine summer days, while indoor customers can browse at leisure in the attractively laid out crafts shop.

Open Easter to late Oct

Coffee, tea and light meals available 10 am - 5 pm Mon to Sat
Unlicensed.
No smoking.

Home-baking with Mrs Pettigrew's lemon cake as a speciality.

No credit cards

Proprietors: Anne Bertram

NEWTON STEWART
148　　　　　　　　　**I5**

Queen's Arms Hotel
22 Main Street
Isle of Whithorn
Newton Stewart
Wigtownshire
DG8 8LF
Tel: 09885 369

A750 south of Newton Stewart.

A small country hotel with a homely atmosphere at the entrance to a small fishing village. Family run, it offers a personal and friendly service. Food is of good Scottish produce prepared in the traditional manner. The atmosphere is relaxed and informal.

Open all year

Rooms: 11, 4 with private facilities
Breakfast 8.30 - 10 am; 9 - 10.30 am winter
Bar Lunch 12.30 - 2 pm (a)
Lunch 12.30 - 2.30 pm (a)
High Tea 4.30 - 6 pm
Bar Supper 9 - 10 pm
Dinner 7.30 - 9.30 pm (c)
No smoking area in restaurant.
Bed & breakfast from £14.50
Dinner B & B from £24.50

Lobster, Galloway steaks and local fresh fish.

RAC 2 Star
AA 1 Star

Credit cards: 1, 3, 5

Proprietor: Donald Niven

OBAN
149　　　　　　　　　**F4**

Alexandra Hotel
Corran Esplanade
Oban
Argyll
PA34 5AA
Tel: 0631 62381

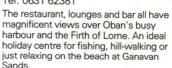

The restaurant, lounges and bar all have magnificent views over Oban's busy harbour and the Firth of Lorne. An ideal holiday centre for fishing, hill-walking or just relaxing on the beach at Ganavan Sands.

Open Apr to Oct

Rooms: 55 with private facilities
Breakfast 8 - 9.30 am
Bar Lunch 12.30 - 2 pm (b)
Dinner 6.30 - 9 pm (c)
Bed & breakfast from £43
Dinner B & B rates on application.

STB 4 Crown
RAC 3 Star
AA 3 Star

Credit cards: 1, 2, 3, 5, 6

Esplanade Restaurant
Esplanade
Oban
PA34 5PW
Tel: 0631 66594

Situated on Oban's waterfront with a view of the island of Kerrera, this cosy à la carte restaurant offers the very best of local seafood and prime Scottish meat. The lounge bar offers a large selection of bar meals throughout the day.

Open all year

Bar Lunch 12 - 3 pm (a)
Bar Supper 5 - 10 pm (a)
Dinner 6 - 10 pm (c)

Credit cards: 1, 3

Proprietor: Colin A Felgate

Manor House Hotel
Gallanach Road
Oban
Argyll
PA34 4LS
Tel: 0631 62087
Fax: 0680 300438

From south side of Oban follow signs to Gallanach and Kerrera Ferry. Past car ferry terminal.

Set in an enviable position in its own grounds on the foreshore of Oban Bay, the Manor House has long held the ▶

reputation for high quality in the comfort of its accommodation and the excellence of its Scottish and French cuisine. All bedrooms have en suite facilities, television, direct dial telephone and central heating.

Open all year

Rooms: 11 with private facilities
Breakfast 8.30 - 9.30 am
Bar Lunch 12.30 - 2 pm (a)
Lunch 12.30 - 2 pm (c)
High Tea (a) by arrangement
Dinner 7 - 8.30 pm (e)
No smoking area in restaurant.
Bed & breakfast from £20
Dinner B & B from £26 (min. 2 night stay)

STB   4 Crown Commended
RAC   2 Star
AA   2 Star

Credit cards: 1, 3

Proprietor: J L Leroy

Sea Life Centre - Shoreline Restaurant

Barcaldine
Oban
Argyll
PA37 1SE
Tel: 063 172 386

On A828 Oban-Fort William road, 10 miles north of Oban.

Seafood and home-baking fare are specialities in the self-service restaurant with a full range of meals and snacks including a salad table. You'll also be enjoying your meal in comfortable surroundings which give you the best possible vantage point to appreciate fully the majestic splendour of the glorious views over Loch Creran to the mountains beyond.

Open Mar to Nov

Meals served from 10 am to 5 pm and till 6.30 pm in Jul and Aug (a). Table licence only.
No smoking area in restaurant.

Seafood lasagne, salmon pie, seafood pie. Local seafood – oysters (fresh), smoked salmon and trout. New coffee shop – with freshly ground coffee and home-baked fare.

No credit cards

Soroba House Hotel

Soroba Road
Oban
PA34 4SB
Tel: 0631 62628

A816 to Oban.

The hotel with its sumptuously appointed dining room stands in a dominant and beautiful site of nine acres above the town, yet close enough to the town facilities, ferry terminal etc.

Open all year

Rooms: 25.
Breakfast 8 - 9.30 am
Bar Lunch 12 - 2.15 pm (a)
Lunch 12 - 2.15 pm (b)
Dinner 7 - 10.15 pm (c)
Bed & breakfast from £20
Dinner B & B from £30

Lunches, dinners, suppers are served from an extensive menu which includes local seafood, Scotch beef and fresh vegetables.

Credit cards: 1, 5, 6

Proprietor: David Hutchison

Willowburn Hotel

Clachan Seil
Isle of Seil
by Oban
PA34 4TJ
Tel: 08523 276

11 miles south of Oban, via A816 and B844, signposted Easdale, over Atlantic Bridge.

Welcome to the Willowburn, a small modern privately owned hotel set in two acres of ground on the sheltered north-east shore of the beautiful unspoilt Hebridean island of Seil – linked to the mainland by the only single span bridge to cross the Atlantic. All bedrooms have full amenities and the restaurant, overlooking Seil Sound, offers table d'hôte and à la carte menus for a relaxing end to your day.

Open Easter to late Oct

Rooms: 6 with private facilities
Breakfast 8.30 - 9.15 am
Bar Lunch 12.30 - 2 pm (b)
Bar Supper 6 - 8.30 pm
Dinner 7 - 8 pm (c)
Dinner B & B from £30

Locally caught Atlantic salmon, squat lobsters, prawns, mussels etc. Herb roast chicken with Drambuie stuffing. Prime Scottish roast beef and steak. Willowburn pâté with whisky and oatmeal.

STB   3 Crown Commended

Credit cards: 1, 3

Proprietors: A M & M Todd

OLD DEER
150   BY MINTLAW   D8

Saplinbrae House Hotel

Old Deer
by Mintlaw
Aberdeenshire
AB4 8PL
Tel: 0771 23515
Telex: 739032

A950 – 10 miles west of Peterhead and 30 miles from Aberdeen.

Welcoming country hotel, set in its own estate, originally the Dower House for the Pitfour Estate. The two bars offer substantial bar suppers, or there is a wide choice on the Stag Restaurant menu. Only top quality local meat is used, plus game (duck, pheasant, grouse, partridge) in season from the estate. Comfortable, modernised bedrooms, and friendly personal service ensure a loyal following.

Open all year

Rooms: 14, 12 with private facilities
Breakfast 7 - 9 am; 8 - 10 am Sun + Sat
Lunch 12 - 2 pm (a)
Bar Supper 6 - 9.30 pm
Dinner 7 - 9 pm (c)
Bed & breakfast from £22.50
Dinner B & B rates on application.

Gamies mushrooms, smoked Pitfour pheasant, game pie, roast mallard duck. Clarty pudding.

STB   Award Pending

Credit cards: 1, 2, 3, 5, 6

ONICH
151   By FORT WILLIAM   E4

Allt-nan-Ros Hotel

Onich
by Fort William
Inverness-shire
PH33 6RY
Tel: 08553 210
Fax: 08553 462

On A82, 10 miles south of Fort William.

The Macleod family welcome you to their Highland country house, set amid landscaped gardens on the shores of Loch Linnhe, midway between Ben Nevis and Glen Coe. All comfortably furnished bedrooms have private facilities, TV, radio, telephone, tea/coffee facilities, electric blankets, central heating, and overlook the loch. Richly furnished lounges and picture windowed Lochview Restaurant complement the stylish cuisine.   ▶

Open mid Mar to late Oct

Rooms: 21 with private facilities
Breakfast 8.30 - 9.30 am
Lunch 12.30 - 2 pm Sun only (b)
Dinner 7 - 8.30 pm (e)
No smoking in restaurant.
No dogs.
Bed & breakfast from £32.50
Dinner B & B from £47.50

A modern style Taste of Scotland menu featuring fruit, vegetables and herbs from the hotel gardens supplemented by home baking and best local produce.

STB 4 Crown Commended
RAC 2 Star R
AA 2 Star

Credit cards: 1, 2, 3, 5, 6
Proprietor: James Macleod

The Lodge On The Loch
Onich
by Fort William
Inverness-shire
PH33 6RY
Tel: 08553 237/238

On A82, 1 mile north of the Ballachulish Bridge.

Rest for a while in a charmed world and discover for yourself the gentle elegance of this renowned family-run hotel. Superbly set above Loch Linnhe and commanding panoramic views to the Morvern mountains, this Highland house is a remarkable discovery. Individually designed bedrooms feature fine woven fabrics from the islands and combine every modern comfort.

Open late Mar to Oct

Rooms: 21, 18 with private facilities
Breakfast 8 - 9.30 am
Bar Lunch 12 - 2.30 pm (a)
Dinner 7 - 10 pm (d)
No dogs.
Facilities for the disabled.
No smoking area in restaurant.
Bed & breakfast £26.50 - £37.50
Dinner B & B £39.50 – £52.50

Local venison, wild salmon, vegetarian dishes and a large variety of Scottish cheeses.

STB 4 Crown Commended
RAC 3 Star H
AA 3 Star H

Credit cards: 1, 3
Proprietors: Norman & Jessie Young

ORKNEY
152   ISLES OF   B7

Creel Restaurant
Front Road
St Margaret's Hope
Orkney
KW17 2SL
Tel: 0856 83 311

13 miles from Kirkwall.

Scottish winner Taste of Britain Award 1986. Voted in AA Top 500 Restaurants in Britain 1989. Scenic 15 mile drive from Kirkwall across the Churchill Barriers. Restaurant on seafront overlooking bay. Charming, homely and friendly atmosphere. Food prepared and cooked by owner/chef. Booking advisable.

Open Feb to Dec

Rooms: 3
Breakfast 8 - 9 am
Dinner 7 -10 pm (c) except Mon, Tue high season and Mon, Tue, Wed low season.
Bed & breakfast from £8
Dinner B & B from £14

Smoked lamb, marinated herring, fish soups. Local crab, scallops, salmon. Prime Orkney beef. Breast of chicken stuffed with smoked salmon.

No credit cards.
Proprietors: Alan & Joyce Craigie

Foveran Hotel
nr Kirkwall
St Ola
Orkney
KW15 1SF
Tel: 0856 2389

On A964 Orphir road, 2½ miles from Kirkwall.

The hotel is set in 20 acres overlooking Scapa Flow and has a reputation for its friendly, personal atmosphere. Open-fired sittingroom for pre-dinner drinks and after-dinner coffee and a bright attractive Scandinavian-style dining room.

Open Mar to Dec except Nov

Rooms: 8 with private facilities
Breakfast
Dinner 7 - 9 pm (c)
Dining room closed to non-residents Sun.
Bed & breakfast rates on application.
Dinner B & B rates on application.

Home-made soups and pâtés; prawns, scallops, lobster, sea trout, lamb, beef, game, farm cheese - all as available. New dishes from traditional raw materials.

Credit card: 3
Proprietor: Norma Gerrard

PATHHEAD
153   G7

The Foresters
107 Main Street
Pathhead
Midlothian
EH37 5PT
Tel: 0875 320273

In the main street of the village just 12 miles south of Edinburgh on the A68.

The Foresters was one of the original horse changeover points on the Edinburgh-York-London route and the character of the time has been maintained. A family-run pub restaurant offering good, inexpensive food.

Open all year

Lunch 12 - 3 pm (a-b); 12.30 - 3 pm Sun.
Dinner 5 - 11 pm (a-b); 6.30 - 11 pm Sun.

Specialities include pastry dishes – five different pies all cooked to order; chicken, pork and steak all wrapped in crisp puff pastry. Local fish and venison.

No credit cards
Proprietor: David Birrell

The Peat Inn

Peat Inn
Fife
KY15 5LH
Tel: 033 484 206

At junction of B940/941, 6 miles south-west of St Andrews.

An 18th century village inn, situated in the village which bears its name, just six miles from St Andrews. An outstanding restaurant now recognised as one of Britain's finest, featuring finest Scottish produce served stylishly in the intimate, beautifully furnished dining rooms. Well worth a detour.

Open all year, except 2 wks in Jan.

Rooms: 8 with private facilities
Continental breakfast served in room.
Lunch 1 pm (d)
Dinner 7 - 9.30 pm (f)
No smoking in restaurant.
Bed & breakfast from £40
Dinner B & B rates on application.

Breast of pigeon in a pastry case with wild mushrooms. Whole lobster in sauce with coriander and ginger. Caramelised apple pastry with a caramel sauce.

AA   Rosette
BTA Commended
Credit cards: 1, 2, 3, 4
Proprietors: David & Patricia Wilson

Cringletie House Hotel

Peebles
EH45 8PL
Tel: 072 13 233

A703 2½ miles north of Peebles.

Scottish baronial mansion set in 28 acres of gardens and woodland, in beautiful and peaceful surroundings. Magnificent views from every room. Scottish meat and fish always used, with fresh fruit and vegetables in season from own two acre walled kitchen garden, and from market. Imaginative home cooking at its best.

Open mid Mar to late Dec

Rooms: 13 with private facilities
Breakfast 8.15 - 9.15 am
Light lunch Mon to Sat
Lunch 1 - 1.45 pm (c) Sun (table d'hôte).

Afternoon Tea 3.30 - 4.30 pm
Dinner 7.30 - 8.30 pm (e)
Smoking discouraged.
Bed & breakfast £32.50 - £35
Dinner B & B £51 - £53.50

Haggis stuffed mushrooms with whisky sauce, hot cheese mousse baked with cream, roast goose with cranberry and apple sauce, casseroled haunch of venison with red wine and prunes. Toffee cheesecake.

STB 3 Crown Commended
RAC 2 Star
AA   2 Red Star
BTA Commended
Credit cards: 1, 3
Proprietors: Stanley & Aileen Maguire

Drummore

Venlaw High Road
Peebles
EH45 8RL
Tel: 0721 20336

In a quiet cul-de-sac off the Edinburgh road (A703) in Peebles.

Hillside house with panoramic views over Peebles and the Tweed Valley. Set among trees on Venlaw Hill, the house is in an ideal situation for walkers, and mountain bikes are available for hire for the more adventurous guest. For the less energetic – the peaceful surroundings are ideal for a relaxing break.

Open Easter to Oct. Advance bookings only Apr and May.

Rooms: 2
Breakfast 8 - 9 am
Dinner 6.30 - 7.30 pm (b)
Unlicensed.
Bed & breakfast from £10.50
Dinner B & B from £18

Fresh local poultry, lamb and beef. Trout fresh from the farm. Variety of salads. Oatcakes and a selection of Scottish cheeses.

STB 2 Crown
No credit cards
Proprietor: Jean Phillips

Kingsmuir Hotel

Springhill Road
Peebles
EH45 9EP
Tel: 0721 20151

On quiet south side of Peebles.

Charming, century-old house standing in own leafy grounds. Family-run hotel, specialising in Scottish cooking, using the best of local produce in a wide variety of dishes, served in restaurant, lounge or bar, lunchtime and evenings. Ideal centre for touring Edinburgh and stately homes of the Borders, golfing and fishing.

Open all year

Rooms: 10 with private facilities
Breakfast 8.30 - 9.30 am; 9 - 10 am Sun
Bar Lunch 12.15 - 2 pm (a)
Lunch 12.15 - 2 pm (a)
Bar Supper 7 - 9.30 pm (a)
Dinner 7 - 8.30 prn (c)
Bed & breakfast from £26
Dinner B & B from £35

Home-made soups (especially Cullen Skink) and pâtés. Kingsmuir steak pie. Salmon – Tweed Kettle a speciality – and trout, seafish and shellfish. Roasts of beef, lamb, venison, chicken (with skirlie).

STB 3 Crown Commended
AA   2 Star
Credit cards: 1, 2, 3
Proprietors: Elizabeth, Norman &
                    May Kerr

Peebles Hotel Hydro

Innerleithen Road
Peebles
Tweeddale
EH45 8LX
Tel: 0721 20602

A large, imposing chateau-style hotel with lofty ceilings, wide corridors and plenty of space, set in 30 acres of ground overlooking River Tweed Valley and Border hills. The hotel's bedrooms are comfortable and up-to-date – all rooms having private facilities, TV, hospitality tray, self-dialling telephones and most with hair-dryers and trouser presses. Leisure centre with pool, jacuzzi, saunas, solarium, steam bath, beauty salon, gymnasium, etc. Tennis, squash, riding.

Open all year

Rooms: 137 with private facilities
Breakfast 7.45 - 9.30 am; 8.30 - 10 am Sun
Bar Lunch 12.30 - 4 pm (a)
Lunch 12.45 - 2 pm (c)
Dinner 7.30 - 9 pm (d)
Bed & breakfast £29.50 - £33.50
Dinner B & B £38 - £43.50

Fresh trout from local fish farm. Best of Scottish smoked salmon, Border lamb, beef and other Scottish produce.

STB 4 Crown Commended
AA   3 Star L
Credit cards: 1, 2, 3, 5

Balcraig House Hotel
by Scone
Perth
PH2 7PG
Tel: 0738 51123

Balcraig is signposted off A94, 1 mile north of Perth.

Former Victorian mansion house tastefully converted to a luxury hotel in 1982. It commands unique unspoilt views over the Perthshire countryside and the city of Perth. The building boasts crystal chandeliers, blazing log fires, and fine antique furniture, complemented by the Victorian style conservatory dining room overlooking the Rose Arbour.

Open all year

Rooms: 10 with private facilities
Breakfast 8 - 9.30 am
Bar Lunch 12 - 2 pm (a)
Lunch 12 - 2 pm (c)
Bar Supper 6 - 8.45 pm (b)
Dinner 7 - 9.30 pm (e)
Facilities for the disabled.
No smoking area in restaurant.
Bed & breakfast from £58
Dinner B & B from £72

Grilled breast of Perthshire pigeon served with a strawberry and port wine sauce. Roast saddle of Invergeldie venison Balcraig.

STB   4 Crown Commended
AA   3 Star

Credit cards: 1, 2, 3, 5, 6
Proprietors: Derek & Lesley Mackintosh

The Bein Inn
Glenfarg
Perthshire
PH2 9PY
Tel: 057 73216

10 minutes south of Perth. Exit M90 (junction 8 northbound or 9 southbound) in the Glen.

Traditional coaching inn set in the beautiful Glenfarg. Character restaurant serving à la carte, Taste of Scotland and vegetarian menus. Cosy lounge bar, 'hideaway' snack bar (May to October). Superbly appointed accommodation, most en suite.

Open all year

Rooms: 13, 11 with private facilities

Breakfast 8 - 9.30 am
Bar Lunch 12 - 2 pm (a)
Dinner 7.30 - 9.30 pm (d)
Bed & breakfast from £19
Dinner B & B from £34

Cullen Skink, Scottish smoked trout and salmon, kipper pâté. Chicken Rabbie Burns. Venison casserole, salmon Ecossaise, pheasant Blairgowrie, clootie dumpling.

STB   3 Crown Commended
RAC   2 Star
AA   2 Star H

Credit cards: 1, 3, 6
Proprietors: Mike & Elsa Thompson

The Coach House Restaurant
8-10 North Port
Perth
PH1 5LU
Tel: 0738 27950

Close to Perth Bridge and North Inch.

Former Georgian town house near Fair Maid's House in cobbled street, dating from 1760. This restaurant has recently changed hands and is now personally run by Simon and Brenda Burns. Finest Scottish ingredients cooked in a modern style. Warm and friendly service – well worth a detour.

Open all year except first 2 wks Jan.

Lunch 12 - 2 pm (c)
Dinner 7 - 10 pm (e)
Closed Sun and Mon
After-theatre meals. Private parties catered for.

Smoked salmon consomme, cream of cucumber and courgette soup. Quenelles of turbot, fillet of beef with bananas and dark rum. Bread and butter pudding, honey and whisky ice cream.

Credit cards: 1, 2, 3
Proprietor: Simon Burns

Murrayshall Country House Hotel
Scone
Perthshire
PH2 7PH
Tel: 0738 51171
Telex: 76197
Fax: 0738 52595

4 miles out of Perth, 1 mile off A94.

Murrayshall Hotel is a sumptuously appointed and elegant country house with high standards of quiet, unobtrusive

efficient service. It is set in 300 acres of parkland and with a challenging 6,240 yards golf course. Bruce Sangster, an award-winning chef, uses produce from the hotel's four acre garden to produce a Taste of Scotland with a hint of French cuisine for the Old Masters Restaurant. Caithness Glass/Taste of Scotland Best Restaurant Award 1988.

Open all year

Rooms: 19 with private facilities
Breakfast 7.30 - 9.30 am
Bar Lunch 12 - 3 pm (b) - Club House
Lunch 12.30 - 1.45 pm (d)
Bar Supper 5.30 - 9 pm (b) - Club House
Dinner 7.30 - 9.30 pm (f)
Gourmet evenings and weekends.
No dogs.
Bed & breakfast rates on application.
Dinner B & B rates on application.

Breast of locally shot pigeon with red cabbage compote. Parcel of wild Tay salmon and turbot with langoustine tails. Perthshire raspberries.

STB   5 Crown Highly Commended

Credit cards: 1, 2, 3, 5, 6

Best Restaurant 1988

Scone Palace
Perth
PH2 6BD
Tel: 0738 52300

On A93 Braemar road, 2 miles out of Perth.

Ancient crowning place of Scotland's kings – now the historic home of the Earl and Countess of Mansfield. See the antique treasures, explore the grounds, enjoy lunch beside the range in the 'Old Kitchen' restaurant, or a snack in the coffee shop. Take home the excellent produce from the shop. To arrange special off-season visits contact the Administrator.

Open Good Friday to mid Oct

Lunch 11.30 - 2 pm (b)
Dinner (f)
Breakfast, High Tea and Dinner by arrangement only. Sun lunches served only during Jul and Aug unless pre-booked.

Fresh Tay salmon, home-made soup always available on the lunch menu. Home-baking, chutney and marmalade a speciality.

No credit cards

Waterside Inn
Fraserburgh Road
Peterhead
Aberdeenshire
AB4 7BN
Tel: 0779 71121

*30 miles north of Aberdeen on A952.
1 mile north of Peterhead.*

Scotland's most north-easterly hotel and
leisure club – swimming pool, spa bath,
sauna, Turkish steam room, keep-fit,
snooker and table tennis. Extensive menu
served all day by award-winning team of
chefs. Ideal for holidaymakers and
businessmen, plus speciality weekend
breaks for all the family.

Open all year

Rooms: 110 with private facilities
Bar Lunch 12 - 2.30 pm (a)
Lunch 12 - 2.30 pm (b)
Dinner 7 - 10 pm (c)
Breakfast and Dinner served all day.
Bed & breakfast £27 - £34.50

*Beef and fish dishes from Europe's
premier fishing port and rich Buchan
hinterland.*

STB　5 Crown Commended
AA　　3 Star B
Credit cards: 1, 2, 3, 5, 6

Pittodrie House Hotel
Pitcaple
Aberdeenshire
AB5 9HS
Tel: 04676 444
Telex: 739935
Fax: 04676 648

*Off A96 near Pitcaple – 21 miles north of
Aberdeen, 17 miles north of airport.*

Originally the family home of the owner,
Theo Smith, rooms retain original
character with antiques and family
portraits. There is also a three acre walled
garden which is at the disposal of guests.

Open all year

Rooms: 26 with private facilities
Breakfast 7.30 - 10 am; 9 -10 am Sun
Lunch 12.30 - 2 pm (b); 12.30 - 1.30 pm
Sun, prior booking essential.

Dinner 7.30 - 9 pm (c)
Bed & breakfast £45 - £60
Dinner B & B rates on application.

*Menu changes daily featuring fresh game
and salmon.*

STB　Award Pending
BTA　Commended
Credit cards: 1, 2, 3, 5
Proprietor: Theo Smith

Airdaniar Hotel
Atholl Roac
Pitlochry
Perthshire
PH16 5AR
Tel: 0796 2266

On old A9 north of town centre

Beautifully situated Victorian stone
building of character with views over
surrounding mountains and countryside
yet close to the centre of Pitlochry and its
many facilities. The Grouse & Claret
Restaurant & Bar overlook the gardens
where lunch may be taken in good
weather. Central heating, tea/coffee tray,
telephone, radio/TV in all rooms –
tastefully appointed throughout.

Open mid Feb to Jan

Rooms: 9 with private facilities
Breakfast 8 30 - 9 am
Bar Lunch 12 - 2 pm (a)
Dinner 6.30 - 9 pm (c)
Bed & breakfast from £22.85
Dinner B & B from £33.35

*Atholl Skewer – pieces of tender lamb
marinaded with fresh ginger and spices,
baked on skewers. Sauté of Scottish
lambs liver with lime and sage butter.*

STB　3 Crown Commended
RAC　2 Star
AA　　2 Star
Credit cards: 1, 3
Proprietors: Andrew & Sue Mathieson

Auchnahyle Farm
Tomcroy Terrace
Pitlochry
Perthshire
PH16 5JA
Tel: 0796 2318

On outskirts of Pitlochry.

Auchnahyle, the family house of Penny
and Alastair Howman is a charming
secluded 18th century farmhouse set
around a traditional stone courtyard. It is a

member of 'Wolsey Lodges' and guests
are treated as friends and offered every
comfort. Elegant, candlelit dinners are
offered for up to six residents.

Open Apr to Sep

Rooms: 3, 1 with private facilities
Breakfast from 8.30 am
Picnic lunches on request (a)
Theatre suppers 6.45 pm (c)
Dinner from 7.30 pm (d)
No smoking in dining room.
Bed & breakfast £18 - £21
Dinner B & B from £28

*Own quail and quail eggs with exclusive
sources for trout and venison. Everything
fresh including garden-grown fruit and
vegetables in season. Menus never
repeated.*

Credit cards: 1, 3
Proprietors: Penny & Alastair Howman

Birchwood Hotel
East Moulin Road
Pitlochry
Perthshire
PH16 5DW
Tel: 0796 2477

*200 yards off the Atholl Road on the Perth
side of Pitlochry.*

Beautiful stone-built Victorian manor
house on wooded knoll surrounded by
four acres of attractive grounds. Noted for
food and hospitality. Open to non-
residents for all meals. Choice of à la carte
and table d'hôte menus with extensive
wine list. All bedrooms with private
facilities, colour TV, telephone and
courtesy trays.

Open mid Feb to mid Dec

Rooms: 16 with private facilities
Breakfast 8.15 - 9 am
Lunch 12 - 1.30 pm (b)
Dinner 6.30 - 8 pm (c)
No smoking in restaurant.
No dogs.
Bed & breakfast rates on application.
Dinner B & B £29 - £38

*Smoked venison with pear, trout Faskally,
Highland steak, sirloin steak with haggis
stuffing, creamed smokie, pork Edradour,
cranachan.*

STB　3 Crown Commended
RAC　2 Star
AA　　2 Star H
Credit cards: 1, 3
Proprietors: Brian & Ovidia Harmon

The Green Park Hotel

Clunie Bridge Road
Pitlochry
Perthshire
PH16 5JY
Tel: 0796 3248

North side of Pitlochry.

Set in its own grounds on the banks of
Loch Faskally, the Green Park Hotel has
37 bedrooms all with private facilities. The
spacious lounges, restaurant and cocktail
bar all boast breathtaking views of the loch
and the hills beyond.

Open late Mar to Oct

Rooms: 37 with private facilities
Breakfast 8.30 - 9.30 am
Bar Lunch 12 - 2 pm (a)
Lunch (b-c) by arrangement only
Bar Supper 7 - 9 pm
Dinner 6.30 - 8.30 pm (c)
No smoking in restaurant.
Bed & breakfast from £32
Dinner B & B from £43

Full Scottish dinner served every Fri.
Choice of over 30 hors d'oeuvres Sat. Cold
buffet table Sun dinner.

AA   3 Star
Credit cards: 1, 3, 6
Proprietors: Graham & Anne Brown

Knockendarroch House Hotel

Higher Oakfield
Pitlochry
Perthshire
PH16 5HT
Tel: 0796 3473

High on hill overlooking village – just off
Atholl Road.

Splendidly confident large Victorian house
standing squarely on its hill looking over
the Tummel Valley and Pitlochry.
Recommended by Karen Brown's Hotel
Guide. Bookings advised and essential for
non-residents.

Open mid Mar to Nov

Rooms: 12 with private facilities
Breakfast 8.15 - 9.15 am
Dinner 6.15 - 7.15 pm (c)
Bed & breakfast from £20.50
Dinner B & B from £30

Good home cooking – pan-fried chicken
with pickled apple and red cabbage,
butterfly of trout, cucumber cream.
Home-made soups and pâtés. Crème
caramel in a sugar nest.

STB 3 Crown Commended
RAC Highly Acclaimed
BTA Commended
Credit cards: 1, 2, 3, 5
Proprietors: Mary & John McMenemie

The Luggie Restaurant

Rie-Achen Road
Pitlochry
Perthshire
PH16 5AM
Tel: 0796 2085

On the way to the famous salmon ladder.
Opposite the west end car park.

Informal eating in the relaxed atmosphere
of an early 18th century stone-built milking
parlour. This restaurant is now in the
hands of Andrew and Sue Mathieson.

Open Mar to early Nov

Morning coffee 9.30 - 11.30 am
Lunch 11.30 am - 2.30 pm
Afternoon Tea 2.30 - 5 pm
Dinner 6 - 9.30 pm (c)

Credit cards: 1, 2, 3, 5, 6

Proprietors: Andrew & Sue Mathieson

Torrdarach Hotel

Golf Course Road
Pitlochry
Perthshire
PH16 5AU
Tel: 0796 2136

On road signposted to golf course at north
end of town.

Muriel and Robert How offer a high
standard of personal service and
traditional home-cooking. The hotel is in a
woodland setting overlooking Pitlochry,
quiet and peaceful. This is a good centre
for touring, walking and fishing, and of
course, the famous Festival Theatre.

Open Easter to mid Oct

Rooms: 7, 3 with private facilities
Breakfast 8.30 - 9 am
Dinner at 6.45 pm (b)
No smoking in dining room.
Residents only.
No dogs.
Bed & breakfast from £15.50
Dinner B & B from £22

Kipper pâté, fresh Scottish salmon, home-
made soups and desserts, together with
local beef and lamb provide interesting
and varied menus.

STB 3 Crown Highly Commended
AA   Listed

No credit cards

Proprietors: Muriel & Robert How

The Haven Hotel

Innes Street
Plockton
Ross-shire
IV52 8TW
Tel: 059 984 223

In the village of Plockton.

In the lochside village of Plockton,
originally a 19th century merchant's
house, the Haven has been carefully
converted into a charming small hotel set
in the centre of one of Scotland's most
beautiful villages. The hotel features three
lounges – one with open fire, two 'no
smoking'. Bedrooms are furnished to the
highest standard.

Open Feb to 20 Dec

Rooms: 13 with private facilities
Breakfast 8.15 - 9 am
Bar Lunch 12.30 - 2 pm (a)
Lunch 12.30 - 2 pm (a) - last order
1.45 pm
Dinner 7 - 8.30 pm (c)
No smoking area in restaurant.
Bed & breakfast from £21
Dinner B & B from £31

Plockton prawns, pheasant, local salmon,
venison, haggis, kippers, local black
pudding, wild duck, Scottish lamb, beef
and pork. Home-made sweets.

STB 4 Crown Highly Commended
RAC 2 Star HR
AA   2 Star HBL
Credit cards: 1, 3
Proprietors: Marjorie Nichols &
                    John Graham

Inverewe Garden Restaurant
(National Trust for Scotland)

Poolewe
by Achnasheen
Wester Ross
IV22 2LG
Tel: 044 586 247

The Garden Restaurant has picture
windows overlooking beautiful Loch Ewe
and the gentle village of Poolewe. The
restaurant is self-service and offers a large
selection of salads. Limited facilities for
the disabled.   ▶

83

Open Apr to mid Oct 10 am - 5 pm
No smoking in dining room.
Facilities for the disabled.

Fresh wild Loch Ewe salmon, dressed crab and lobster, when available, home-made soups, garden produce when possible, variety of dishes using meat from the Black Isle. Fresh baked cakes and pastries.

No credit cards

PORT-NA-CON
162   B5

Port-na-Con House
Loch Eriboll
Altnaharra
Lairg
Sutherland
IV27 4UN
Tel: 097 181 367

7 miles east of Durness on A838, signposted 'Portnacon'.

Situated on the west shore of Loch Eriboll, amidst beautiful tranquil surroundings, this former custom house built about 200 years ago has recently been tastefully converted by the Frazers to a comfortable centrally heated guest house. All rooms overlook the Loch. Good selection of wines. New nine-hole golf course nearby.

Open Easter to early Oct

Rooms: 4
Breakfast 8 - 8.30 am; 8.30 - 9 am Sun.
Dinner from 7 pm (b)
No smoking in restaurant.
Dinner B & B £21 - £22.50

Home cooking, all freshly prepared. In season: Loch Eriboll lobster and giant prawns, locally caught salmon and lemon sole, or try Port-na-Con's very popular seafood platter, advance booking essential.

STB 2 Crown
AA Listed
Credit cards: 3
Proprietor: Sheila Frazer

PORTPATRICK
163   I4

The Fernhill Golf Hotel
Heugh Road
Portpatrick
nr Stranraer
DG9 8TD
Tel: 077681 220

Spectacularly situated house built in 1872 now a modern comfortable hotel.
Victorian conservatory, newly constructed, enjoys superb view, seats 30 and is a no smoking area. Fine selection of food and wine in both restaurant and popular local bar restaurant. Large grounds and garden with ample overnight parking.

Open all year

Rooms: 15 with private facilities
Breakfast 8 - 9 30 am
Bar Lunch 12 - 2 pm (a)
Lunch by special arrangement
Bar restaurant meals 6 - 10 pm
Dinner 7 - 9 pm (c)
No smoking area in conservatory restaurant.
Bed & breakfast from £23
Dinner B & B from £32.50

Only finest meat, fish and local produce used in season and when available. All meals are cooked to order.

STB 4 Crown Commended
RAC 3 Star
AA 3 Star

Credit cards: 1, 2, 3, 5
Proprietors: Anne & Hugh Harvie

RAASAY
164   ISLE OF   D3

Isle of Raasay Hotel
Raasay Island
by Kyle of Lochalsh
IV40 8PB
Tel: 047 862 222/226

Between Skye and mainland. Easy access by car ferry from Sconser (Skye).

Small, comfortable hotel situated in woodlands on the totally unspoiled beautiful Isle of Raasay, overlooking the Sound of Raasay to the mountains of Skye. The hotel itself is a remarkable blend of old and new with modern wings added to the renovated old stone mansion house. Ideal for bird-watching, hill-walking

and geology. The food is good and wholesome. Spectacular views of the Cuillins.

Open Apr to Sep

Rooms: 12 with private facilities
Breakfast 8.15 - 9 am
Bar Lunch 12.30 - 2 pm (a)
Dinner from 7 pm (d)
No smoking area in restaurant.
Bed & breakfast from £24
Dinner B & B from £37

Home-made soups and sweets a speciality. Fresh Raasay salmon in season, best Scottish beef, local fish, cranachan, Strathbogie mist, Raasay wild brambles and apple crumble with cream.

STB 3 Crown Commended
AA 2 Star

No credit cards

Proprietor: Isobel Nicholson

ROTHES
165   D7

Rothes Glen Hotel
Rothes
Morayshire
IV33 7AF
Tel: 034 03 254

On north side of Rothes, on road to Elgin.

A delightful turreted and compact Victorian mansion, standing in 40 acres of grounds maintaining a herd of long-haired Highland cattle. The public rooms are imposing, with marble fire places and 18th century furniture.

Open Feb to Dec

Rooms: 16, 13 with private facilities
Breakfast 8 - 9.30 am
Bar Lunch 12.30 - 2 pm (a)
Lunch 12.30 - 2 pm (c)
Dinner 7.30 - 9 pm (e)
Bed & breakfast from £50.25
Dinner B & B from £69.50

Fresh fish and shellfish from the Moray Firth and salmon from the River Spey.

BTA Commended

Credit cards: 1, 2, 3, 5, 6
Proprietors: Donald & Elaine Carmichael

ROY BRIDGE
166   E4

Stronlossit Hotel & Restaurant
Roy Bridge
Inverness-shire
PH31 4AG
Tel: 0397 81 253

On A86 between Spean Bridge and Loch Laggan.

Small, family-run hotel near Fort William with views of the Nevis range of mountains. Stronlossit offers comfortable accommodation and a warm welcome in the restaurant. Relax in the lounge bar/games room by an open log fire.

Open all year

Rooms: 9, 4 with private facilities
Dinner 7 - 9.30 pm (c)
No smoking area in restaurant.
Bed & breakfast from £16
Dinner B & B from £23

Seafood, home-made soups and pâtés, River Roy salmon, Lochaber lamb; fresh Loch Lochy trout, prime Scotch beef, local pheasant and rabbit.

Credit cards: 1, 3, 5

Proprietor: Maurice Vallely

ST ANDREWS
167   F7

The Grange Inn
Grange Road
St Andrews
Fife
KY16 8LJ
Tel: 0334 72670

Grange Road is off A917 to Crail on exit from St Andrews.

Charming old world inn beautifully situated on a hillside overlooking the town, St Andrews Bay and the Tay estuary. The restaurant features the best of local produce in season, such as East Neuk salmon, Tay salmon, Perthshire venison, local beef and lamb. A daily selection of home-cooked bar meals.

Open all year

Rooms: 2 with private facilities
Bar Lunch 12.30 - 2 pm (b)
Lunch 12.30 - 2 pm except Mon (c)
Bar Supper 7 - 10 pm (b)
Dinner 7.30 - 9.30 pm except Mon (e)

Restaurant closed Mon - only Bar Meals available. Dinner menu changes monthly. No smoking in restaurant.
Dinner B & B rates on application.

Baked filo parcels with smoked haddock in a cream sauce. Ramekin of lamb's kidneys with port and rosemary. King prawns and wild mushrooms in chablis sauce. Hot chocolate pudding with chocolate sauce.

Credit cards: 1, 2, 3, 5

Proprietors: Ann Russell & Peter Aretz

Parkland Hotel & Restaurant
Kinburn Castle
Double Dykes Road
St Andrews
Fife
KY16 9DS
Tel: 0334 73620

Near centre of St Andrews.

Parkland Hotel occupies part of a fine castle-style mansion, set in its own grounds. Close to all amenities of the town. Golf course, beach and shopping are all within a few minutes walk.

Open all year

Rooms: 15, 9 with private facilities
Breakfast 8 - 9 am
Lunch 12.30 - 2 pm except Sun (b)
Dinner 7.30 - 8.30 pm except Sun Mon - reservations essential.
Dinner 6.30 pm daily, table d'hôte for residents.
Bed & breakfast £21 - £28.75
Dinner B & B from £29.50 - £37.85

STB 3 Crown Commended
RAC 2 Star
AA 2 Star

Credit cards: 1, 3

Proprietors: Brian & Rosemary
            MacLennan

Rufflets Country House Hotel
Strathkinness Low Road
St Andrews
Fife
KY16 9TX
Tel: 0334 72594

On B939 1½ miles west of St Andrews.

Rufflets Country House Hotel is situated in ten acres of beautiful gardens, 1½ miles from the town centre and famous golf courses. All bedrooms with private bath/shower, radio, TV, tea/coffee-making facilities and hair-dryers. Restaurant renowned for Scottish specialities using fresh local produce.

Open all year except 7 Jan to 19 Feb inclusive.

Rooms: 21 with private facilities
Breakfast 8 - 9.30 am; 8.30 - 10 am Sun.
Bar Lunch 12.30 - 2 pm (b)
Lunch 12.30 - 2 pm (b)
Dinner 7 - 9 pm (e)
Dinner (Flints) 7 - 10 pm (c)
Bed & breakfast from £36.50
Dinner B & B from £38

Collops of Aberdeen Angus fillets with garlic butter and lobster. Poached darne of Tay salmon in a light vinegar and basil cream sauce. Brandy snap baskets filled with hot cherries and Kirsch.

STB 4 Crown Commended
RAC 3 Star
AA 3 Star HBL
BTA Commended

Credit cards: 1, 2, 3, 5

Proprietor: Ann Russell.

St Andrews Golf Hotel
St Andrews
Fife
KY16 9AS
Tel: 0334 72611

Forth Bridge/M90, take A91 for St Andrews. Turn left for golf course.

Situated on seafront with magnificent views of beaches, golf links and rock pool. 23 bedrooms with bath, colour TV, phone, and central heating. Lift available. Elegant cocktail bar, lounge with panoramic view of sea. Conference facilities available.

Open all year

Rooms: 23 with private facilities
Breakfast 7.30 - 9.30 am
Bar Lunch 12 - 2.30 pm (a)
Lunch 12.20 - 2.30 pm Sun only (b)
High Tea for residents only.
Dinner 7 - 9.30 pm (d)
Bed & breakfast from £32
Dinner B & B from £46

Creamed watercress and Stilton soup; grilled salmon with fresh oysters and pastry in stout-based sauce; breast of chicken in creamed groundnut sauce, with a fresh fruit salad. Loch Fyne langoustines.

STB 4 Crown Commended
RAC 3 Star C
AA 3 Star L

Credit cards: 1, 2, 3, 5, 6

Proprietors: Maureen & Brian Hughes

Eastertown Farm
Sandilands
Lanark
ML11 9TX
Tel: 055588 236

2½ miles from M74, taking A70 Edinburgh/Ayr exit.

Tastefully modernised traditional stone-built farmhouse on working sheep farm, set in commanding situation in beautiful countryside. TV, tea/coffee making facilities in all rooms. Seven miles from Lanark, convenient to M74 road link. Scottish Farmhouse of the Year Winner 1987.

Open all year

Rooms: 5, 2 with private facilities
Breakfast at 8.30 am
Dinner at 6.30 pm
Bed & breakfast rates on application.
Dinner B & B from £17

Home-made Scottish dishes using home-produced lamb, pork and vegetables.

STB 2 Crown Highly Commended
AA Approved
Scottish Farmhouse Holidays
No credit cards
Proprietor: Janet Tennant

Philipburn House Hotel
Selkirk
TD7 5LS
Tel: 0750 20747
Fax: 0750 21690

A707 Moffat-Peebles. 1 mile from A7.

Award-winning country house hotel and restaurant, set in the heart of the romantic Scottish Borders. Imaginative bar meals, home-baked afternoon teas. 1751 Georgian house with swimming pool and five acres of beautiful grounds – garden gained 'Grounds for Delight' Award 1989. Special breakaway packages available.

Open all year

Rooms: 16 with private facilities
Breakfast 8.30 - 9 am

Bar Lunch 12 - 2 pm (a)
Lunch 12.30 - 2 pm (a)
Children's High Tea 5.30 - 6 pm
Dinner 7.30 - 9.30 pm (c)
No smoking area in restaurant.
Bed & breakfast from £37
Dinner B & B from £44

Medallions of roe deer Monanie (with a blueberry sauce and poached pear). Fillet of Border lamb Philipburn (cooked rosy pink on a crisp potato galette with gooseberry and mint sauce).

STB 4 Crown Commended
Credit cards: 1, 2, 3, 5
Proprietors: Jim & Anne Hill

Busta House Hotel
Busta
Brae
Shetland
ZE2 9QN
Tel: 080622 506

On the Muckle Roe road – 1 mile off the A970 Hillswick road.

Explore beautiful Shetland and relax in the tranquil comfort of 16th century Busta House. Fresh flowers and peat fires welcome you, superb food, fine wines and a choice of 120 malt whiskies await you in the charming old house. All bedrooms are en suite and have TV, hair-dryer, trouser press, tea/coffee making facilities and direct dial telephones.

Open all year

Rooms: 21 with private facilities
Breakfast 7.30 - 9 am
Bar Lunch 12 - 2 pm (a)
Dinner 7 - 9.30 pm (e)
No smoking area in restaurant.
Bed & breakfast from £37
Dinner B & B from £34 (min 3 nights stay).

Shetland lamb and salmon, Orkney beef and ale, home-made Shetland soups, fish dishes and gravadlax.

STB 4 Crown Commended
RAC 3 Star
AA 3 Star L

Credit cards: 1, 2, 3, 5, 6
Proprietors: Peter & Judith Jones

St Magnus Bay Hotel
Hillswick
Shetland
ZE2 9RW
Tel: 080623 372

36 miles north of Lerwick.

Historic Norwegian-built hotel erected at the turn of the century. Ideal base for wildlife enthusiasts. Dining room with carvery and bistro/coffee house offer a high standard of food and extensive wine list. Fresh local seafood is a speciality. Children always welcome.

Open all year.

Rooms: 26 with private facilities
Breakfast 6.30 - 9 am
Bar Lunch 12.30 - 1.45 pm (a)
Lunch 12.30 - 2 pm (b)
High Tea 4 - 6 pm
Dinner 7.30 - 9 pm (c)
Bed & breakfast £23 - £26
Dinner B & B £35 - £38

Fresh seafood – lobster, scallops, etc.

STB 3 Crown
Credit cards: 1, 3, 6
Proprietor: Lysbeth Calland

Manor Park Hotel
Skelmorlie
Ayrshire
PA17 5HE
Tel: 0475 520832

Off A78 halfway between Largs and Wemyss Bay piers.

Gracious Victorian manor situated on hillside overlooking Firth of Clyde. Panoramic views from all public rooms. Luxuriously furnished throughout. Hair-dryer, tea-making facilities. First class cuisine. Unique cocktail bar with renowned malt whisky collection.

Open Mar to early Jan

Rooms: 23, 22 with private facilities
Breakfast 7.30 - 10 am
Bar Lunch 12.45 - 2.30 pm (a)
Lunch 12.45 - 2.30 pm (c)
Dinner 7 - 9.30 pm (d)
Bed & breakfast from £44
Dinner B & B from £61

The best of local meat and fish predominate. Scampi Laphroaig, venison Macallan.

STB 4 Crown Commended
RAC 3 Star HC
AA 3 Star BL
No credit cards
Proprietor: Clifford Sebire

Ardvasar Hotel
Ardvasar, Sleat
Isle of Skye
IV45 8AS
Tel: 04714 223

Opposite Mallaig – ½ mile from Armadale ferry.

Small white, traditional, whitewashed stone building overlooking mountains and Sound of Sleat water to Mallaig. Cosy small rooms, sittingroom with log fire. Traditionally furnished to give warm homely atmosphere.

Open Mar to Dec

Rooms: 10 with private facilities
Breakfast 8.15 - 9.30 am
Bar Lunch 12 - 2 pm (b)
Bar Supper 5 - 7 pm
Dinner 7.30 - 8.30 pm (d)
Bed & breakfast from £22
Dinner B & B from £36

Fresh lobster, scallops, prawns. Princess scallops. All locally caught – on availablility. Daily changing menus.

RAC 2 Star
AA 2 Star

Credit cards: 3

Proprietors: Bill & Gretta Fowler

Atholl House Hotel
Dunvegan
Isle of Skye
IV55 8WA
Tel: 047 022 219

A863 Dunvegan Village.

Small family-run hotel in the village of Dunvegan with magnificent views of mountains and loch. The tastefully decorated bedrooms, all have colour TV, direct dial telephones, tea/coffee making facilities and duvets. Ideal centre for touring the Isle of Skye.

Open all year except Nov

Rooms: 9, 6 with private facilities
Breakfast 8 - 9 am
Morning Coffee 10 - 11.30 am
Lunch 12 - 2 pm (a)
Afternoon Tea 3 - 5 pm
Dinner 7 - 9.30 pm (d)
Restricted licence.
No smoking in restaurant.
Bed & breakfast £21 - £24
Dinner B & B £34 - £37

Scottish beef steaks, local seafoods. Skye lamb, trout and venison. Home-made soups and sweets. Highland wines, jellies and cheeses.

STB 3 Crown Commended
AA 1 Star H

Credit cards: 1, 3

Proprietors: Cliff & Barbara Ashton

Glenview Inn
Culnacnoc
by Portree
Isle of Skye
IV51 9JH
Tel: 047 062 248

13 miles north of Portree on A855.

Fine example of a traditional Skye house, pleasantly converted to a small and friendly family-run inn, 13 miles north of Portree in one of the loveliest areas of Skye. The proprietors take great enjoyment in their cooking and helping guests' waistlines expand in comfort. Calorie counters beware.

Open Mar to Oct

Rooms: 6, 4 with private facilities
Breakfast 8.30 - 10 am by arrangement
Bar Lunch 12.30 - 2.30 pm (a)
Dinner from 8 pm (d)
Bed & breakfast from £22
Dinner B & B from £35

Fresh bread with unusual soups; rich pâtés; skewered scallops, roast lobsters and Skye oysters; whiskied steaks; crab stuffed chicken; calorie-laden puddings.

STB 3 Crown Commended
AA 1 Star + Rosette

Credit card: 1

Proprietors: Harper Family

Harlosh Hotel
by Dunvegan
Isle of Skye
IV55 8ZG
Tel: 047 022 367

4 miles south of Dunvegan off A863.

Perfectly positioned on the shores of Loch Caroy the Harlosh commands one of the finest views of the Cuillins, MacLeods Tables and the Islands of Loch Bracadale. This small cosy hotel offers an elegant but homely atmosphere with an emphasis on peace and tranquillity.

Open Easter to Oct

Rooms: 8, 2 with private facilities
Breakfast 8.30 - 9 am
Dinner 6.30 - 9 pm (c)
No dogs.

No smoking area in restaurant.
Bed & breakfast from £21
Dinner B & B from £32

Local fish and shellfish – fresh whenever possible on a constantly changing menu dependent on what is available. Cooked sympathetically to any requirement.

STB 2 Crown Commended
AA 1 Star H

Credit cards: 1, 3

Proprietor: Peter Elford

Kinloch Lodge
Sleat
Isle of Skye
IV43 8QY
Tel: 047 13 214

6 miles south of Broadford on A851 and 8 miles north of Armadale on A851.

Kinloch Lodge is an isolated converted shooting lodge at the south end of the island. It is set a mile from the main road at the foot of a mountain at the head of a sea loch. Spectacular panoramic views of the mainland at one side and the Cuillin range at the other. Personally run by Lord and Lady Macdonald.

Open Mar to mid Jan except 11 to 27 Dec

Rooms: 10 with private facilities
Breakfast 8.30 - 9.30 am
Dinner from 8 pm (e)
Residents only.
Bed & breakfast £35 - £48
Dinner B & B £56 - £70

Lady Macdonald pays particular attention to the food served both at breakfast and on the small dinner menus, using the very best of the wide range of ingredients available locally.

AA 2 Star + Rosette
BTA Commended
Credit cards: 1, 3

Proprietors: Lord & Lady Macdonald

CREDIT/CHARGE CARDS

1 Access/Mastercard/Eurocard
2 American Express
3 Visa
4 Carte Bleu
5 Diners Club
6 Mastercharge

Portree House
Home Farm Road
Portree
Isle of Skye
IV51 9LX
Tel: 0478 2796

5 minutes walk from the centre of Portree village.

Bar-Restaurant within Georgian mansion house with views over Portree Loch to the Cuillins – open all year round to residents and non-residents, serving lunches and evening meals seven days a week. Families welcome – large garden area including children's playground.

Open all year
Bar Lunch 12 - 4.30 pm; 12 - 2.30 pm winter (a)
Dinner 5.30 - 10 pm (a-b)
Home-made soups, pâté and delicious real ice-cream. Local fish, Highland venison, Aberdeen Angus steaks, Ross-shire lamb – all beautifully served with freshly baked potatoes.
5 self-catering cottages.
STB 3 Crown Commended to
       4 Crown Highly Commended
No credit cards
Proprietors: N & M Wilson and
             P & F Gooch

Skeabost House Hotel
Skeabost Bridge
Isle of Skye
IV51 9NP
Tel: 047 032 202

4 miles north of Portree on Dunvegan road.

Built in 1870 – the hotel, a former hunting lodge, stands in 12 acres of secluded woodland and garden with glamorous views over Loch Snizort. It is a comfortable, relaxing family run hotel with three lounges, billiard room, cocktail bar and fine restaurant, with a young staff who endeavour to make your stay a memorable one. The hotel has a small nine-hole golf course, par 31, and salmon fishing on the eight miles of the River Snizort.

Open Apr to mid Oct
Rooms: 26 with private facilities
Breakfast 8.30 - 9.30 am; 9 - 10 am Sun.
Bar Lunch 12 - 1.30 pm (a)
Buffet Lunch 12 - 1.30 pm (a)
Dinner 7 - 8 pm (c)
Bed & breakfast £28 - £36
Dinner B & B £42 - £49

Fresh salmon, venison, Skye lamb.
STB 4 Crown Commended
RAC 3 Star
AA   3 Star L
BTA Commended
No credit cards
Proprietors: Stuart/McNab/Stuart

Three Chimneys Restaurant
Colbost
nr Dunvegan
Isle of Skye
IV51 9SY
Tel: 047 081 258 (Glendale)

4 miles west of Dunvegan on B884 road to Glendale. Look out for Glendale Visitor Route signs.

Very old crofter's cottage with cosy, candlelit, stone-walled interior, beamed ceilings and open fires. Widely acclaimed restaurant, close by the sea on the shores of Loch Dunvegan. Remote and beautiful spot on scenic road to Glendale and most westerly point of Skye. Spectacular views and glorious sunsets over the Outer Isles. Excellent accommodation within walking distance, as well as in and around Dunvegan village.

Open Easter to mid Oct
Lunch 12.30 - 2 pm (b)
Dinner from 7 pm (d)
Closed Sun.
No smoking.

Local shellfish – fresh Skye oysters, langoustine and lobster; fresh fish and wild Skye salmon; fresh Scottish beef, lamb and venison dishes, including steaks; vegetarian selection.
Credit cards: 1, 3
Proprietors: Eddie & Shirley Spear

Toravaig House Hotel
Knock Bay
Teangue
Isle of Skye
IV44 8RJ
Tel: 04713 231

On A851 – 5 miles north of Armadale.

Family run country house hotel set in eight acres of mature gardens. Enjoy some of the finest scenery to be found in Scotland in this the south or, as it is better known, the garden of Skye. The hotel is noted for its hospitality and excellent cooking. Visitors are assured of the personal attention of the proprietors Jenny and Grant Abernethy.

Open Easter to Oct
Rooms: 10 with private facilities
Breakfast 8.30 - 9 am
Bar Lunch 12.30 - 2 pm (a)
Dinner 7 - 8 pm (d)
No smoking area in restaurant.
Bed & breakfast rates on application.
Dinner B & B £34 - £38.

Local lamb, venison, salmon, trout and vegetables from hotel garden in season. Home-made soups and desserts.
STB 3 Crown Commended
RAC 2 Star H
AA   2 Star H
Credit cards: 1, 3, 5
Proprietors: Jenny & Grant Abernethy

Ullinish Lodge Hotel
Struan
Isle of Skye
IV56 8FD
Tel: 047 072 214

Off A863 between Sligachan and Dunvegan.

Eighteenth century country house beautifully set overlooking the Cuillins and the shores of Loch Bracadale. Ideally situated for walking and climbing. Brown-trout fishing in the three lochs, salmon fishing in two rivers. Rough shooting over 27,500 acres. You are assured of a warm welcome by John and Claudia Mulford.

Open Easter to mid Oct
Rooms: 8, 5 with private facilities
Breakfast 8 - 9 am
Lunch 12 - 2 pm (a-b)
Bar Supper 6 - 9 pm (a-b)
Dinner 7 - 9 pm (d) or by arrangement
No smoking area in restaurant.
Bed & breakfast £17 - £23
Dinner B & B £29.50 - £35.50

Fresh local seafood – salmon, prawns, scallops, lobster. Traditional steaks and roasts. Venison, pheasant, grouse, served with home-made sauces, fresh vegetables in season. Clootie dumpling.
STB 3 Crown Approved
No credit cards
Proprietors: John & Claudia Mulford

Hawes Inn
Newhalls Road
South Queensferry
West Lothian
EH30 9TA
Tel: 031 331 1990

A90 from Edinburgh city centre following signs for Forth Bridge. Turn off B924 to South Queensferry.

This fine old building with marvellous views across the Firth of Forth dates from the 16th century. It has literary connections with Sir Walter Scott and it was immortalised by Robert Louis Stevenson in 'Kidnapped'. A traditional inn – it offers a fine range of food from bar snacks to haute cuisine in the elegant restaurant.

Open all year
Rooms: 5
Breakfast 7.30 - 9.30 am
Bar Lunch 12 - 2 pm (a)
Lunch 12.30 - 2 pm except Sat (b)
Dinner 6.30 - 10 pm (d)
Bed & breakfast £28.50 - £39.50
Dinner B & B rates on application
STB Award Pending
AA   2 Star
Credit cards: 1, 2, 3, 5, 6

Chapeltoun House Hotel
Stewarton
Ayrshire
KA3 3ED
Tel: 0560 82696

On B769 Stewarton-Irvine road (access via A77 Glasgow-Kilmarnock road).

Chapeltoun – a gracious country house hotel set in beautiful Ayrshire countryside. The hotel has an inviting restaurant renowned for its excellent cuisine and service, complemented by an extensive cellar of fine wines. The chef selects only the finest fresh produce to create interesting and appetising menus.

Open all year except first 2 wks Jan.
Rooms: 6 with private facilities
Breakfast from 7.45 am
Bar Lunch 12 - 2 pm (b)
Lunch 12.30 - 2 pm (c)

Dinner 7 - 9.15 pm (e)
Bed & breakfast £42.50 - £65
Dinner B & B £62.50 - £85

Best of local meat, fish, game and vegetables.
STB 4 Crown Highly Commended
RAC 3 Star HCR
AA   3 Star + Rosette
BTA Commended
Credit cards: 1, 2, 3
Proprietors: Colin & Graeme McKenzie

Lochend Farm
Carronbridge
Denny
Stirlingshire
FK6 5JJ
Tel: 0324 822778

6 miles from Stirling; 5 miles from junction 9 of M80/M9 motorway.

An upland sheep farm in delightful situation beside Loch Coulter with panoramic views all around. The 18th century Listed farmhouse is modernised with full central heating and tastefully furnished. Tea/coffee making facilities in both bedrooms. Guests own bathroom, dining room and sittingroom with colour TV. Excellent base to explore Stirling, Edinburgh, Trossachs, Loch Lomond, St Andrews, and Glasgow with its famous Burrell Collection.

Open Easter to late Oct or by arrangement.
Rooms: 2
Breakfast from 8.30 am or by arrangement.
Dinner from 6.30 pm except Sun (c)
No smoking in dining room.
Residents only.
Unlicensed.
Bed & breakfast from £11
Dinner B & B rates on application
Full Scottish breakfast with oatmeal porridge. Home-made traditional Scottish dishes, using home-produced lamb and beef.
STB 2 Crown Commended
AA   Listed
No credit cards
Proprietor: Jean Morton

The Topps Farm
Fintry Road
Denny
Stirlingshire
FK6 5JF
Tel: 0324 822471

On B818 Denny-Fintry road, off M80.

New farmhouse in superb scenic position. Working sheep and cashmere goat farm in easy reach of Glasgow, Edinburgh, Perth, Trossachs and Loch Lomond. Fishing, walking. Nine and 18 hole golf courses nearby. Also horse riding by arrangement. Non-smokers only.

Open all year
Rooms: 8 with private facilities
Breakfast from 7 am
Dinner from 7 pm (b)
No smoking throughout.
Residents only.
Unlicensed.
Bed & breakfast from £10
Dinner B & B from £20
Breakfast trout, porridge, local haggis, black pudding,etc. Glenmorangie gateau, rosewater meringues. Grumphies and neeps. Roast garlic lamb.
STB 3 Crown Commended
Credit cards: 1, 3
Proprietors: Jennifer & Alistair Steel

Tolbooth Restaurant
Old Pier
Stonehaven Harbour
Stonehaven
Tel: 0569 62287

Off A92 10 miles south of Aberdeen.

Situated in 16th century old building, the Tolbooth is the oldest building in Stonehaven, with picturesque views of Stonehaven harbour. This restaurant specialises in seafood. There is a permanent exhibition of Royal Academy artists on the whitewashed stone walls. Afghan rugs enhance the beautifully polished wooden floors.

Open Apr to Dec. Closed Christmas to Easter.
Lunch 12 - 2.30 pm (b)
Dinner 7 - 9.30 pm (b)
Apr to Oct open Tue to Sun.
Nov and Dec open weekends only. ▶

North Sea bouillabaisse – local fish, mussels and prawns simmered in a saffron broth, Dublin Bay prawns, Orkney scallops, langoustines. Organic herbs and vegetables used.

Credit cards: 1, 3

Proprietor: Moya Bothwell

STRACHUR
177   F4

The Creggans Inn
Strachur
Argyll
PA27 8BX
Tel: 0369 86 279

1½ hours from Glasgow on A83 then A815.

This is an inn with a difference! The food is superb and the atmosphere in the friendly comfortable luncheon bars delightful. At night in the pretty dining room looking down the loch, dinner is more formal, with a large selection of original Scottish country house dishes from Lady MacLean's cookbooks.

Open all year

Rooms: 9, 7 with private facilities
Breakfast 8 - 9.30 am
Bar Lunch 12.30 - 2.15 pm (a)
Lunch 12.30 - 2.15 pm (b)
Dinner 7.30 - 9.30 pm (e)
Bed & breakfast from £38
Dinner B & B from £52

Loch Fyne oysters, smoked salmon, local langoustine, herring and shrimps.

RAC   3 Star HR
AA   3 Star
BTA   Commended
Credit cards: 1, 2, 3, 5, 6

STRANRAER
178   I4

The Bay House Restaurant & Bar
Cairnryan Road
Stranraer
Wigtownshire
DG9 8AT
Tel: 0776 3786

Overlooking Loch Ryan on A77 – 200 yards from Sealink Ferry terminal, Stranraer.

Bay House Restaurant – originally the golf clubhouse – is situated on the shores of Loch Ryan. This family owned and run establishment welcomes children and aims to cater for individual tastes and appetites.

Open all year
Bar Lunch 12 - 2.15 pm (b)
Bar Supper 6 - 9.15 pm (b)
Dinner 6 - 9.15 pm (d)
No meals served on New Year's Day.
Facilities for the disabled.
Credit cards: 1, 2, 3, 6
Proprietor: T Pearson

North West Castle Hotel
Portrodie
Stranraer
DG9 8EH
Tel: 0776 4413
Telex: 777038
Fax: 0776 2646

Seafront – opposite harbour.

Seafront hotel overlooking Loch Ryan and surrounding countryside. Situated in own grounds. Facilities include indoor swimming pool, saunas, sunbeds, bowls, curling rink, table tennis, darts, pool, snooker. Conference facilities for 60. Most inclusive rates include free golf at two local courses. Bedrooms have bath, shower, colour TV, radio, trouser press, hairdryer and coffee-making facilities. Pianist playing during dinner.

Open all year
Rooms: 88 with private facilities
Breakfast 7.45 - 9.45 am
Bar Lunch 12 - 2.30 pm (a)
Lunch 12 - 2.30 pm (b)
Dinner 7 - 9.30 pm (c)
Bed & breakfast from £28
Dinner B & B from £42

Prime Scottish beef, wild Cree salmon, Drummore lobster, scallops, smoked salmon and home-made sweets.

STB   5 Crown Commended
RAC   4 Star
AA   3 Star L
No credit cards
Best Town Hotel 1989
Proprietor: H C McMillan

STRATHLACHLAN
179   G4

Inver Cottage Restaurant
Strathlachlan
by Cairndow
Argyll
PA27 8BU
Tel: 036 986 396/275

B8000, 6 miles past Strachur.

A charming restaurant in delightful surroundings on the shores of Loch Fyne overlooking the ruins of old Castle

Lachlan. A warm welcome always awaits you at the restaurant with its friendly atmosphere and open log and peat fires.

Open Mar to Oct
Bar Lunch 11.30 am - 2.30 pm (a)
Lunch 11.30 am - 2.30 pm (b)
High Tea 6 - 10 pm
Dinner 6 - 10 pm (c)

Wide variety of home-made bar meals. In the evenings also an à la carte menu specialising in local seafood. Only fresh produce used. Renowned for its pudding trolley, home-made tablet and truffles.

Credit cards: 3
Proprietor: Rosemary MacInnes

STRATHTUMMEL
180   F6

Queen's View Hotel & Restaurant
Strathtummel
by Pitlochry
PH16 5NR
Tel: 0796 3291

Turning from A9 at Pitlochry junction (north) on B8019.

Discover this delightful hotel on 'The Road to the Isles' commanding beautiful views overlooking Loch Tummel. The restaurant 'The Room with a View' is the perfect Highland setting in which to relax and enjoy good food and wine.

Open Easter to Oct
Rooms: 11, 6 with private facilities
Breakfast 8.30 - 9.45 am
Bar Lunch 12 - 2.30 pm (a)
Lunch 12 - 2 pm (a-b)
Dinner 7 - 8.30 pm (b-c)
Bed & breakfast from £22.70
Dinner B & B from £37.20

All dishes – Scottish and classic – cooked to order. Renowned for its sizzling steaks.

Credit cards: 1, 2, 3, 5, 6
Proprietors: Jim & Valerie Torry

STRATHYRE
181   F5

Creagan House
Strathyre
Perthshire
FK18 8ND
Tel: 087 74 638

On A84, ¼ mile north of Strathyre.

In a lovely country setting, Creagan is a family owned 17th century farmhouse with five charming bedrooms. The   ▶

baronial dining hall with its grand open fire provides a unique setting in which to enjoy good food and fine wines. A mixture of experience, caring and friendliness makes the recipe for that special occasion.

Open Mar to Jan

Rooms: 5, 3 with private facilities
Breakfast 8 - 9.30 am
Lunch from 1 pm Sun only (c)
Lunch parties on other days by arrangement.
Dinner 7.30 - 8.30 pm (c-d)
No smoking area in restaurant.
Bed & breakfast £15 - £18.50
Dinner B & B £24.50 - £28

Mushrooms Dunsyre, ragout of seafood, venison Beananach, wee collops. Flora McDonald steamed pudding, strawberry and chestnut roulade.

Credit cards: 3

Proprietors: Gordon & Cherry Gunn

STRONTIAN
182   E3

Kilcamb Lodge Hotel
Strontian
North Argyll
PH36 4HY
Tel: 0967 2257

Strontian, south-west of Fort William.

Kilcamb Lodge is in the centre of an area renowned for its scenic excellence, in 30 acres of private parkland on the shores of Loch Sunart.

Open Easter to Oct

Rooms: 9 with private facilities
Breakfast 8.30 - 9.15 am
Bar Lunch 12 - 2 pm (b)
Dinner 7 - 8 pm (d)
No smoking area in restaurant.
Bed & breakfast from £30
Dinner B & B from £42

Traditional Scottish cuisine with prime Scottish beef and lamb, venison and locally caught salmon and trout, seafood and game.

STB   3 Crown Commended
RAC   2 Star HCR
AA   2 Star H

No credit cards

Proprietors: John & Suzanne Bradbury

Loch Sunart Hotel
Strontiar
Argyll
PH36 4HZ
Tel: 0967 2471

A82 to Corran Ferry. A861 to Strontian.

Delightful, family-run 18th century country house, overlooking loch in a magnificent area. An ideal base for touring, walking, bird-watching or just "getting away from it all". Take advantage of the 4/7 day breaks. Fresh local produce prepared and cooked on the premises.

Open Easter to Oct

Rooms: 11, 8 with private facilities
Breakfast 8.30 - 9.30 am
Bar Lunch 12 - 2 pm (a)
High Tea 2 - 6.30 pm
Bar Supper 7.30 - 8.45 pm
Dinner 7 - 7.30 pm (c)
No smoking in dining room.
Facilities for the partially disabled.
Bed & breakfast from £19
Dinner B & B from £34

Renowned for home-cooking to a high standard of both traditional and unusual dishes. Specialities include soups and ice cream.

STB   3 Crown Approved
AA   2 Star

No credit cards

Proprietors: Peter & Mildred Renton

TAIN
183   D6

Morangie House Hotel
Morangie Road
Tain
Ross-shire
IV19 1PY
Tel: 0862 2281

Just off A9 Inverness to Wick road.

A fine old Victorian mansion set on the northern outskirts of the Highland town of Tain, Scotland's oldest Royal Burgh. The hotel has been extensively modernised but still maintains the character of the building with its superb collection of Victorian stained glass windows. Award winning chefs prepare meals unsurpassed in the area and served by the friendly but efficient staff.

Open all year

Rooms: 11 with private facilities
Breakfast 7 - 9.30 am
Bar Lunch 12 - 2.30 pm (a)

Lunch 12 - 2.30 pm (b)
Bar Supper 5 - 10 pm (a)
Dinner 7 - 10 pm (d)
No dogs.
Bed & breakfast £22 - £35
Dinner B & B £36 - £49

Extensive à la carte menu specialising in local beef and seafood dishes. Mussel and onion stew. Beef Wellington. Game soup. Lobster thermidor. Moules marinière.

STB   4 Crown Commended
RAC   3 Star
AA   3 Star

Credit cards: 1, 2, 3, 5

Proprietor: John Wynne

TARBERT
184   G3

The Anchorage Restaurant
Quayside, Harbour Street
Tarbert
Argyll
PA29 6UD
Tel: 08802 881

On A83 (situated on Tarbert quayside).

Unique restaurant on the quayside at Tarbert not far from Tarbert Castle. Seafood is the order of the day offering a good selection from Arran, Islay, Gigha, Jura and numerous other places along the west coast. The owner personally selects fish from the evening sale on the quayside. The restaurant also has a direct line to a fishing boat for a resumé of the day's catch.

Open Mar to Dec

Lunch 11.30 am - 2.30 pm (b)
Dinner 6.45 - 10.30 pm (d)
Closed Sun + Mon
Facilities for the disabled.

Seafood is the speciality of this restaurant, all personally selected, direct from boat and the quayside. Brought in from Kintyre and the islands. Aberdeen Angus beef. Vegetarian dishes available.

Credit cards: 1, 3

Proprietors: David & Fiona Evamy

Barmore Farm

Tarbert
Argyll
PA29 6YJ
Tel: 08802 222

2 miles north of Tarbert.

Charmingly restored Listed farm steading providing bar and restaurant facilities. Self-catering accommodation. Three properties tastefully furnished, fully equipped. Children and dogs very welcome. Large play area.

Open all year

Bar Lunch 12 - 2 pm (a)
Bar Supper 6 - 7 pm
Dinner 7.30 - 9.30 pm (c)

Emphasis on fresh, simple food using local produce. Everything home-made, crofters pie, game in season, fish and shellfish straight from Tarbert Quay. Clootie dumpling always available.

3 self-catering cottages -
STB 4 Crown Commended

No credit cards

Proprietors: Elizabeth & Graeme Scott

The Columba Hotel

East Pier Road
Tarbert
Argyll
PA29 6UF
Tel: 08802 808

On East Pier Road, ½ mile to the left around harbour.

Superbly positioned at entrance to Tarbert Harbour. Warm, comfortable lounge bar with log fire, providing good wholesome bar meals daily. Restaurant with beautiful views over Loch Fyne. Menus with emphasis on local produce – shellfish, venison, locally supplied fish and fresh vegetables. Twelve bedrooms centrally heated, sauna, mini-gym, solarium.

Open all year

Rooms: 12, 9 with private facilities
Breakfast 8 - 9.30 am
Bar Lunch 12 - 2 pm (a)
Bar Supper 6 - 7.30 pm (a)
Dinner 7 - 9 pm (c)
Dinner not available Mon - Thu, 1 Nov to Easter.
Bed & breakfast from £17.50
Dinner B & B from £27

Lobster and king prawns – when available. Jura venison, local fish, only fresh vegetables.
STB 3 Crown Commended
Credit cards: 1, 2, 3, 5
Proprietors: Alistair Wilkie & Kenneth Tod

THORNHILL
185   H6

Trigony House Hotel

Closeburn
Thornhill
Dumfriesshire
DG3 5EZ
Tel: 0848 31211

A76 – 13 miles north of Dumfries.

Trigony makes an excellent base for exploring this magnificent untouched part of Scotland. An attractive secluded country house hotel under the personal supervision of the owners. There is a friendly and welcoming atmosphere with open wood-burning fires in the bar and lounge. Enjoy home cooking and comfortable bedrooms.

Open all year

Rooms: 12, 8 with private facilities
Breakfast 8.30 - 9.30 am
Bar Lunch 12 - 2 pm (a)
Bar Supper 7 - 9 pm except Sun;
7 - 10 pm Fri + Sat
Dinner 7 - 8.30 pm (c)
Bed & breakfast £11.50 - £23
Dinner B & B rates on application.

Roast Galloway beef, local pheasant and venison, Nith salmon, steak stuffed with haggis.
STB Award Pending
RAC 2 Star R
AA 2 Star

No credit cards

Proprietors: Doreen & Ron Seekins

TIREE
186   ISLE OF   F2

The Glassary

Sandaig
Isle of Tiree
Argyll
PA77 6XQ
Tel: 08792 684

West coast of island.

Guest house and licensed restaurant situated on the picturesque west coast of the island close to white, sandy beaches. Guest house, all on one level, includes residents' lounge with TV, and tea/coffee making facilities. Adjacent is the restaurant which is a pine-lined converted byre, with panoramic views of shore and Atlantic Ocean. Guest house open all year – restaurant open Easter to October.

Open all year

Rooms: 3
Breakfast 8 - 9.30 am
Lunch 12 - 2.30 pm (a-b)
Afternoon Tea 2.30 - 4.30 pm
Dinner 7 - 9 pm (b-d)
Bed & breakfast from £12.50
Dinner B & B from £19.50

Local meat and seafood, including lobster to order. Scottish salmon, home-made soups and sauces, home-baking with home-made jam. Carrageen pudding.

No credit cards

Proprietors: Mabel & Donny Macarthur

TORRANYARD
187   NEAR IRVINE   G4

Montgreenan Mansion House Hotel

Montgreenan Estate
Torranyard, Kilwinning
Ayrshire
KA13 7QZ
Tel: 0294 57733
Telex: 778525.

Off A736 Glasgow to Irvine road near Torranyard.

The character of this former country seat has remained gracious with the history of the estate dating back to 1310. All the late 18th century features, including attractive marble and brass fireplaces, decorative ceilings and plaster work, have been retained. Montgreenan has a heliport facility and a snooker room, tennis court, lawn croquet and golf course.

Open all year   ▶

Rooms: 16 with private facilities
Breakfast 7 - 11 am
Bar Lunch 12 - 2.30 pm (b)
Lunch 12 - 2.30 pm (b)
Dinner 7 - 10 pm (e)
Bed & breakfast £44 - £100
Dinner B & B £50 - £69

Scottish lobster Montgreenan, Montgreenan game and whisky pie. Locally caught salmon, trout and shellfish.

STB 4 Crown Commended
RAC 3 Star HCR
AA   3 Star L

Credit cards: 1, 2, 3, 4, 5, 6
Proprietors: The Dobson Family

TROON
188   G5

Marine Highland Hotel
Troon
Ayrshire
KA10 6HE
Tel: 0292 314444
Telex: 777595
Fax: 0292 316922

South end of Troon overlooking golf course and sea.

This magnificent four star hotel overlooks the 18th fairway of Royal Troon Championship Golf Course with breathtaking views across the Firth of Clyde to the Isle of Arran. An atmosphere of quiet elegance exists throughout the hotel combined with a standard of service and hospitality second to none. The Marine Leisure & Sports Club is a first class addition to the present facilities. A very special hotel which has admirably blended style and tradition with outstanding facilities.

Open all year

Rooms: 70 with private facilities
Breakfast 7.30 - 12 noon
Bar Lunch 12 - 3 pm (a)
Lunch 12 - 3 pm (b)

Dinner 6 - 11 pm (d)
Bed & breakfast from £43
Dinner B & B from £40 (min. 2 nights stay)

Wild boar, local wild salmon, fresh scallops, Scotch lamb, fresh vegetables.

STB 5 Crown Commended
RAC 4 Star
AA   4 Star

Credit cards: 1, 2, 3, 5

Piersland House Hotel
Craig End Road
Troon
Ayrshire
KA10 6HD
Tel: 0292 314747

South corner of Troon.

Piersland House, c.1899, built for Sir Alexander Walker of Johnnie Walker whisky fame. Set in four acres of grounds – the gardens and interior wood panelling are special features.

Open all year.

Rooms: 19 with private facilities
Breakfast 7.30 - 10 am
Bar Lunch 12 - 2 pm (a)
Lunch 12 - 2 pm (d)
Afternoon Tea 3 - 5 pm
Bar Suppers 5 - 10 pm
Dinner 7 - 9.30 pm (d)
Bed & breakfast from £37
Dinner B & B rates on application.

A la carte includes fish and shellfish, chicken supreme, collops in the pan. Bar meals include local Ayrshire ham, gammon, salmon, lamb and beef.

STB 4 Crown Commended
RAC 3 Star
AA   3 Star

Credit cards: 1, 2, 3, 5, 6
Proprietor: J A Brown

TURNBERRY
189   H4

Malin Court Hotel
Turnberry
Girvan
Ayrshire
KA26 9PB
Tel: 0655 31457/8

On A719 south of Maidens.

Situated between Ayr and Girvan, on the west coast of Scotland and ideal for touring the 'Burns Trail'. Central to a lot of major golf courses, including the famous Turnberry. All bedrooms have full amenities, including colour television and

full central heating. Table d'hôte or full à la carte menus are available in the splendid restaurant with views of Arran and the hills beyond. Fully refurbished.

Open all year

Rooms: 8 with private facilities
Breakfast 7 - 10.30 am
Bar Lunch 12.30 - 2.30 pm (a)
Lunch 12.30 - 2.30 pm (b)
Afternoon Tea 2 - 5 pm
High Tea 5.30 - 7 pm
Dinner 7.30 - 9.30 pm (c)
Bed & breakfast £27.95 - £31.95
Dinner B & B £40 -£47

Hotel enjoys more or less all year round availablility of fresh local beef, lamb and pork, salmon and fresh sea produce.

STB .4 Crown Commended
RAC 3 Star

Credit cards: 1, 2, 3, 5, 6

The Turnberry Hotel & Golf Courses
Turnberry
Ayrshire
KA26 9LT
Tel: 0655 31000
Telex: 777779
Fax: 0655 31706

A77 – 17 miles south of Ayr.

Turnberry Hotel is situated overlooking Scotland's south-west Ayrshire coast. Within its 360 acres are a luxury 115-bedroom hotel, two championship golf courses, all weather tennis courts, swimming pool and a billiards room amongst other amenities. The excellent restaurant combines elegance and gracious service with most magical views of Ailsa Craig and Arran.

Open all year

Rooms: 115 with private facilities
Breakfast 7.30 - 9.30 am
Bar meals served in Clubhouse all day.
Lunch 1 - 2.30 pm (d)
High Tea served in the Clubhouse.
Dinner 7.30 - 9.30 pm (f)
Bed & breakfast £70 - £170
Dinner B & B rates on application.

Collops of venison with a farce of hazelnuts and two sauces.

RAC 5 Star
AA   4 Star HL

Credit cards: 1, 2, 3, 4, 5, 6

TYNDRUM
190 F4

Clifton Coffee House & Craft Centre
Tyndrum
Perthshire FK20 8RY
Tel: 08384 271
Fax: 08384 330

On A85 just east of junction with A82.

A popular staging post at the eastern end of Glen Coe. A family-run roadside restaurant and shopping complex surrounded by scenic splendour. The busy self-service restaurant has special facilities for the disabled and there are adjacent shops in which to browse.

Open mid Mar to late Dec

Meals and snacks served all day from end of Mar to end of Nov.
No smoking area in restaurant.

Fresh local produce, vegetables, game, salmon, trout and venison, brought together to give good food at budget prices.

Credit cards: 1, 2, 3, 5

Proprietors: D D & L V Wilkie, L P Gosden

UPHALL
191 G6

Houstoun House Hotel
Uphall
West Lothian
EH52 6JS
Tel: 0506 853831

Just off A89 (Edinburgh-Bathgate) at Uphall.

This 16th century Tower House stands in its own 26 acres of grounds, with the dining room in the old part of the building. The best of Scottish produce is used to create daily changing menus, with herbs and vegetables from the garden. An extensive wine list is offered to complement your meal, whilst there is also an excellent range of malt whiskies in the vaulted bar.

Open all year except 1 and 2 Jan (incl).

Rooms: 30 with private facilities
Breakfast 7.30 - 9.30 am
Bar Lunch 12.30 - 2 pm Sat only
Lunch 12.30 - 2pm (d)
Dinner 7.30 - 9.30 pm (e)
Bed & breakfast £63 - £96
Dinner B & B from £48 (weekend break)

Crayfish and scallops with a leek tartlet on a basil flavoured sauce. Creative desserts.

STB 4 Crown Commended
RAC 3 Star
AA 3 Star

Credit cards: 1, 2, 3, 5, 6

WALKERBURN
192 G7

The George Hotel
Galashiels Road
Walkerburn
Peeblesshire
EH43 6AY
Tel: 0896 87 219

On A72 midway between Peebles and Galashiels.

A comfortable village inn serving Taste of Scotland food. The restaurant overlooks the River Tweed and surrounding hills. A friendly atmosphere giving an insight into country life in the Scottish Borders.

Open all year

Rooms: 4
Breakfast from 8.30 am
Bar Lunch 12.15 - 3 pm (a)
Lunch 12.30 - 3 pm (b)
Bar Supper 7 - 9.30 pm (a)
Dinner 7 - 9.30 pm except Tue (c)
Bed & breakfast from £11.50
Dinner B & B rates on application.

Traditional home-made pies all made on premises. Fillet steak with fresh oysters. Scottish salmon.

No credit cards

Proprietor: Ian W Mackay

Tweed Valley Hotel & Restaurant
Walkerburn
near Peebles
EH43 6AA
Tel: 089 687 636
Fax: 089 687 639

A72 at Walkerburn – 7 miles east of Peebles. 32 miles south of Edinburgh.

A complete Taste of Scotland awaits you with scenic views overlooking the River Tweed and hills. After sightseeing or country pursuits, including fishing, golf and birdwatching, log fires in the lounge add that extra glow while you quietly relax with a drink before enjoying à la carte dishes including local trout, salmon and game.

Open all year

Rooms: 15 with private facilities
Breakfast 8 - 9.30 am
Bar Lunch 12 - 2 pm (a-b)
Lunch 12 - 2 pm (a-c)
High Tea - by prior arrangement only.
Dinner 7 - 9.30 pm (c-d)
No smoking area in restaurant.
Bed & breakfast from £31.50
Dinner B & B from £37.50

Trout, salmon, venison and game dishes including grouse, pheasant, duck in season and as available.

STB 4 Crown Commended
RAC 3 Star R
AA 2 Star H

Credit cards: 1, 2, 3, 5

Proprietor: Charles Miller

WEST LINTON
193 G6

The Leadburn Inn
Leadburn
West Linton
Peeblesshire
EH46 7BE
Tel: 0968 72952

On junction of A701, A702 and A720.

Small family run hotel, set in beautiful countryside between Edinburgh and the Borders. One of the oldest inns in Scotland – records date back to August 1777. A menu which is as extensive as any in the Borders is served all day in the lounge, the conservatory or the bar. In the evening, dinner is served in the attractive Carriage Restaurant – a luxuriously converted railway carriage. Carefully planned table d'hôte menu includes a selection of traditional Scottish dishes.

Open all year except 25 to 27 Dec and 1 to 3 Jan.

Rooms: 6, 2 with private facilities
Breakfast 7 - 10 am
Bar meals 12 - 6 pm (a)
Lunch 12 - 6 pm (b)
High Tea/Supper 6 - 10 pm (a-b)
Dinner 6 - 10 pm (d)
Bed & breakfast £15 - £20
Dinner B & B rates on application.

Local game and fish a speciality.

STB Listed Commended

Credit cards: 1, 2, 3, 5, 6

Proprietors: Linda & Alan Thomson

WHITEBRIDGE
194   **E5**

Knockie Lodge
Whitebridge
Inverness-shire
IV1 2UP
Tel: 045 63 276

*On B862 – 8 miles north of Fort Augustus.
26 miles south of Inverness.*

Formerly a shooting lodge, this very comfortable country house hotel, owned and run by Ian and Brenda Milward, is set in magnificent scenery high above Loch Ness and offers an exceptional experience. Reading/writing room and billiard room.

Open Apr to Oct

Rooms: 10 with private facilities
Breakfast 8.30 - 9.15 am; 9 am Sun.
Bar Lunch 12.30 - 1.30 pm (a)
Dinner from 8 pm (e)
Booking essential for non-residents.

Licensed for residents only.
No smoking in restaurant.
Bed & breakfast rates on application.
Dinner B & B £50 - £72
STB   3 Crown Highly Commended
AA   2 Red Star
BTA   Commended
Credit cards: 1, 2, 3
Proprietors: Ian & Brenda Milward

WORMIT
195   **F7**

Sandford Hill Hotel
nr Wormit
Newport-on-Tay
Fife
DD6 8RG
Tel: 0382 541802

Junction of A 914 and B946.

Situated close to a A914 road linking the Tay and Forth Bridges. Picturesque country house hotel designed by London architect Baillie Scott in a style unique to the area.

Quaint narrow corridors lead to bright modernised bedrooms most with views over the six acres of gardens. Open-air courtyard restaurant with its old fashioned wishing well is popular in summer.

Open all year except 1 and 2 Jan.

Rooms: 15, 13 with private facilities
Breakfast 7.15 - 9 am
Bar Lunch 12 - 2 pm (b)
Lunch 12 - 2 pm (d)
High Tea 4.45 - 6 pm Sun only
Bar Supper 5 - 6.45 pm except Sun + Sat, and 9 - 10 pm except Sat.
Dinner 7 - 9 pm (d)
Bed & breakfast £25 - £28
Dinner B & B £30 - £33

Soups – mussel and onion – cock-a-leekie; Fife coast fish, sole, local lamb, game, pheasant, duck, pigeon. All in season.

STB   3 Crown Commended
RAC   2 Star
AA   2 Star
Credit cards: 1, 2, 3, 5
Proprietor: A B Robertson

LATE ENTRY LATE ENTRY LATE ENTRY LATE ENTRY LATE ENTRY LATE ENTRY LATE ENTRY

EDINBURGH
78   **G7**

The Magnum
1 Albany Street
Edinburgh
EH1 3PY
Tel: 031 557 4366

On corner of Dublin Street (continuation of North St Andrew Street) and Albany Street.

There has always been a dearth of good eating places north of St Andrew Square, but now The Magnum fills the void. This is a first class up-market restaurant and bar beautifully appointed and drawing on the business and financial centre around it for its lunch time clientele, but with a wider catchment area in the evenings. The restaurant exudes an atmosphere of elegant relaxation and the food is prepared carefully and presented with appeal.

Open all year except Christmas & Boxing Days, 1 to 4 Jan.
Bar Lunch 12 - 2.30 pm (a)
Lunch 12 - 2.30 pm except Sat (d)
Bar Supper 6.30 - 9.45 pm (a)
Dinner 6.30 - 10 pm (d)
Closed Sun.

Menus change regularly dependent on availability of good fresh fish and shellfish, lamb, beef.

Credit cards: 1, 2, 3, 5

The 1991 TASTE OF SCOTLAND GUIDE
is scheduled to be published in November 1990.

To reserve a copy at the 1990 price of £2.70 (including post & packaging), complete the coupon on page 141 and send it with your cheque or postal order, made payable to TASTE OF SCOTLAND, to
     Taste of Scotland (Guide Sales),
     33 Melville Street, Edinburgh EH3 7JF.

You will be placed on the priority list to receive the Guide as soon as it is published.

ELIE
79A   **F7**

Bouquet Garni Restaurant
51 High Street
Elie
Fife
KY9 8BD
Tel: 0333 330374

A delightful little restaurant in the centre of this charming East Neuk town. With ample supplies of fresh fish and seafood on its doorstep the Bouquet Garni naturally specialises in high quality fish dishes but with a complementary range of other typical Scottish fare. The intimate and cosy candlelit dining room is almost certain to appeal to the connoisseur of good food. Well worth a detour. Re-opening early 1990 after alterations.

Open Feb to Dec. Closed first wk Nov.
Dinner 7.30 - 9.30 pm; 7.30 - 10.30 pm Jul to Sep (d)
Closed Sun + Mon

Shellfish, wholemeal pastry case with smoked bacon, cheese and leeks served with crayfish sauce. Trio of fresh market fish (catch of the day).

Credit cards: 1, 3

Taste of Scotland

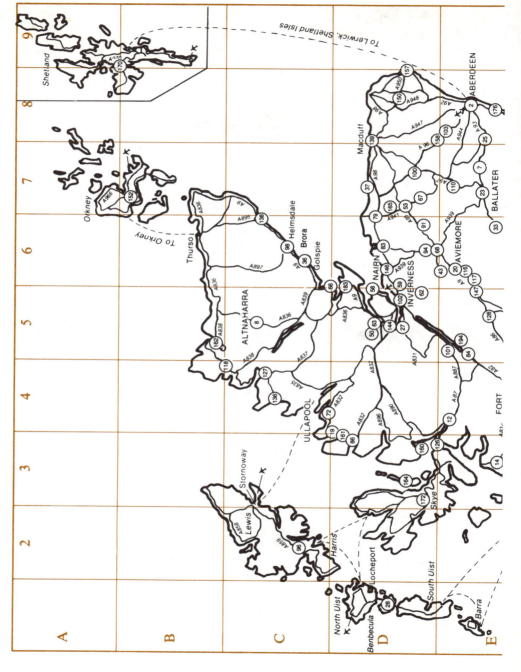

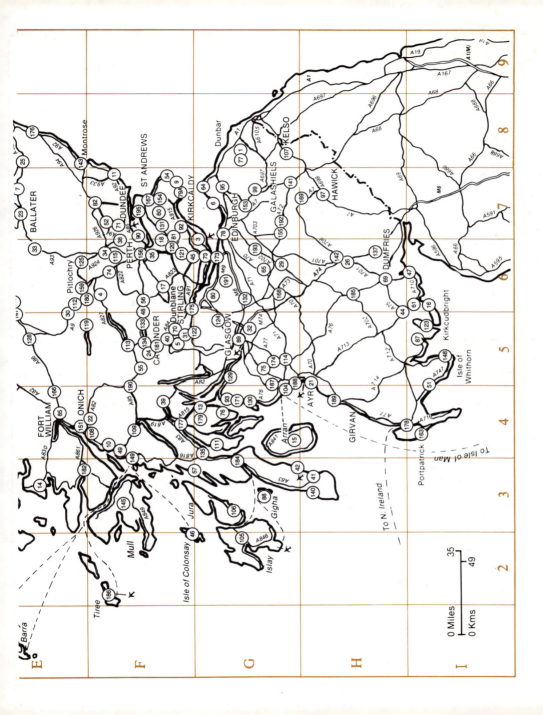

97

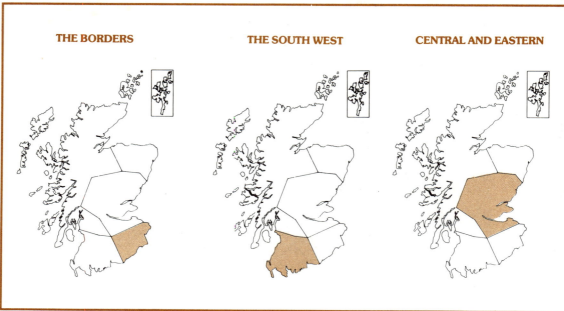

THE BORDERS

THE SOUTH WEST

CENTRAL AND EASTERN

For more details about the locations of hotels and restaurants, car touring routes and general holiday information, contact the Area Tourist Board for the area you are planning to visit. Details on page 104.

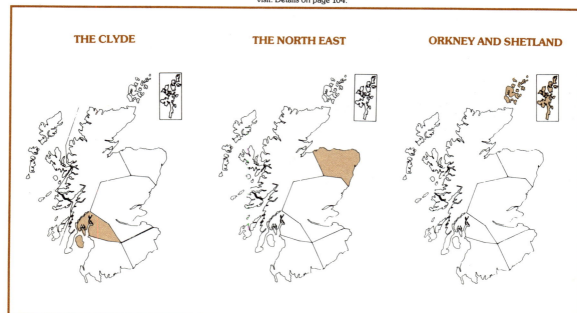

THE CLYDE

THE NORTH EAST

ORKNEY AND SHETLAND

THE BORDERS

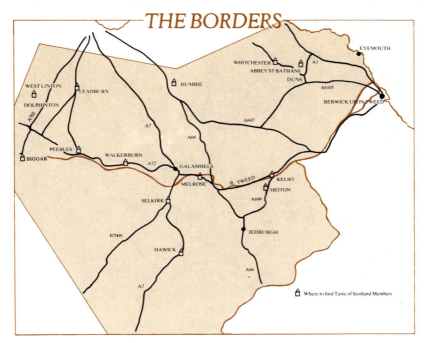

EYEMOUTH

WHITCHESTER
ABBEY ST BATHANS
DUNS
A1

WEST LINTON
LEADBURN
HUMBIE
A6105
BERWICK UPON TWEED

DOLPHINTON
A702

A697

A7

A68

PEEBLES
WALKERBURN
A72
GALASHIELS
R. TWEED
KELSO

BIGGAR
MELROSE
HEITON

SELKIRK
A698

B7009
JEDBURGH

HAWICK
A68

A7

🏠 Where to find Taste of Scotland Members

THE SOUTH WEST

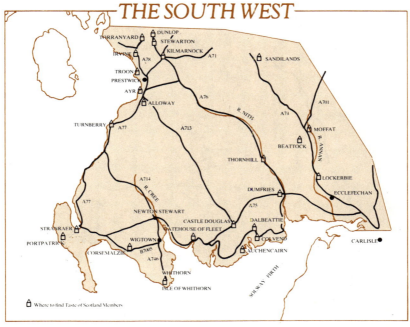

TORRANYARD
DUNLOP
STEWARTON
KILMARNOCK

IRVINE
A71
SANDILANDS

A78

TROON
PRESTWICK
AYR
A76
A701

ALLOWAY
R. NITH
A74

TURNBERRY
A77
A713
MOFFAT
R. ANNAN

BEATTOCK

THORNHILL

A714
LOCKERBIE

R. CREE
DUMFRIES
ECCLEFECHAN

A77
A75

NEWTON STEWART
CASTLE DOUGLAS
DALBEATTIE

STRANRAER
GATEHOUSE OF FLEET
COLVEND

PORTPATRICK
WIGTOWN
AUCHENCAIRN
CARLISLE

CORSEMALZIE
B7005

A746

WHITHORN
SOLWAY FIRTH

ISLE OF WHITHORN

🏠 Where to find Taste of Scotland Members

99

CENTRAL AND EASTERN

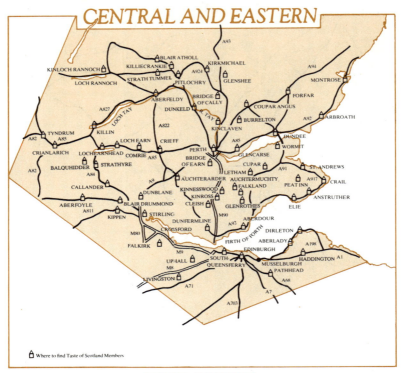

KINLOCH RANNOCH
LOCH RANNOCH
BLAIR ATHOLL
KILLIECRANKIE
STRATH TUMMEL
KIRKMICHAEL
GLENSHEE
A93
A924
PITLOCHRY
A94
MONTROSE
ABERFELDY
BRIDGE OF CALLY
FORFAR
A827
LOCH TAY
DUNKELD
R. TAY
COUPAR ANGUS
A92
ARBROATH
TYNDRUM
KILLIN
LOCH EARN
CRIEFF
A822
BURRELTON
KINCLAVEN
A82
A85
CRIANLARICH
LOCHEARNHEAD
COMRIE
A85
PERTH
A85
DUNDEE
WORMIT
BALQUHIDDER
STRATHYRE
BRIDGE OF EARN
GLENCARSE
ST ANDREWS
A82
A84
CALLANDER
LETHAM
AUCHTERARDER
AUCHTERMUCHTY
CUPAR
A91
A917
CRAIL
PEAT INN
ANSTRUTHER
ABERFOYLE
A811
DUNBLANE
BLAIR DRUMMOND
KINNESSWOOD
KINROSS
CLEISH
FALKLAND
GLENROTHES
ELIE
KIPPEN
STIRLING
DUNFERMLINE
CROSSFORD
M90
ABERDOUR
A92
DIRLETON
M80
FALKIRK
FIRTH OF FORTH
ABERLADY
A198
M9
EDINBURGH
UPHALL
SOUTH QUEENSFERRY
MUSSELBURGH
HADDINGTON A1
M8
PATHHEAD
LIVINGSTON
A71
A68
A7
A703

⌂ Where to find Taste of Scotland Members

THE CLYDE

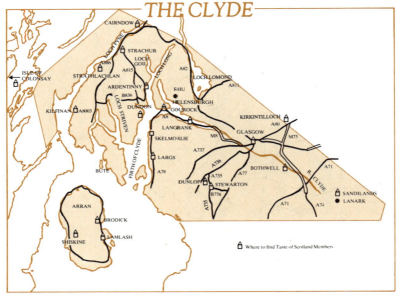

CAIRNDOW
LOCH FYNE
STRACHUR
LOCH GOIL
LOCH LONG
A886
A815
A82
LOCH LOMOND
ISLE OF COLONSAY
STRATHLACHLAN
A811
ARDENTINNY
B836
RHU
HELENSBURGH
KILFINAN A8003
LOCH STRIVEN
DUNOON
GOUROCK
A8
KIRKINTILLOCH
A80
LANGBANK
M8
GLASGOW
M73
SKELMORLIE
FIRTH OF CLYDE
A737
BUTE
A78
LARGS
A736
BOTHWELL
A77
R. CLYDE
A71
DUNLOP
A735
STEWARTON
SANDILANDS
LANARK
ARRAN
B778
A735
A71
A74
BRODICK
SHISKINE
LAMLASH

⌂ Where to find Taste of Scotland Members

100

ORKNEY AND SHETLAND

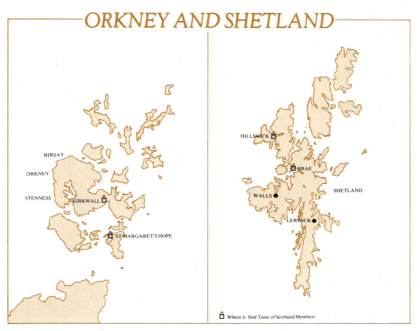

BIRSAY

ORKNEY

STENNESS

KIRKWALL

ST MARGARET'S HOPE

HILLSWICK

BRAE

WALLS

SHETLAND

LERWICK

⌂ Where to find Taste of Scotland Members

THE NORTH EAST

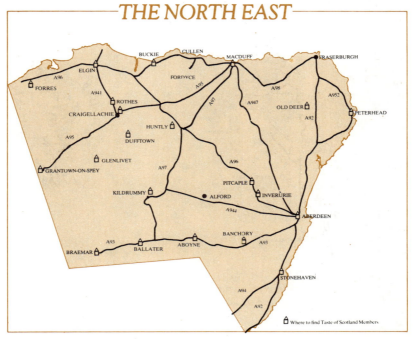

BUCKIE CULLEN MACDUFF FRASERBURGH

ELGIN

A96

FORRES

FORDYCE

A95

A941

ROTHES

A97

A98

A947

OLD DEER

A952

CRAIGELLACHIE

HUNTLY

A92

PETERHEAD

A95

DUFFTOWN

GLENLIVET

A97

A96

GRANTOWN-ON-SPEY

PITCAPLE

KILDRUMMY

ALFORD

INVERURIE

A944

ABERDEEN

BANCHORY

BRAEMAR

A93

BALLATER

ABOYNE

A93

A944

STONEHAVEN

A94

A92

⌂ Where to find Taste of Scotland Members

101

THE HIGHLANDS

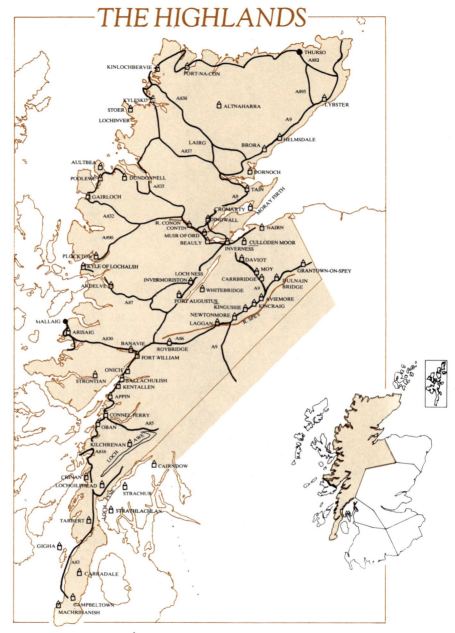

KINLOCHBERVIE
PORT-NA-CON
THURSO
A882
A838
A895
KYLESKU
STOER
ALTNAHARRA
LYBSTER
LOCHINVER
A9
LAIRG
BRORA
A837
HELMSDALE
AULTBEA
POOLEWE
DUNDONNELL
DORNOCH
A835
TAIN
GAIRLOCH
A9
MORAY FIRTH
A832
CROMARTY
R. CONON
DINGWALL
NAIRN
A890
CONTIN
MUIR OF ORD
BEAULY
CULLODEN MOOR
PLOCKTON
INVERNESS
KYLE OF LOCHALSH
DAVIOT
GRANTOWN-ON-SPEY
ARDELVE
LOCH NESS
MOY
INVERMORISTON
CARRBRIDGE
DULNAIN BRIDGE
A87
WHITEBRIDGE
A9
FORT AUGUSTUS
AVIEMORE
KINGUSSIE
KINCRAIG
MALLAIG
NEWTONMORE
ARISAIG
LAGGAN
R. SPEY
A830
BANAVIE
A86
ROYBRIDGE
A9
FORT WILLIAM
ONICH
STRONTIAN
BALLACHULISH
KENTALLEN
APPIN
CONNEL FERRY
OBAN
A85
KILCHRENAN
LOCH AWE
A816
CAIRNDOW
CRINAN
LOCHGILPHEAD
STRACHUR
STRATHLACHLAN
LOCH FYNE
TARBERT
GIGHA
A83
CARRADALE
CAMPBELTOWN
MACHRIHANISH

Where to find Taste of Scotland Members

102

THE HEBRIDES

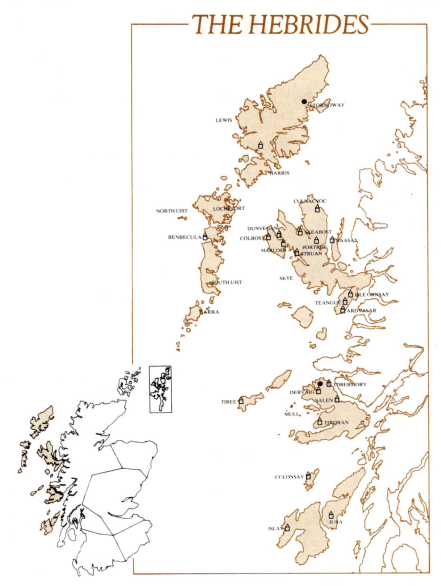

STORNOWAY

LEWIS

HARRIS

CULNACNOC

NORTH UIST   LOCHBORT

BENBECULA   DUNVEGAN   SKEABOST
                COLBOST   RAASAY
                HARLOSH   PORTREE
                              STRUAN

SOUTH UIST   SKYE

BARRA   ISLE ORNSAY
                        TEANGUE
                              ARDVASAR

                              TOBERMORY
                DERVAIG
TIREE   SALEN

                MULL
                        TIRORAN

        COLONSAY

                              JURA
        ISLAY

Where to find Taste of Scotland Members

LOCAL TOURIST INFORMATION

*For specific information on a particular part of Scotland
contact the following:*

Angus Tourist Board
Arbroath
Angus DD11 1HR
Tel: (0241) 72609/76680

Aviemore and Spey Valley Tourist Board
Aviemore
Inverness-shire PH22 1PP
Tel: (0479) 810363

Ayrshire and Burns Country Tourist Board
39 Sandgate, Ayr KA7 1BG
Tel: (0292) 284196

Ayrshire Valleys Tourist Board
Kilmarnock
Ayrshire KA1 1ER
Tel: (0563) 39090

Banff and Buchan Tourist Board
Banff AB4 1AU
Tel: (026 12) 2419

Caithness Tourist Board
Wick
Caithness KW1 4EA
Tel: (0955) 2596

City of Aberdeen Tourist Board
Aberdeen AB9 1DE
Tel: (0224) 632727

City of Dundee Tourist Board
4 City Square
Dundee DD1 3BY
Tel: (0382) 27723

City of Edinburgh District Council Tourism Dept.
3 Princes Street
Edinburgh EH2 2QP
Tel: (031) 557 1700

Clyde Valley Tourist Board
Lanark ML11 7LQ
Tel: (0555) 2544

Cunninghame District Council
Largs
Ayrshire KA30 8BG
Tel: (0475) 673765

Dumfries and Galloway Tourist Board
Whitesands
Dumfries DG1 2SB
Tel: (0387) 53862

Dunoon and Cowal Tourist Board
Dunoon
Argyll PA23 8AB
Tel: (0369) 3755

East Lothian Tourist Board
Musselburgh EH21 6AE
Tel: Dunbar (0368) 63353

Fort William and Lochaber Tourist Board
Fort William
Inverness-shire PH33 6AJ
Tel: (0397) 3781

Forth Valley Tourist Board
Linlithgow
West Lothian EH49 7AH
Tel: (0506) 84 4600

Gordon District Tourist Board
Aberdeen AB9 1DE
Tel: (0224) 632727

Greater Glasgow Tourist Board
35 - 39 St.Vincent Place
Glasgow G1 2ER
Tel: (041) 227 4880

Inverness, Loch Ness and Nairn Tourist Board
Inverness IV1 1EZ
Tel: (0463) 234353

Isle of Arran Tourist Board
Brodick
Isle of Arran KA27 8AU
Tel: (0770) 2140

Isle of Bute Tourist Board
Rothesay
Isle of Bute PA20 9AQ
Tel: (0700) 2151

Isle of Skye and South West Ross Tourist Board
Portree
Isle of Skye IV51 9BZ
Tel: (0478) 2137

Kincardine and Deeside Tourist Board
Banchory
Kincardineshire AB3 3XX
Tel: (033 02) 2066

Kirkcaldy District Council
South Street, Leven
Fife KY8 4PF
Tel: (0333) 29464

Loch Lomond, Stirling and Trossachs Tourist Board
Stirling FK8 2LQ
Tel: (0786) 75019

Mid Argyll, Kintyre and Islay Tourist Board
Campbeltown
Argyll PA28 6EF
Tel: (0586) 52056

Moray District Council
17 High Street
Elgin IV30 1EG
Tel: (0343) 2666/3388

Oban, Mull and District Tourist Board
Argyll PA34 4AN
Tel: (0631) 63122

Orkney Tourist Board
Kirkwall
Orkney KW15 1DH
Tel: (0856) 2856

Perthshire Tourist Board
George Inn Lane
Perth PH1 5LH
Tel: (0738) 27958

Ross and Cromarty Tourist Board
North Kessock
Inverness IV1 1XB
Tel: (0463 73) 505

St Andrews and North East Fife Tourist Board
St Andrews
Fife KY16 9TE
Tel: (0334) 72021

Scottish Borders Tourist Board
Selkirk TD7 4JX
Tel: Jedburgh (0835) 63435/63688

Shetland Tourist Organisation
Lerwick
Shetland ZE1 0LU
Tel: (0595) 3434

Sutherland Tourist Board
Dornoch
Sutherland IV25 3SD
Tel: (0862) 810400

Western Isles Tourist Board
Stornoway
Isle of Lewis PA87 2XY
Tel: (0851) 3088

AUCHTERARDER
H O U S E

One of Scotland's finest country mansions, set in 17½ acres of scenic grounds, Auchterarder House reflects the elegance and splendour of the Victorian era. Guests are offered the highest standards of personal service, comfort and cuisine, in magnificent surroundings. All 10 bedrooms and one suite have en suite bathrooms. Shooting, fishing and golf can be arranged. Only one hour's drive from Edinburgh and Glasgow and one mile from Gleneagles golf courses.

Owned and managed by two generations of the Brown family, Auchterarder House is not just a hotel, it is an experience in gracious living. Experience the pleasures of a real Scottish country house – experience the magic of Auchterarder House.

For brochure, tariff and reservations write, telephone or fax . . .

**Auchterarder House
Auchterarder, Perthshire PH3 1DZ
Telephone 0764 63646. Fax 0764 62939.**

See entry page . . . 31

If you have a taste for somewhere different — it's time you visited Dumfries and Galloway.
Follow the Solway Coast Heritage Trail, and discover the refreshing flavour of South-West Scotland.
Castles, abbeys, gardens and visitor centres — open all year.
Hills, forests and beaches — with room to breath.

Dumfries and Galloway

Scotland's Surprising South West

Full details from Tony Stevens, Dumfries and Galloway Tourist Board, Whitesands, Dumfries DG1 2SB. Tel. 0387 53862 (24 hours).

THE ROMAN CAMP
COUNTRY HOUSE HOTEL

Nestling in the heart of the beautiful Trossachs, the Roman Camp Hotel offers a magical mixture of gracious living and historic atmosphere.

Surrounded by 20 acres of superb gardens on the banks of the River Teith, the hotel's picturesque interior reflects the original charm of this 17th century building.

All bedrooms have private bathrooms, and facilities which make for a welcoming, comfortable stay. Guests can enjoy peace and tranquillity in a truly unique style.

Fresh produce and fine wines will tempt the most discerning diner and friendly personal service creates an atmosphere of leisured living.

The Roman Camp invites you to relax and enjoy the warmest of welcomes and the greatest of pleasure.

For brochure, tariff and reservations write telephone or Fax.

**The Roman Camp Hotel
Callander FK17 8BG
Telephone 0877 30003. Fax 0764 62939.**

See entry page . . . 39

FREE GOLF at
North West Castle Hotel

Seafront, Stranraer
AA*** Egon Ronay ****RAC
5 Crown STB award winning hotel for food, welcome and hospitality

TASTE OF SCOTLAND
PRESTIGE AWARD WINNER 1989
FOR BEST TOWN HOTEL

All bedrooms with private bath, colour TV and telephone. Hotel facilities include curling rink, indoor heated swimming pool, sauna, sunbeds, table tennis, bowls, snooker and pool tables.

Elegant dining-room with views overlooking the harbour and Loch Ryan. Food is international with added traditional Scottish dishes.

ASK ABOUT OUR WEEKLY
FAMILY SUMMER RATES
WHICH INCLUDE FREE GOLF

*For Further Details
Telephone (0776) 4413 or Fax 0776 2646*

See entry page . . . 90

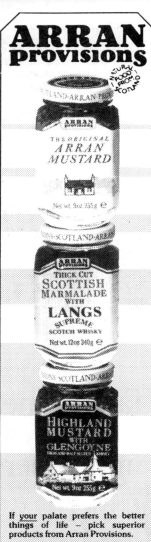

Dunrobin Castle

△ Ochil Hills, Tillicoultry

Brig o' Balgownie, Old Aberdeen ▽

△ Dunvegan, Isle of Skye

Loch Eilt, Inverness-shire ▽

△ *Caledonian Canal, near Fort William*   *Inverness-shire* ▽

Castle Campbell, Dollar

△ *Rogie Falls, near Strathpeffer*

Ullapool ▽

Pittenweem Harbour, Fife

Glen Coe, Argyll

△ Sutherland

Drumadoon Point, Isle of Arran ▽

Findhorn Gorge

Eigg, Muck, Rhum

Some interesting Recipes selected from a range submitted by Taste of Scotland members

Langoustine Tails in an apple and stem ginger cream sauce

(From Jean Michel Gauffre, Executive Chef, Edinburgh Sheraton)

Ingredients

24 langoustine tails
½ pint cream
1 fl oz fish stock
½ oz butter
½ oz stem ginger
2 red apples (julienne)

½ oz chives
1 fl oz Noilly Prat
Dill, chervil for garnish
1 oz shallots
½ fl oz olive oil
Seasoning

Serves 4

Method

1. Peel langoustine tails, season and dust with flour.
2. Reduce shallots, Noilly Prat and fish stock by one quarter, add cream and reduce by one third: season and pass.
3. Heat olive oil till hot, add half butter and quickly pan-fry tails till golden brown: keep warm.
4. Add apple and ginger julienne to sauce with a little stock syrup from the ginger. Slowly, add rest of butter.
5. Add chives and place tails in a shallow bowl or dish, coat with sauce and garnish.

Edinburgh Sheraton
1 Festival Square
Edinburgh EH3 9SR

Tel: (031) 229 9131

Spinach Roulade with Dunsyre Blue Cheese

(From Susan Blockey, Tiroran House)

Ingredients

2 lbs fresh picked spinach (wash well and trim stalks)
1 oz butter
1 oz flour
½ pint milk
2 eggs (separated)
salt, pepper
3 oz Dunsyre blue cheese
4 tablespoons single cream
4 shallots (finely chopped)

Serves 6 as a starter or 4 as a main vegetarian course.

Method

1. Cook spinach fast in lightly salted water until just tender and beautifully green. Drain well.
2. Make a sauce with the butter, flour and milk.
3. Stir in cooked spinach.
4. Beat egg yolks into the sauce.
5. Line a Swiss roll tin with silicone paper.
6. Whisk egg whites until stiff and fold lightly into sauce mixture. Pour into the prepared tin.
7. Bake at (GM 6/200°C/400°F) for about 10 minutes until lightly set.
8. Meantime combine cheese and finely chopped onion.
9. Turn out the roulade and spread with cheese mixture. Roll up and leave to settle for 5 minutes.
10. Sprinkle with freshly grated parmesan and pour over a little warmed and seasoned cream. Put under grill for a minute or two.
11. Serve with a tomato salad and mild garlic bread.

Tiroran House
Tiroran, Isle of Mull
Argyll PA69 6ES

Tel: (06815) 232
Proprietors: Robin & Susan Blockey

Savoury Apple
with Tarragon Cream

*(From Tony Kersley, Head Chef,
Invercreran Country House Hotel)*

Ingredients

4 medium size eating apples
1½ oz flaked almonds
2½ oz red pepper
1½ oz butter
2 pinches fresh (or dried) herbs
4 fl oz single cream
¼ oz fresh tarragon (or dried) chopped finely

Serves 4

Method

1. Peel apples and dice.
2. Saute in butter with diced red peppers.
3. Add flaked almonds and mixed herbs.
4. Cook until the apple and peppers are still crunchy, stirring all the time.
5. Keep warm.
6. Add the tarragon with the cream, then reduce to the correct consistency.
7. Place apple mixture equally on four plates and pour over tarragon cream.

Invercreran Country House Hotel
Glen Creran, Appin
Argyll PA38 4BJ

Tel: (063 173) 414/456
Proprietor: John & Mary Kersley & Family

Arbroath Smokie Soup

(From Bill Morrison, Chef, Newton House Hotel)

Ingredients

2 large or 3 small Arbroath smokies
2 onions finely chopped
3 pints fish stock
2 pints milk
parsley stalks
3 oz flour
3 oz butter

Serves 10

Method

1. Put smokies, onion, fish stock, milk and parsley stalks in a pot.
2. Bring to the boil.
3. Simmer for half an hour.
4. Melt butter. Add flour and make a roux. Cook for approx 2 minutes.
5. Strain stock from the fish and onion and add slowly to the roux.
6. Take the smokie flesh from the bones and add to the soup. Cook for about half an hour.
7. Put through a liquidiser.
8. Finish with fresh cream, chopped parsley or chives.

Newton House Hotel
Glencarse
By Perth PH12 7LX

Tel: (073 886) 250
Proprietors: Geoffrey & Carol Tallis

Jellied Salmon with Dulse

(From David McCrae,
Chef, Martins Restaurant)

Ingredients

1 × 12 oz salmon fillet
1 pint strong, clear fish stock
2 oz dried dulse
24 green peppercorns
1 few drops Ricard
a few drops lemon juice
sea salt

Sauce
2 tablespoons creme fräiche
Chopped dill
Tomatoes

Serves 4

Method

1. Cook dulse in the fish stock for 3 minutes. Remove dulse from liquor and allow to cool.
2. Add Ricard, lemon juice and sea salt to fish stock, pass through muslin and allow to cool.
3. Slice salmon fairly thinly and put one slice into each of 4 ramekin dishes. Strew some dulse and ⅔ green peppercorns over salmon, and cover with some fish stock.
4. Repeat until salmon and dulse are used up, making sure that there is enough stock to cover.
5. Poach in a bain-marie for 20 minutes in an oven, temperature low-medium.
6. Chill for 5 hours.
7. To unmould, dip ramekins in hot water.

For Sauce

1. Add 2 tablespoons creme fräiche, chopped dill and chopped deseeded and peeled tomatoes to the remaining fish stock.

Martins Restaurant
70 Rose Street North Lane
Edinburgh EH2 3DX

Tel: (031) 225 3106
Proprietors: Martin & Gay Irons

Scots Potatoes

(From Helen Broughton, Chef/Proprietor Broughtons Restaurant)

Ingredients

1lb peeled, sliced raw potatoes (¼ inch thick)
Seasoned flour
1 egg mixed with 2fl oz of milk, salt and pepper
Plate of medium oatmeal

Serves 4

Method

1. Slice raw potatoes to quarter inch thick, but do not rinse.
2. Dip the potatoes in the flour seasoned with salt and pepper, then in the egg mix and finally in the oatmeal.
3. Deep fry for about four minutes.

   A simple but interesting way to serve potatoes.

Broughtons of Blair Drummond
Stirling
FK9 4XE

Tel: (0786) 841897
Proprietor: Helen Broughton

A Sauce for Salmon

(From Anita Steffen, Cuilmore Cottage)

Ingredients

1 onion
1 large clove garlic

For Sauce

4 oz double cream
4 oz white wine
1 teaspoon Dijon mustard
1 tablespoon anchovy essence

pinch dried dill and tarragon
pinch sugar
1 teaspoon white wine vinegar
salt, pepper
⅓ cucumber (finely diced)

Method

1. Chop onion and garlic and fry in butter.
2. Add sauce ingredients (with the exception of cucumber) to onion and garlic and simmer for 10 minutes. The texture of this sauce improves if made in advance and left to stand.
3. Warm cucumber through in sauce, shortly before serving.
4. Serve around or over grilled salmon steaks.

Cuilmore Cottage
Kinloch Rannoch
Perthshire PH16 5QB

Tel: (08822) 218
Proprietor: Anita Steffen

Mrs McGillvray's Pheasant

(From Penny Howman, Auchnahyle Farm)

Ingredients

2 pheasants
3 onions
1 carrot
3 oz butter
4-5 sticks celery
bouquet garni
clove garlic
1 tablespoon plain flour
1½ tablespoons Mrs McGillvray's Scotch Apple Liqueur
2 green dessert apples
3-4 tablespoons soured cream
salt and pepper

Serves 6

Method

1. Put pheasants in large casserole and add 1½ pints water, a carrot, a stick of celery, an onion roughly chopped up and a bouquet garni.
2. Cover and pot roast in oven GM4/180°C/350°F for approx 1¼ hours depending on size of pheasants.
3. Take out and when cool strip meat off birds and put in oven proof dish.
4. Slice remaining onions and chop celery and garlic and saute in butter until soft.
5. Add flour and ¾ pint stock from casserole and bring to boil.
6. Take off heat and add soured cream, the apple liqueur and salt and pepper to taste.
7. Pour over pheasant.
8. Slice dessert apple and decorate top.
9. Brush with melted butter and re-heat in oven of GM2/150°C/300°F for 30 minutes.

Auchnahyle Farm
Tomcroy Terrace, Pitlochry
Perthshire PH16 5JA

Tel: (0796) 2318
Proprietors: Alastair & Penny Howman

Steak with Dunsyre Blue Cheese and Walnut Sauce

(From Marian Campbell, Braemar Lodge)

Ingredients

2 oz butter
2 shallots (finely chopped)
4 sirloin steaks
salt
1 carrot (peeled and finely chopped)
1 sprig fresh thyme
1 bay leaf
7 oz dry white wine
3 oz Dunsyre blue cheese
4 tablespoons double cream
3 oz walnut halves
2 tablespoons chopped parsley
¼ pint milk

Serves 4

Method

1. Fry steaks as desired, keep warm.
2. Lower heat under frying pan add shallots, carrot, thyme and bay leaf. Cook for 2-3 minutes.
3. Turn heat up to moderate and add wine.
4. Mash cheese with fork, add to pan with cream. Cook until reaches a syrupy consistency. Strain.
5. Reheat, salt and pepper to taste.
6. Meanwhile put walnuts into boiling water, bring back to boil, drain.
7. Leave to soak in cold milk for 10 minutes.
8. Add walnuts to sauce.
9. Spoon over steaks, sprinkle with parsley and serve.

Braemar Lodge
Braemar
Royal Deeside AB3 5YQ

Tel: (03397) 41627
Proprietors: Trevor & Marian Campbell

"Sound of Gigha" Turbot with Wild Highland Herbs and White Wine Sauce

*(From Tom Ewing, Chef,
The Anchorage Restaurant)*

Ingredients

1lb fresh turbot fillets
6 oz finely chopped shallots
2 oz chopped parsley
1 oz tarragon
1 oz sorrel
2 pints fish stock
6 oz dry white wine
3 oz double cream
3 oz unsalted butter
Seasoning
Juice of ½ lemon
Sprigs of parsley

Serves 2

Method

1. Fillet the turbot and place washed fillets in white wine with chopped herbs.
2. Lightly butter the base of a poaching tray, lightly season and sprinkle with chopped shallots.
3. Place the turbot fillets (approx 6 oz portions) in the poaching tray. Cover with fish stock, white wine and herbs.
4. Bring to a slight tremble and poach gently for four to five minutes.
5. Remove fillets when gently cooked. Place on a warm tray. Cover with foil, then place in a hot oven.
6. Reduce the cooking liquor by half. Gently blend in the butter with the fresh cream and whisk in herbs. Correct the seasoning.
7. Remove the turbot from oven. Place on warm presentation plates.
8. Coat the fish with sauce and garnish with sprigs of parsley.

**The Anchorage Restaurant
Harbour Street, Tarbert,
Argyll PA29 6UD**

**Tel: (08802) 881
Proprietors: David & Fiona Evamy**

Veal Kerrera

(From George Wilson, Head Chef,
Leadburn Inn)

Ingredients

4 × 5 oz veal escalopes
4 teaspoons Scottish whole grain mustard
1 freshly squeezed lemon
½ teaspoon freshly chopped basil

¼ pint fresh double cream
Salt and pepper to season
Butter

Serves 4

Method

1. Pan-fry veal in butter, do not brown. Remove veal and keep warm.
2. Drain butter, add lemon juice, mustard, basil, cream and season to taste.
3. Reduce till correct consistency is achieved.
4. Serve veal coated with sauce and garnish with fresh basil and a twist of lemon.

The Leadburn Inn
Leadburn, West Linton
Peeblesshire EH46 7BE

Tel: (0968) 72952
Proprietors: Linda & Alan Thomson

Pork Fillet in Drambuie and Clove Sauce

(From George Aitken, Chef
Allt-Chaorain Country House)

Ingredients

6 × 4 oz portions diced pork fillet
4 oz butter
ground cloves to taste
¾ pint double cream
2 liqueur/sherry glasses of Drambuie

1 teaspoon mixed herbs
24 mangetout
24 slices tomato
salt and pepper

Serves 6

Method

1. Melt butter in large pan and saute pork for approx 10-15 minutes.
2. Remove pork and put in a dish then put in oven and cover.

For Sauce

3. Gently heat cream, cloves and Drambuie. Add herbs and season.
4. Blanche mangetout.

To serve

5. Place pork in centre of heated plate and cover with sauce.
6. Garnish with mangetout and slices of tomato and sprinkle with parsley.

Allt-Chaorain Country House
Crianlarich
Perthshire FK20 8RU

Tel: (083883) 283
Proprietor: Roger McDonald

Rack of Lamb baked with a Pine Kernel and Garlic Crust

(From Richard Sturgeon, Executive Chef, Marine Highland Hotel)

Ingredients

1 × 8 cutlet bone dressed best end lamb
4 oz white breadcrumbs
2 cloves crushed garlic
¼ oz pine kernels
1 teaspoon mixed herbs
1 teaspoon chopped parsley
2 fl oz garlic oil
2 oz butter (soften)
2 oz French mustard
seasoning
1 whole tomato
sprigs watercress
2 oz butter to finish sauce
½ pint brown stock

Serves 2

Method

1. Place garlic oil and butter in pan; when butter begins to colour add crushed garlic, white breadcrumbs, herbs and parsley. Mix well and add pine kernels. Mix again and season. Mixture should bind together when pressed – if not, add a little more oil.
2. Remove eye of tomato, cut in half, cover with breadcrumb mix. Place under grill until golden brown. Remove and keep warm.
3. Season lamb and put on to roast in hot oven for approximately 30 minutes, turn lamb after 15 minutes. Five minutes before required degree of cooking, remove lamb from oven and spread thin layer of French mustard over top of lamb and cover with remainder of breadcrumb mix. Return to oven until breadcrumbs are golden brown. Place lamb on serving dish and keep warm.
4. Pour off all excess fat from roasting tin, add stock, bring to boil and reduce stock by half. Remove pan from stove and add softened butter stirring all the time until butter dissolves. Do not boil sauce. Season sauce, strain through fine sieve, pour sauce around lamb, garnish with tomatoes and sprigs of watercress and serve.

Marine Highland Hotel
Troon
Ayrshire KA10 6HE

Tel: (0292) 314444
Propietor: Scottish Highland Hotels

Dunsyre Stuffed Partridges

*(From Roy Ellis, Executive Head Chef,
Dolphinton House Hotel)*

Ingredients

4 young partridges (boned)
4 rashers of Ayrshire bacon
Butter to baste
Salt and pepper

Stuffing

4 oz breadcrumbs
4 oz pork sausagemeat
2 oz chopped pears
2 oz Dunsyre blue cheese (crumbled)
1 tablespoon chopped mint
2 oz melted butter
cream to mix

Mix all ingredients thoroughly

Sauce

4 oz redcurrant jelly
1 oz port
1 tablespoon coarse mustard
1 pinch caraway seeds

Melt jelly with port and other ingredients and keep warm.

Serves 4

Method

1. Bone partridges and stuff.
2. Cover with bacon and baste liberally with butter.
3. Cook at GM4/200°C/400°F for approx 25 minutes.
4. Place on serving dish and surround with port and redcurrant sauce.
5. Decorate with mint leaves, serve with seasonal vegetables and gravy.

**Dolphinton House Hotel
Dolphinton, near West Linton
Peeblesshire EH46 7AB**

Tel: (0968) 82286

Cranachan

*(From Jeff Bland, Executive Chef,
Caledonian Hotel, Edinburgh)*

Ingredients

4 oz soft berries
(e.g. strawberries, brambles, blackcurrants or raspberries)
5 oz crushed shortbread and Scottish toasted pinhead oatmeal
3 fl oz whisky or Glayva
1½ pints whipped double cream
4 oz sugar
1 oz honey

Serves 4

Method

1. Whip the double cream and sugar together.
2. Crush the shortbread and wash the fruit. Drain well
3. Add the whisky etc to the cream as well as the shortbread, oatmeal, fruit and honey. Fold in with a wooden spoon.
4. When nicely mixed in, put into a large bowl and decorate, or pipe into Paris goblets and decorate, or shape with spoons.
5. Serve with a blackcurrant puree.

Caledonian Hotel
Princes Street
Edinburgh EH1 2AB

Tel: (031) 225 2433
Proprietor: Norfolk Capital Hotels

Cloutie Dumpling

(From Jean Morton, Lochend Farm)

Ingredients

10 oz plain flour
6 oz finely chopped beef suet
3 oz sugar
½ teaspoon baking soda
1 teaspoon cream of tartar
8 oz sultanas
6 oz currants
1 teaspoon cinnamon
½ teaspoon ground ginger
½ teaspoon mixed spices
¼ teaspoon all spice
¼ teaspoon salt
shake of black pepper
milk to mix approx ½ pint

Method

1. Have a large pot boiling water, with an old dinner plate on bottom.
2. Scald a suitable cloth, wring out and dredge with flour.
3. Mix all the dry ingredients well and bind to a firm scone dough with milk.
4. Place mixture in the centre of cloth, draw ends of cloth together and tie, leaving enough space to expand.
5. Lower into enough boiling water to cover, keep pot boiling gently, topping up as required from a boiling kettle.
6. After at least 3 hours lift out dumpling – remove cloth and dry off in the oven till skin is shiny.

Serve hot with custard or cream

Serve remaining dumpling cold, buttered, or fry and serve with bacon and tomato for breakfast.

Lochend Farm
Carronbridge, Denny
Stirlingshire FK6 5JJ

Tel: (0324) 822778
Proprietor: Jean Morton

Hot Filo Pastry Parcel of Pears and Bananas with a Duo of Sauces

(From Bruce Sangster, Executive Chef Murrayshall)

Ingredients

Parcels

4 sheets of filo pastry
3 peeled and sliced pears
3 sliced bananas
Pinch cinnamon
Icing sugar for dusting

Sauces

Vanilla – served warm

1 pint milk
1 split vanilla pod or
    ½ teaspoon vanilla essence
7 egg yolks
4 oz sugar

Caramel – served hot

4 oz butter
6 oz soft brown sugar
4 oz golden syrup
2 tablespoons condensed milk
8 fl oz double cream

Serves 4

Method

1. Take one sheet of filo paste, lightly butter and fold in half.
2. Put two spoonfuls of the sliced pears, bananas and cinnamon in centre.
3. Cut the corners of the pastry and fold the sides together to make parcel.
4. Do the same with the other three, then bake at GM5/190°C/375°F for about 15 minutes.

The Sauces

Caramel: Put all the ingredients apart from cream into a heavy based pan and slowly bring to the boil. When boiling whisk in cream and return to heat. Bring back to boil then sieve and put to one side.

Vanilla: Bring milk and vanilla pod to boil. Whisk egg yolks and sugar together, pour milk onto eggs, continue whisking. Put back into heavy based pan and return to heat. Slowly cook out until it covers back of spoon. Sieve and leave to one side.

Presentation: Serve with the caramel sauce around the outside of the plate and the vanilla sauce in the centre. Place the parcel on the vanilla sauce and dust with icing sugar. Place three single strawberries around the plate with sprigs of mint and serve.

Murrayshall Country House Hotel
Scone
Perthshire PH2 7PH

Tel: (0738) 51171
Proprietors: MacOlsen Ltd

Highland Clouds

(From Chris Bentley, Head Chef, Coul House Hotel)

Ingredients

8 egg whites
8 oz fresh Scottish strawberries
1 lb fresh Scottish raspberries
2 tablespcons icing sugar
1 fl oz Glayva

Serves 4

Method

1. Whip the egg whites until stiff.
2. Puree the raspberries with the icing sugar and Glayva, then pass through a sieve to remove the seeds.
3. Hull the strawberries and slice: put to one side.
4. In a hot omelette pan or oiled frying pan, spoon quarter of the egg whites and cook until set and lightly coloured on the bottom.
5. Slide onto a metal tray and repeat cooking for three more 'clouds'.
6. Place the tray in the oven GM 4/180ºC/350ºF for five minutes.
7. Remove from oven and place on four plates.
8. Top with the sliced strawberries and pour over the sauce.
9. Serve immediately.

Coul House Hotel
Contin, by Strathpeffer
Ross-shire IV14 9EY

Tel: (0997) 21487
Proprietor: Martyn Hill

Raspberry and almond roulade

(From Ruth Hadley, The Cross)

Ingredients

4 eggs – separated
4 oz sugar
4 oz ground almonds
1 teaspoon baking powder
1 teaspoon orange flower water
1 lb Scottish raspberries
1 oz sugar (icing)
10 oz double/whipping cream
Drambuie

Serves 4-6

Method

1. Whisk egg whites, add 2 oz sugar slowly and whisk to stiff.
2. Beat egg yolks with remaining sugar to white, add flower water.
3. Fold in almonds and baking powder then egg whites.
4. Transfer to swiss roll tin, lined with bakewell paper. Spread evenly.
5. Bake GM4/180⁰C/350⁰F for 20-25 minutes until firm to touch. Allow to cool.
6. Meanwhile blend half the raspberries with the icing sugar. Press through a sieve to remove pips. Whip cream till thick and flavour to taste with Drambuie.
7. Invert sponge onto a sheet of greaseproof paper which has been sprinkled lightly with sugar. Carefully remove bakewell paper from sponge. Neaten edges if necessary.
8. Spread with the cream and remaining raspberries.
9. Using the greaseproof paper, carefully roll sponge into a "swiss roll" and lift, via the paper, onto a serving dish. Refrigerate.

To serve, remove paper, serve in slices with the raspberry sauce and fresh raspberries.

The Cross
High Street,
Kingussie PH21 1HX

Tel: (0540) 661762
Proprietors: Tony & Ruth Hadley

Millefeuille of Bitter Chocolate Mousse flavoured with Glayva and Honeycomb on a Glayva Creme Anglaise Sauce

(From Colin John Bussey, Head Chef, Auchterarder House)

Ingredients

4½ oz butter
8¼ oz extra bitter chocolate
1½ oz cocoa
3 egg yolks
3 oz caster sugar
2 tablespoons good quality coffee powder
6 fl oz whipped cream
2 oz fresh honey
1 measure Glayva

Sauce

2-3 egg yolks
½ vanilla pod
2 oz caster sugar
½ pint milk
1 oz honey
1 measure Glayva

Serves 8

Method

1. Melt together butter, cocoa and 2¼ oz of the chocolate and mix well.
2. Beat egg yolks and sugar until thick and creamy, add coffee.
   (While adding coffee, taste, as too much will spoil the flavour of the mousse).
3. Beat in the chocolate base and when mixed well, beat in the whipped cream and add the honey and Glayva liqueur.
4. Leave to set in the refrigerator.
5. Melt and spread the remaining 6 oz of chocolate onto silicone paper.
6. Allow to set then cut out 24 even sized circles or squares.
7. Allow 3 tiers per portion. Pipe mousse onto the first, top with second tier, pipe more mousse, then add the top tier.
8. Dust with icing sugar.

Sauce

9. Bring milk to the boil, infuse vanilla pod.
10. Cream egg yolks and sugar, whisk in the milk.
11. In a clean pan, stir this mixture over a low heat until it thickens (do not allow to boil).
12. Add honey and liqueur, strain and set aside to cool.

To serve

13. Pour sauce onto plate, gently set the millefeuille onto the sauce.
14. Decorate with chocolate shavings and a sprig of mint.

**Auchterarder House
Auchterarder,
Perthshire PH3 1DZ**

**Tel: (0764) 63646
Proprietors: Ian & Audrey Brown**

Carradale Hotel

CARRADALE, ARGYLL, SCOTLAND PA28 6RY
Telephone: Carradale (05833) 223

Our brochure is only a phone call away!

Standing in its own gardens high above the quaint fishing harbour our family-owned hotel offers you a unique combination of personal friendly service, great dining experiences and a host of modern hotel amenities. Visit us in 1990 and be enchanted by Carradale's beautiful hills, glens and beaches!

If sport is your forte, indoors and outdoors there's always lots to do at Carradale – the hotel even boasts its own indoor leisure centre, featuring two international standard glass-backed squash courts, sauna, solarium and table tennis. Outdoors, the scenic and challenging 9-hole golf course has its first tee right alongside the hotel and we can arrange river and sea fishing, pony trekking and dinghy sailing at a moment's notice to name but a few!

Children are especially welcome here at Carradale Hotel, and of course there is no accommodation charge for them when sharing a family room or suite with their parents.

Finally watch out for some great value packages in 1990 – details available in our brochure!

See entry page . . . 39

KINGSMUIR HOTEL
PEEBLES   **Borders**

Charming century-old country house, in leafy grounds, on quiet, south side of Peebles, yet only 5 minutes' walk through parkland to High Street.

There are 10 bedrooms, all en suite, with TV, telephone, tea-maker and hairdrier. The very best of local produce is used in preparing the Restaurant, Bar Lunch and Bar Supper dishes.

Ideal centre for touring Edinburgh and the stately homes of the Borders.

Open all year. Personally run by Elizabeth, Norman & May Kerr.

Tel: 0721-20151

STB Commended 👑👑👑   *AA***

See entry page . . . 80

IN ASCENDING ORDER (LEFT TO RIGHT) ON THE STAIR
CAITHNESS GLASS/TASTE OF SCOTLAND PRESTIGE AWARD WINNERS 1989
WITH MAGNUS MAGNUSSON:

Ruth Hadley, The Cross
Amanda Graham, Ostlers Close
Colin Terris, Caithness Glass
Ian Brown, Auchterarder House
Alistair Mair, Caithness Glass
Hamilton McMillan, North West Castle Hotel
Peter Fairlie, Smugglers, Glenturret Distillery
Grant Howlett, Cromlix House

The 1991 TASTE OF SCOTLAND GUIDE

is scheduled to be published in
November 1990.

To reserve a copy at the 1990 price of £2.70 (including post & packaging), complete the coupon below and send it with your cheque or postal order, made payable to TASTE OF SCOTLAND, to

Taste of Scotland (Guide Sales)
33 Melville Street
Edinburgh EH3 7JF.

You will be placed on the priority list to receive the Guide as soon as it is published.

- ✂ →

To: TASTE OF SCOTLAND (GUIDE SALES)
    33 MELVILLE STREET
    EDINBURGH EH3 7JF

Please send_____copy/copies of
the 1991 Guide.
Cheque / Postal Order enclosed for_____

NAME:_____

ADDRESS:_____

              _____

              _____Post Code_____

BLOCK CAPITALS, PLEASE!

GUIDE
1991

Overseas prices including post & packaging:
Ffr50 : Bfr325 : Dm15 : NLfl15 : US$10 : CAN$13

*On your travels have you visited
a restaurant or hotel which you
feel merits inclusion in the
Taste of Scotland Guide?*

We welcome your recommendations.

INDEX TO GUIDE ENTRIES

in alphabetical order
by establishment

INDEX

144

COMMENTS on meals in places listed in
The Taste of Scotland Guide are welcomed.
Send to: Taste of Scotland, 33 Melville Street, Edinburgh EH3 7JF.

Establishment visited _____

Date _____ Meal _____

Comments _____

_____

_____

_____

_____

Name _____

Address _____

_____

COMMENTS on meals in places listed in
The Taste of Scotland Guide are welcomed.
Send to: Taste of Scotland, 33 Melville Street, Edinburgh EH3 7JF.

Establishment visited _____

Date _____ Meal _____

Comments _____

_____

_____

_____

_____

Name _____

Address _____

_____

Send to: Taste of Scotland, 33 Melville Street, Edinburgh EH3 7JF

Caithness Glass *Prestige Award*

I nominate_____[ESTABLISHMENT]
for a Caithness Glass Prestige Award for the following category:

(Categories)   (Please tick <u>one</u> category only)

☐   Best Hotel   ☐   Best Hospitality & Welcome

☐   Best Restaurant   ☐   Best Newcomer to Taste of Scotland

☐   Best Country House Hotel

Name_____

Address_____

_____

Date of visit_____

Meal (if appropriate)_____

Closing date for entries: 15 September 1990.

✂ -

Send to: Taste of Scotland, 33 Melville Street, Edinburgh EH3 7JF

Caithness Glass *Prestige Award*

I nominate_____[ESTABLISHMENT]
for a Caithness Glass Prestige Award for the following category:

(Categories)   (Please tick <u>one</u> category only)

☐   Best Hotel   ☐   Best Hospitality & Welcome

☐   Best Restaurant   ☐   Best Newcomer to Taste of Scotland

☐   Best Country House Hotel

Name_____

Address_____

_____

Date of visit_____

Meal (if appropriate)_____

Closing date for entries: 15 September 1990.

TASTE OF SCOTLAND GUIDE 1990

Editor : **Nancy K. Campbell, BA**

Published by : **Taste of Scotland Scheme Ltd,**
a non-profit making company limited
by guarantee trading as Taste of
Scotland
Registered in Scotland No. 90836

Typeset and printed in Scotland by : **Inglis Allen**
Kirkcaldy

Inside colour photography : Courtesy of
Scottish Tourist Board, Paul Tomkins
Aberdeen Tourist Board
Dunoon & Cowal Tourist Board
Edinburgh District Council, Department of
    Public Relations & Tourism
Loch Lomond, Stirling & Trossachs Tourist
    Board, Ronnie Weir
Moray District Council, Department of
    Recreation
St Andrews & North-East Fife Tourist Board
Scottish Borders Tourist Board
J D Calum Campbell (Auld Brig o' Doon;
    Drumadoon Point)
William McDonald Dunn (Ochil Hills)

□□□□□□□□□□□□

□□□□□□□□□□□□

TASTE OF SCOTLAND SCHEME LTD
33 Melville Street
Edinburgh
EH3 7JF
Telephone: 031 220 1900

ISBN 0 9510250 9 0

Notes